1996

ENTHUSIASMS

ENTHUSIASMS

BERNARD LEVIN

CROWN PUBLISHERS, INC.
NEW YORK

Published in the United States of America in 1984
by Crown Publishers, Inc., One Park Avenue,
New York, New York 10016

Published originally in Great Britain in 1983 by
Jonathan Cape Ltd., 39 Bedford Square, London
WC1

Manufactured in the United States of America

Library of Congess Cataloging in Publication
Data
Levin, Bernard.
  Enthusiasms.

  Includes index.
  I. Title.
PN5123.L44A25   1984   824'.914   83-25181
ISBN 0-517-55352-X

10 9 8 7 6 5 4 3 2 1
First American Edition

For Arianna
with much more than enthusiasm

Acknowledgments

Once again, I am most grateful for the assistance and encouragement of my secretary, Sally Chichester, and for the sharp-eyed proof-reading of Brian Inglis. The index was compiled by Mrs Oula Jones of the Society of Indexers; this is the third of my books to have, in this difficult and exacting labour, the benefit of her outstanding professional skill, to which she adds a no less valuable sympathetic understanding.

The quotations on pages 4 and 9 are by G. K. Chesterton. They are taken from the epigraph to *The Man Who Was Thursday*, which is reproduced in Chesterton's *Collected Poems* (London, 1933) and appear by permission of Miss D. E. Collins of Methuen & Co. Ltd. The lines from Xenophon, *The Persian Expedition*, which appear on pages 113–14, are quoted from the Rex Warner translation, copyright © 1949 by Rex Warner, and are reprinted by permission of Penguin Books Ltd. The Ruskin passages reproduced on pages 125–6 are taken from *Modern Painters* (George Allen, London, 1907). The Oliver Lodge quotation on page 231 is from the Proceedings of the Society for Psychical Research, Vol. 38, 1928–9.

One

We live in a querulous age; more, we live in an age in which it is argued that to be happy is frivolous, and expecting to be happy positively childish. To be passionate in a cause provokes widespread embarrassment, and to be passionate in appreciation of the good things of life, especially the non-material good things, is to court on the one hand stern denunciation as an irresponsible hedonist, and to set off on the other the squealing and tittering of those whose motto is 'Surtout, Messieurs, point de zèle'.

It is, of course, worse than that; behind much of the contempt for joy lie a deep fear and hatred of enjoyment. 'In Xanadu did Kubla Khan a stately pleasure-dome decree . . .'; the pleasures to be found there were of the most innocent kind – gardens bright with sinuous rills, trees bearing incense, forests ancient as the hills enfolding sunny spots of greenery, a deep romantic chasm – yet Kubla none the less heard from far ancestral voices prophesying war.

It was the war on pleasure that they prophesied, and it has been going on ever since. The intensity of the disapproval has obviously been greater in some eras than in others, and the phenomenon has been variously explained – climate and religion are two of the favoured versions of the reason – but the terrible truth is that the hatred of pleasure is for some an end in itself.

Throughout history there have been those who have hated pleasure irrespective of its nature; it began, I suppose, with the serpent in Eden, whispering his doubts about its enjoyment until Adam and Eve became so inhibited by self-

1

consciousness that they took the steps which led to their expulsion from that innocent realm. Macaulay's famous summation of the pleasure-haters' motives – 'The Puritan hated bear-baiting not because it gave pain to the bear, but because it gave pleasure to the spectators' – has never lost its force; the members of the League Against Cruel Sports would not abate their detestation of fox-hunting in the least even if they were assured that the foxes enjoyed it by the foxes themselves.

The hatred of pleasure, the origins of which go back centuries but which has grown vastly powerful in our own day, has almost entirely ceased to be rooted in moral or ethical grounds. It is, of course, not difficult to make a conclusive case against pleasures which depend on the harming of other people or of animals. But apart from the dubious nature of the zeal which animates our modern puritans when they contemplate respectively the bear-baiter (whom they hate) and the bear (whom they do not love), the proof that a new basis has been established for the disapproval of others' pleasure can be found in the fact that that disapproval is excited, sometimes in its most intense form, by pleasures which cannot be said to cause harm of any kind to any sentient creature.

Our age, in which ideology is king, is the first to condemn pleasures, from good food to opera, which, though in practice enjoyed by the few, are readily accessible to the many. (A man of modest means cannot sit in the most expensive seats at Covent Garden, but he can sit in the cheapest ones; he cannot eat at the Gavroche, but he can eat at the Gay Hussar.) What has happened is that, for the first time, pleasure itself has become – along with almost everything else – politicized. The attack on excellence, stigmatized as 'elitism', has never been more intense, and since excellence in most of its concrete forms gives great pleasure, it follows that the fruit of a rotten tree must itself be rotten, and the pleasure it gives condemned.

Once, revolutionaries and peaceful reformers alike sought

to bring the good things of life to those deprived of them by poverty or by an arbitrary exclusion imposed by the selfish few who refused to share their possession. The vicious game-laws were designed to prevent the villagers eating the squire's pheasants, and Cobbett's campaign against such laws was aimed at enabling them to do so; today, the steel man-traps have gone from the coverts, but those who now hate the squire for hating's sake would deny the villagers also the taste of pheasant, and not at all out of consideration for the pheasant's feelings.

The hatred of excellence, and of the pleasure it gives, has nothing to do, any longer, with considerations of shared burdens and shared benefits. On the contrary, it is now self-contained. There is a short story by Ray Bradbury which sums up this attitude and what it implies, for it describes a society not very different from ours – indeed, it is clearly meant to *be* ours a few years hence – which has turned the hatred of excellence and pleasure into a guiding principle, and its destruction, wherever it can be found, into a consistent policy.

On the day of the story, a crowd has gathered to destroy an object which, because it enshrines beauty and art, civiliza-tion and the things of the spirit, cannot be allowed to survive. The people hurl themselves upon the thing; this, it gradually transpires, is a painting, and the mob tears it to pieces; only in the last sentence does the reader discover that the painting is the Mona Lisa, as one of the crowd goes off clutching her smile.

The active hatred of pleasure and excellence, however, though more important, and certainly more sinister, than the indifference which is so fashionable today, deserves a study in itself, though one which I am not much inclined to embark upon, if only because I would find it too depressing. But I never cease to be fascinated by the strange fact that ours is the first era in history in which enthusiasm is widely suspect, and the expression of it even more so.

At all times, of course, there have been individuals who

3

have felt nothing for anything, and others who have thought it a mark of the highest cultivation to affect indifference and boredom as their outlook on life; the Earl of Chesterfield, indeed, went so far as to maintain that 'there is nothing so illiberal and so ill-bred, as audible laughter'. Very occasionally, this philosophy of indifference produces a masterpiece; Huysmans's *A Rebours* comes to mind. More often, though, it leads to something like a cult, as in England at the end of the nineteenth century, when poor Wilde discovered that it wouldn't do just as the prison gates were swinging open for him; it surfaced again in the 1920s, among the Bright Young Things with their 'dyes and drugs and *petits verres*', and to a lesser extent (made to look greater by the puffing of the newspapers and television) in the 1960s. But hitherto such fashions have always been brief:

> And the Green Carnation withered, as in forest fires that
>   pass,
> Roared in the wind of all the world ten thousand leaves of
>   grass.

Many would say that the attitude derives from the eighteenth century, but that is great nonsense, for the Age of Reason was also the Age of Sensibility, and did not care who knew it; Diderot was one of the least cerebral men who ever lived, and Rousseau must have spent half his waking hours in tears. But imagine a man – and a philosopher, too – weeping today! No, one cannot quite see Sir Alfred Ayer in floods, though one can certainly conjure up the look of horror and embarrassment on the face of the bystanders if it were to happen.

Is there no fundamental difference between weeping and expressing an intensity of feeling? Not really, no. To be moved – by a symphony, the plight of a friend, a sunset, a sudden stab of unsought happiness – and to express the emotion thus generated, is held today, more widely than ever before (and, it seems, more tenaciously, for there is no sign of the attitude diminishing) to be a mark of weakness.

4

This can be taken to remarkable lengths; Senator Barry Goldwater, the unsuccessful Republican candidate for the US Presidency in 1964, was the subject, during the campaign, of a magazine article in which his mind and character were publicly analysed by a substantial number of psychiatrists, none of whom, incidentally, had ever examined him. (It was felt that he needed such analysis because only some mental imbalance could explain his rejection of then fashionable liberal political views.) There was general agreement among a number of these charlatans that the candidate's trouble was that he hated his wife, and their views to this effect were duly published. Whereupon, Senator Goldwater sued the magazine for libel and, when giving evidence, said, without circumlocution, 'I love my wife. I always have and I always will.' He won the case, but among the *bien-pensants* he has never lived down his statement; it is acceptable (though less so than it once was) for a man to love his wife, but to say as much in public is to invite derision.

But that is not because if such behaviour were to spread it might loosen the bonds of infidelity; it is because such statements are too charged with feeling, and it is feeling itself that is the enemy.

It is now generally agreed by almost all who saw it, on both sides of the Atlantic, that the Royal Shakespeare Company's adaptation and production of *Nicholas Nickleby* was one of the most successful, enjoyable and memorable theatrical productions to be seen for some decades. It is *now* agreed; but it was not so agreed among the London theatre critics, most of whom, when it began its ultimately triumphant career, were at best lukewarm and in some cases distinctly hostile. That is not a particularly rare, surprising or blameworthy state of affairs, but what, though neither rare nor surprising, *is* blameworthy was the attitude that plainly informed many of the adverse reviews: it was one of embarrassment at the unashamed enthusiasm of Dickens, and a consequently strengthened determination among the embarrassed not to make matters worse by being enthusiastic on their own account.

Mark, however, what followed. I saw *Nicholas Nickleby* shortly after the production opened, and was entirely carried away, again and again to the point of tears, by its enormous, richly Dickensian force of feeling; in this I was certainly not alone, for throughout the theatre (no more than two-thirds full) my fellow-members of the audience were plainly experiencing the same willing submission to a justified and indeed inescapable emotion. I was not at that time a theatre reviewer myself; but in my regular column in *The Times* I had no limitations on my choice of subject. A few days after seeing the production I published an account of it and of its effect upon me; the article has already been published elsewhere,★ but I may perhaps be permitted to quote briefly from it again to explain what follows:

> this . . . captures the spirit of Dickensian morality by divining that Dickensian morality is . . . the spirit of universal moral truth . . . Dickens, in addition to all the other things he is doing in his novels, is rooting all those things in a foundation built from a clear distinction between right and wrong . . . to show that there is good and bad and a choice between them for all of us. The huge and glorious pageant . . . never loses sight of this central truth . . . If you miss out love from Dickens you cut out his heart, and only if you understand the part it plays with him will you understand him truly . . . It is a celebration of love and justice that is true to the spirit of Dickens's belief that those are the fulcrums on which the universe is moved, and the consequence is that we come out not merely delighted but strengthened, not just entertained but uplifted, not only affected but changed.

Within two days of the article appearing, every seat for every remaining scheduled performance had been sold, and the continuing demand was such that the R.S.C. was

★ *Speaking Up* (Cape, London, 1982)

obliged, naturally to its great delight, to embark on the logistically appalling labour of planning a long season of further performances.

Now it would be absurd to maintain or believe that my article had had that effect because, even though I was not a critic, the public preferred my opinion to the opinions of the regular reviewers. Many of those who had written of it adversely were critics of real distinction, experience and judgment, with a well-deserved following among their readers; it was not surprising, on the face of it, that their readers had stayed away from the play. Yet my article did have the effect I have described. What had happened?

What had happened was, put simply, that *I had legitimized enthusiasm*. By being enthusiastic without reservation, without apology and plainly without embarrassment, I had encouraged otherwise reluctant playgoers to release in themselves feelings that had been trapped beneath the fashion for decrying enthusiasm altogether – a fashion so powerful, apparently, that it had persuaded many people to stifle in themselves their normal and natural responses. Once they got to the play, of course, they had no problem; Dickens swept them away as he had swept me away. But they apparently needed, in order to give him the chance, someone who was not in the least ashamed to express unqualified enthusiasm in public. I find it odd that anyone should need such encouragement, and the fact that many people clearly do is a measure of the extent to which the assault on feeling and its expression has been successful; I received a very large number of letters from those who had gone to see *Nicholas Nickleby* because of what I had written about it, and I was much struck by the fact that the note that ran through a very large proportion of them was one of *relief* – relief that someone had said plainly that he felt what the correspondents were longing to feel.

I think it was at that moment that the idea of this book was born. I reflected thus: if I am right, and there is a potential for enthusiasm in people who for too long have found it difficult to articulate such feelings, then – irrespective of any effect it might have on them – it is possible that they would find interesting and enjoyable a book composed entirely of someone else's enthusiasms. Naturally, I would not expect to find any single person whose enthusiasms exactly matched mine; but might not an account of his own loves, by a man long accustomed to feeling enthusiastic and expressing the feeling, have some validity beyond his own experiences?

I was not at all sure of the answer to that question, nor am I even now. But the more I thought about a lifetime of enjoying my enthusiasms, the more enthusiastic I felt about writing of them. To start with, I was surprised to discover how many subjects, let alone individual examples of them, arouse enthusiasm in me and provide me with pleasure. And very few of these are in any way odd or eccentric choices; I am not, after all, the first man to take pleasure in opera, Shakespeare, painting and *haute cuisine*, or even in walking, reading and cities. True, I also take pleasure in the smell of the igniting strip on the side of a box of safety matches, but for all I know many other people secretly share this liking, and even if I am alone in it there must be others with likings of their own that are entirely foreign to me.

We live in a world which not only fears and distrusts joy but which goes far towards denying its existence. It would, of course, be a very odd newspaper which, the day after an aeroplane crash, headlined the news '3,795 flights out of 3,796 land safely', or, on publication of the annual tables of mortality, 'Almost fifty-five million people in Britain not killed by lightning last year.' Such a newspaper would not stay long in business. Nevertheless, it would reflect the truth about the world. And the truth about disaster itself reflects a much greater and more important truth, which is that most people are happy most of the time, and this even applies to the people of those nations which are oppressed by tyranny, war or hunger. (Since the bombing and killing began in Northern Ireland, the incidence of nervous and mental disease in the province has gone *down*.) Nor does it need

8

extensive sociological surveys to establish this; it accords with the experience and observation of anyone not hypnotized by the fashion for denying the obviously true. Yet the air is full of precisely such denials:

> A cloud was on the mind of men, and wailing went the
>   weather,
> Yea, a sick cloud upon the soul when we were boys
>   together.
> Science announced nonentity and art admired decay;
> The world was old and ended: but you and I were gay.
> Round us in antic order their crippled vices came –
> Lust that had lost its laughter, fear that had lost its
>   shame.
> Like the white lock of Whistler, that lit our aimless gloom,
> Men showed their own white feather as proudly as a
>   plume.
> Life was a fly that faded, and death a drone that stung;
> The world was very old indeed when you and I were
>   young . . .

A vast quantity of public comment – in such areas as the modern theatre the denial encompasses almost everything that is done – consists of incessant reiteration of a palpable falsehood: that nothing and no one is enjoyable, admirable, brave, loyal, inspiring, worthy of praise, sustaining, hopeful, beautiful or true. This is not the place for me to consider the question of how deep the happiness of most people goes, nor is it necessary to do so in order to counter the argument – or more usually the unargued assumption – that none but fools (or the rich) are happy at all, or have any cause to be, or even any right to be. Imagine, for instance, the report that a Martian, or for that matter a Trobriand Islander, sent to examine the mood of Britain, would take back to his superiors if the only evidence he studied was the correspondence page of the *Guardian*: he would report that the entire country was convulsed with rage and hatred, that govern-

9

ment and all other institutions – schools, the law, the press, the arts, the churches, business, industry, marriage – were corrupt, mendacious and oppressive, that the people were poor, frightened, maltreated and enslaved, that the chief quality of Britain was irremediable evil and the chief occupation of its people whining, and that no discernible trace of a sense of humour existed anywhere. (He would also conclude that practically everybody in the country was illiterate, but that is not relevant to my present point.)

If I am right, I am not alone; indeed, in this question that is a definition of being right. Enthusiasm can take a thousand forms, but is of one nature: it means the taking of great pleasure, the feeling of great ardour, the experiencing of great excitement, in the presence or contemplation of the object that arouses the enthusiasm. It is not to be confused with a hobby, though the two may overlap; it is not to be confused with love, though again the two are not mutually exclusive; it is certainly not to be confused with fanaticism, though the original meaning of the word was coloured by a sense of religious frenzy; it may perhaps be said that the word 'interest' is the inert form of the organic 'enthusiasm', so that the tongue-tied dinner-guest who asks his neighbour, 'Have you read any good books lately?' is showing interest, and the neighbour who promptly waxes rapturous about his bedside reading is showing enthusiasm.

My own enthusiasms are numerous and mostly long-rooted. Like other people's, some grow greater with the passage of time, and some recede, though some which appear to have vanished are only lying dormant; I used, for instance, to play a lot of chess when I was young – it was indeed a passionate enthusiasm – and have played only a handful of games these many years past, but whenever I have taken the pieces out I have instantly felt all the old excitement and pleasure, the eagerness to start and to enjoy. But a quick count when I began to think seriously about what this book might contain revealed an alarmingly large number of enthusiasms, which would require a no less alarmingly fat volume to accommodate them,* and I have been obliged to omit many more than I have included.

History, for instance; I am no historian, but I love to wander in the past conjured up by those who are. My favourite game among friends is history-based; the players in turn pick a historical place and era, and imagine themselves set down in it with no advantages whatever other than the knowledge and skill they carry in their heads (it is assumed only that they speak the language of the society they have chosen). The object of the game is not simply to survive, or even to survive in comfort, but to become one of the most prominent and powerful figures in the land, solely by the use of the modern knowledge which the chosen society does not have; but the players can take no tools, equipment or even books into the time machine.

Newcomers to the game start with a rush: 'Caesar's Rome – and I'll teach him about guns.' 'But could you actually *make* a gun?' 'Ah, I suppose not. I know – I'll warn him against the assassins.' 'But why should he believe you – he didn't believe the soothsayer, after all.' The first confidence wears off, and is replaced by a salutary realization of how little we actually know that is of any use. But that is one of the delights of history, to match our own understanding against those who lacked the advantage of our hindsight, which would have been their foresight.

Then again, there is no chapter on travel, though if I had included one I would have had to start with a strange disclaimer, not normally found in a discussion of enthusiasms: I detest *all* forms of travel with an unassuageable loathing that grows greater, not less, with the passing years. But by 'travel' in that sentence I mean the action of getting from X to Y, not the state of being *at* Y, which I take to be not travel but the aim of travel. Every kind of transport, from the car to the Concorde, I find unbearable, which is

* I had something of a 'dry run' in the summer of 1982, when I gave a series of radio broadcasts on 'Pleasures'; I have even incorporated a few passages from these talks in my accounts of my enthusiasms.

why I normally fly everywhere I can, since the agony is over more quickly. But being in strange places, amid strange sights and sounds and people, is an enthusiasm with which few can compare.

Leaving out my enthusiasm for language – the English language, that is, for I am no linguist – was hardest of all. I have two enthusiasms for it, and one of them – books – I have included (though even that chapter omits any discussion of book collecting, which in my case is not so much an enthusiasm as a disease). But I have a quite separate (not *quite* separate, I suppose, for there must be a connection) enthusiasm for language in its lexicographical, grammatical and syntactical forms, with a corner in my heart for punctuation as well; I fully expect to be, and quite soon now, the last living man who knows the difference between a colon and a semi-colon.

Architecture, philosophy, gadgets, darkness, coffee, argument, law, stationery, elections (as spectator, not candidate), clocks, newsprint, solitude – all these and more might well have made a chapter each, for every one of them ranks among my enthusiasms; it is a mercy I have only a mild taste for crossword puzzles and none for detective stories, and cannot abide the ballet. There is, of course, one other, very obvious, omission, but it is not for writing about: at any rate it is not for *me* to write about, though that must be a minority view, as rather more than half the world's novels and three-quarters of its poetry are on the subject.

On the other hand, there is its gentler cousin friendship, which is not a substitute for it but a different experience, though naturally a neighbouring and overlapping one. Certainly, it has been the greatest of all my enthusiasms, and although I have not devoted a chapter to it, I must discuss it here, for the story of my friendships is in effect the story of my life. As I indicate at several points in this book, however, my life did not begin at the beginning, least of all the part that friends have played in it.

To start with, I have always been suspicious of those

whose childhood friendships endure throughout their lives; true friendship is surely inseparable from maturity, for true friendship is a union of two fully-formed personalities, and of the deepest and most inward part of those personalities, too, and the child's unawakened heart, unrealized self, cannot rise to such occasions. I have found that those who make their friends in infancy and cleave to them thereafter are commonly those who are also apt to dwell in their school-days as the time of their greatest happiness, an even surer clue to emotional immaturity.

Or so I say, but it is probably all a rationalization, a salve for the remembered pain of childhood friendlessness. Certainly there were boys I would have called friends. There was a neighbour's son, of my own age, with whom I played when very young, but I cannot remember any shared adventures, worlds of childish fantasy constructed together, joint conclusions about the world and grownups, blood-brotherhood sworn or futures planned, and some such union of mind or purpose must be involved in even the least mature friendship. At school there was no one to whom I felt really close; I had no homosexual phase, and the nearest I ever got to friendship was through shared interests such as chess, which a group of us played incessantly, and, later – I now find myself amazed to write the word – bridge.

The bridge club had its headquarters in the air-raid shelters, its sessions during the Alert. Beneath the school ran a tunnel, which had previously been used only in wet weather, to enable the boys to get from their Houses to classroom, dining-hall or chapel. At the outbreak of war, which is when I went away to school, it was divided at intervals by sandbags, each section being big enough to hold a House of some fifty boys, together with staff. For a long time, before it was decided that the Luftwaffe had no designs upon the school (though its staring red brick must have been visible from Berlin, never mind from the sky above), everyone trooped down to the shelter as soon as the sirens sounded; moreover, at first no arrangements for study or lessons were made, and even when they were they were largely informal, undemanding and laxly supervised. We discovered bridge.

The standard-issue civilian gas mask came in a brown cardboard box, a cube some nine inches each way, suspended by a cord for carrying on the shoulder; the public were exhorted to carry it with them always, lest the lethal clouds expected to pour down upon the country at any moment should catch us unawares. I think carrying the gas mask may have been compulsory by law; in any case, I can remember that the King and Queen were invariably photographed with their gas masks in position, thus setting an example in this as in all matters. (The public being called upon, in the interests of conserving fuel stocks, to bathe in no more than five inches of hot water, it came to be known that the baths at Buckingham Palace had had a tide-line loyally painted round the inside, exactly five inches from the bottom.) For us, the idea of gas raids seemed strangely remote, though there were blankets suspended, rolled, from the roof of the tunnel at each end of each section, ready to be unfurled and soaked with water, this being supposed, according to the official instructions (largely indistinguishable from old wives' tales) to keep the gas out. But the outside of the cardboard gas mask containers made perfect scoring-pads for a surreptitious game of bridge, since all we had to do if disturbed by authority was to throw the cards under a seat and look innocent; nobody would think of examining the boxes for tell-tale figures. (Much later, it transpired that if poison gas had been used in raids on Britain the masks would have been useless anyway, and some poor souls went far towards proving the point by donning them and putting their heads in the oven, despite the fact that even the official instructions had emphasized from the start that they would be no use against coal gas.) We had thus discovered the only useful purpose of the standard-issue gas mask, though another was added later by my mother; she used to wear hers while peeling onions.

So I was part of a chess school and a bridge school, and

later of a play-reading circle and a band of amateur actors, and later still of a political coven and finally of a group which succeeded, without intending to (legend says to the contrary), in setting the place on fire. But in none of these collectives could I say that I made friends, though relations were friendly enough all round.

Things were not very different at the university, for by then I had acquired a shyness so paralysing that I would cross the road if I saw a fellow student, particularly one of the opposite sex, approaching, and it took the whole of the first year for me to break out of this absurd prison into the realization that there was a fundamental difference between school and university. But I was still very young indeed, and the emotional confusion that would have made enduring friendships unlikely was great enough to make even temporary ones slow to achieve. Some of my dearest friends today were among my college contemporaries, but with one exception – the first true love of my life – only became really close later, and perhaps that is largely true even of the exception, for it took time, and her marriage, to fashion new links, though for nearly thirty years now they have been links of gold and iron.

Very gradually, and even within the gradualness very slowly, I began to make real friends. To make a friend we must open our hearts, for me the hardest thing of most of my life, yet not to be escaped unless we want to live among acquaintances only. It must seem absurd, at least to those who have never had any difficulty in the matter, but there are people who fear friendship as inexplicably as a phobic (I am one of those too) dreads some harmless creature or condition. What fear of revealing, of vulnerability, of being human, grips us so fiercely, and above all why? What unhealing wound, struck by what act of unimaginable betrayal, bleeds afresh when a hand of a loving friend is held out? What is it that, down there in the darkness of the psyche, cries its silent No to the longing for Yes?

There are answers to these questions, of course, though

15

they are not to be discovered easily or quickly. But it is possible, and I have demonstrated as much in my own life, to make friends even before facing the truths about our difficulty in doing so. In the introduction to the first chrestomathy of my journalism, *Taking Sides*,★ I confessed that my friends had justice on their side when they complained that by reading me regularly they could find out everything about me except what was important, and that what was important was fenced off even from them. I added (and in a footnote, too!) words which now astonish me, though they were written in March 1979, hardly a lifetime ago:

> There is nothing here on the subject of friendship itself. But to discuss in public what has hitherto been the most important thing in my life is, I have found, quite impossible. I beg my friends' pardon, if not my readers'.

But surely the most important thing in our lives cannot be something to shut away in the attic like Mr Rochester's poor mad wife? Evidently it can; well, the attic door has creaked open at last, and no mad wives, or bogeymen, or unhappinesses, have come forth to harm me, and such pain as there has been has been the rare, precious kind, accepted gladly, that comes with healing.

Why there should ever have been a need for such healing I cannot imagine, for I believe that I am fortunate above most of mankind in the steadfastness of my friends. I have sorely tested their love at times; again and again, pain has caused me to retreat into the darkest lair of depression (and as anyone who has ever suffered from real depression – the 'black dog' – will know, that lair is dark indeed), where the sick soul's desire for solitude turns into misanthropy, with invitations refused, meetings cancelled, and outstretched hands spurned.

Shaw said of William Archer that he was a friend '. . . whom I was never sorry to see or unready to talk to'. If you

★ Cape, London, 1979

take that test literally – *never* sorry to see, *never* unready to talk to – I have absolutely no friends at all, and never have had. But that is a definition of depression and the withdrawal to which it leads, and my good fortune lies in the fact that as far as I know – and by now I know very far indeed – my friends are indeed never sorry to see me or unready to talk to me.

Besides, I am not depressed all the time, and for several years now have been hunted less and less often by the black dog. More to the point, it is apparent that my friends don't care; they have repeatedly made it plain that they would go on extending the hand of friendship even if I were to bite it off at the wrist, and indeed some of them are a finger or two short.

I said, of the passage I have quoted above, that I am now astonished at my earlier reluctance to discuss friendship. But I do not in the least wish to question the more important statement that I there made; friendship has been, and is, the most important thing in my life, and I do not think I am cheating when I say that I include *amitiés amoureuses*, if only because almost without exception the women with whom I have shared more than friendship have remained among my closest friends thereafter.

Measured against friendship, everything else dwindles. My work, in which I have had much success, as the world counts success; the causes, great and small, in which I have laboured; the varied passions I have chronicled in this book; as soon as the comparison is made, the answer is plain. What opera, what book, would I not see unwritten instead of a friend lost? What professional *réclame* (Dead Sea fruit anyway) can offer drink from a spring as fresh as that of friendship? What balmy evening when the world is still, what triumph of justice over wickedness, what lovely flower or tree, what mundane pleasure, however rarefied, what ambition, achievement or worldly power, what precious memento, what sack of gold, can be compared with that twinning of souls – for anything from an evening of food and laughter to a lifetime of shared experience – which surely, if any such mirror exists anywhere in the universe, reflects the universe's meaning and strengthens the certainty that it has one?

I remember a walk with a friend, after a quiet dinner, through the deserted streets of the City of London, talking of everything in the world; suddenly we caught sight of the hideous bulk of a new building unknown to us, and came simultaneously to the conclusion that the monstrous shadow ahead of us must be Hell Cathedral, only to discover on getting closer to it that we were right, and that we stood before the recently built and just opened Stock Exchange. There was nothing special about the evening – we had had many others like it – but it lingers in my memory, in an almost unbelievably rich gallery of such memories, as a few hours of happiness with a friend, in which hours the true nature of friendship, though not defined and indeed indefinable, stood revealed.

It stood revealed again in an evening spent trying to comfort a friend whose marriage was breaking up and who wanted someone to believe it was all his fault; in what followed a telephone conversation, in the small hours, with a friend who ended it convinced that I was near suicide and who drove through the streets of London at, as I afterwards learned, eighty miles an hour, ready and armed to batter down my door; in another late-night phone call from a friend who had already determined to take her own life, though she did not say so, and with whom I talked for two hours, altogether unaware of her intention, only to discover long afterwards that I had instinctively found the words to turn her thoughts lifewards; on a drive in Provence with two friends, after a gigantic meal, in which a tiny joke grew and grew and grew, until we were all three of us so infected with uncontrollable laughter that we were obliged to stop the car, get out and roll helplessly upon the verge; in a wholly unexpected encounter, in a Swiss museum, with a friend who shared with me a memory of another and very different visit to Switzerland fully thirty years before; in a day of rain and gloom when, on a long train journey to an uninviting destination, I suddenly realized that I was passing the home of a friend, and experienced a lifting of the spirits that drove away thoughts of the wretched weather and the boredom ahead; in an alfresco lunch beneath a lime tree in Austria when I exchanged with a friend confidences deeper and more startling, on both sides, than any we had previously shared; in a cry of welcome across a hotel foyer; in journeys shared with friends on foot, on wheels or in the air; in talk and argument with friends, in visiting the sickbeds of friends, in saying nothing to friends when no words are needed, in the farewell clasp of a friend's hand, and the no less affecting handshake that marks a meeting with a friend after a long absence; in a sound, a scent, a phrase that brings a friend to mind, and brings to mind at the same moment the knowledge that there is another human being, man or woman, near me or far away, in the past or in the present, whose soul is contiguous with mine. Surely St Paul would not begrudge me an emendation to help me convey my meaning and the depth of the lifelong gratitude that informs it:

> Friendship suffereth long, and is kind; friendship envieth not; friendship vaunteth not itself, is not puffed up, doth not behave itself unseemly, seeketh not her own, is not easily provoked, thinketh no evil; rejoiceth not in iniquity, but rejoiceth in the truth; beareth all things, believeth all things, hopeth all things, endureth all things.

One of the important qualities of enthusiasm is the desire to communicate it; indeed, it is a very good test of the strength of any enthusiasm, for who, enjoying in more than common measure something that is readily available, does not wish others to enjoy it too? It has been my aim throughout this book to try to convey what I feel for my enthusiasms; I realize, of course, that it is impossible, even impermissible, to proselytize – if it were not, balletomane friends would long ago have converted me. But there is an important clue there; although I remain entirely untouched by the ballet, I am by no means indifferent to the enthusiasm others have for it, for enthusiasm itself can be enjoyed at second hand, which is why I can even listen to enthusiastic and knowledgeable golfers talking about their passion, though I think I would rather spend a week at the ballet than try to share it.

I hope, therefore, that no one who lacks enthusiasm for, say, music or walking, painting or cities, will feel excluded from the chapters on those subjects; it has been my purpose to try to convey my enthusiasm, not to lecture my readers or to provide them with useful knowledge or instruction. It follows, or should, that those who have ever experienced enthusiasm for anything will recognize the feeling in my pages, even if their list hardly overlaps mine at all. As for those who have never been enthusiastic, I am sorry for them, but at least I shall not have to feel guilty also, for they will hardly be inclined to buy a book with the title of this one.

Two

Books were my first friends; for a long time my only friends, apart from a teddy bear called Onjie (that being the nearest my infant tongue could get to his colour, a vivid orange). I can remember almost nothing at all of my life at first hand – that is, without the help of the family stories I have heard until the memories of the events they depict have become my own – from before I was about nine years old; even Onjie is there only because he survived long past that point. This absence of memories from early childhood is, I have learned, unusual; there is a reason for it, of course, and a fairly obvious one. I was certainly not the first child to flee from traumatic and incomprehensible events around him, and to blot out the events themselves while fleeing. Nor was I unique in choosing to escape into books, though I have spent most of my life slowly discovering, with pain, amazement and ultimately joy, that there can be human friends, too, who never fail us. But it is to those first, vanished, years that I owe what Gibbon called 'my early and invincible love of reading', and like him, I would not exchange that love for the treasures of India.

There is another, stranger, debt that I think I owe to my infancy also. When the mists of that self-imposed amnesia lift, I find myself possessed, for as long as I *can* remember, of a freak memory, which must be analogous in my case to the sharpening of the remaining senses in one who has become blind or deaf. Given the right cross-reference, I can recite whole pages of books I have not opened for thirty years, and I have sometimes astonished and alarmed my friends by quoting remarks of theirs that go back decades.

21

I turned this trick to good account early on. One of the minor punishments, for minor transgressions, at my public school, was to be set to learn by heart a passage of poetry. For most of my fellow-sinners this was a labour of agony, to which they would have much preferred chastisement with whips and scorpions; for me, however, it was a ludicrously light burden – a fact which I had just enough sense to keep to myself. Ordered to learn, within a fixed time-limit (usually a couple of days), Wordsworth's 'On Westminster Bridge' or John of Gaunt's apostrophe to England, I would compose my features in a suitably doleful expression and retire as soon as possible to a remote hedge or haystack, accompanied by the allotted task and *The Hotspur*, knowing that I could accomplish the former in ten minutes and wallow in the latter for an hour or more. Only much later did I realize that my head was in consequence stuffed with the poetic treasures of India; it still is.

When the trigger that fires off memory is that of the most evocative of the senses, smell, my feats of memory astonish even me. There is one scent that I have not come across for many years now – not surprisingly, for it is that of a 'mantle', the glowing pipeclay lattice which surrounds a burning gas-jet to give light, and I have not been in a house lit by gas for a long time. But when my nose stumbles across a scent close enough to the gas mantle for it to unlock the same door (the striking of a safety match will do) the entire scene of my gaslit childhood home is reproduced in my mind's eye with such profusion of detail that I yearn for a magic camera that can photograph memories.

I have just struck the match, and the picture is before me as though I had walked into a darkened room and switched the light on. I can see the exact pattern, red and blue dentils, of the linoleum; the furniture, including the Windsor chairs which, the collective family memory has told me, I once beat all over with a hammer when my mother was out, so that they were ever afterwards pitted with dents; the heavy sideboard with its fringed 'runner', and the massive bronze pestle and mortar standing on it beside the samovar, these being the only physical possessions my maternal grandparents had brought with them on the long trek from the pogroms of late nineteenth-century Russia; the view from the window – not much of a view in those rows of back-to-backs; and, high up on the wall, the gas burning with a gentle sizzling sound in its little cage. (I have often promised myself that when I am a millionaire I shall have a room in my house lit by gas, regardless of expense – including, presumably, the cost of hiring a craftsman to reproduce the apparatus – just so that I can have the pleasurable smell whenever I want it. I also plan to be followed about the streets by a man pushing a hurdy-gurdy, which will play the hurdy-gurdy tune from *Petrushka* over and over again.)

There are never any human figures in the childhood scenes thus conjured into being by the appropriate scent, at any rate until I make a conscious effort to summon them up, though there is always a cat; indeed, nothing at all is actually happening, and certainly I can never see myself. But I can see very clearly the battered armchair in which I used to settle myself with a book, and find oblivion.

The cat is Tim, a handsome Persian of whom I have written elsewhere; he is the first cat I can remember, though not the first cat in my life, for there is another family story, from well before Tim, that on a hot summer's day with the windows open, in the room with the pitted chairs, I was whirling a towel round my head and caught the cat, sunning itself on the window sill, a glancing blow, causing it to fall three storeys to the ground. It survived the experience, I learned, but got into the habit of sitting on the stairs and spitting at me as I went past on my way to bed.

There was much more to Tim than I have hitherto related. He was a long-haired Persian; at least, most of him was, but I think there are no authentic tabby Persians, and Tim had the traditional tabby markings, though not the customary white patch on the chest. He had the Persians' broad forehead, but not their perpetual cross look; on the contrary, he exuded a

23

remarkable benignity, clearly the fruits of a settled wisdom that had tested the world, with all its other creatures, and decided that it was worth making the best of.

That sounds like sentimental anthropomorphism, but I do not feel it like that; I have loved many cats, and Tim most deeply, but I respected them before I loved them, and have never thought of them as four-legged human beings, or believed that they are on earth to amuse us, or that they see the world through our eyes, or think in our categories. Certainly I have never addressed a cat I know by anything but its name, or a stranger cat as anything but 'Cat'. Perhaps that sounds even more whimsical, and I cannot prove that it is not, but if I think back to my feelings for Tim or any of the other cats in my life, it is true affection I relive, not amusement.

It is not difficult for me to guess why I acquired so early a love of cats. Cats will let us love them, in fact they plainly wish us to, but they will not love us in return, though many of us delude ourselves that they do. On the other hand, they do not pretend to reciprocate our feelings, they make no promises that they cannot or will not keep, and they swear no empty vows; better so, much better.

I never saw Tim hurry; nobody did, even when he was catching mice, though long before he died he had given up trying to do so. It was not that he was a lazy cat; I think he had come to the conclusion that the mice had just as much right to live as he had, and since he bore them no enmity and was always far too fastidious to eat one, he could see no point in stretching out a soft, liquid paw to bring it down on a struggling back. I do believe that Tim had a soul, and though I know that that is heresy to the Christians I can think of no other explanation for his truly noble nature. His bearing was proud but gentle; I remember as a child putting my knuckle to his mouth to feel his warm breath, and despite the fact that he normally eschewed any form of demonstrative affection, he licked my finger slowly, so that I felt for the first time that curious roughness that all cats' tongues have. He would never play in the ordinary sense; a dangling ball on the end of a string he ignored, and though he would occasionally go after a marble rolled across the floor he would not, having retrieved it, repeat the action as soon as he realized it was only a game. Nor would he ever beg; it was beneath his dignity, and besides, his wants were few.

Tim was the only cat I have ever known who understood what a mirror was. In my grandfather's shop there was a full-length mirror, too big and heavy to hang or even fix, so it stood against the wall, its base a few inches out from the wainscot. Tim's successors, like all other cats I have ever seen before a mirror, were perplexed; they either failed to see their reflection or, seeing it, would think it was another cat, and, after putting out an exploratory paw, would run round behind the mirror, into the space made by the angle at which it leaned against the wall. Tim was plainly aware that it was his own self that he saw in it, but he lacked all vanity; he was obviously aware of his own fineness – his carriage proved as much – but did not need to have it confirmed; it is generally only the man or woman who lacks confidence who needs to bolster it by constantly looking in the mirror, and doubtless the same applies to cats. Tim lived to a great age.

What is it that I love about cats? Whatever it is, it is something both deep and strong, because apart from those overbred pedigree types, which have become toys rather than living creatures, I have never met a cat I could not warm to. People talk of the independence of cats, their pride, their self-sufficiency, their fastidiousness; I talk of these things, too, and I am sure they are valid. But I do not think that is why I love cats, any more than I think I do so because of their obvious kinship, seen even in the tiniest kitten, to the greatest cats of the jungle, and in particular the tiger. Nor is it their extraordinarily ancient lineage and the way that they have never allowed themselves to forget it, as we can see every time a cat goes to sleep in our presence, first making those obligatory turns which once flattened the grass of the primeval jungle to clear a space for its ancestors. Nor is it even their

25

mysteriousness, which can also be found in some men and women with a secret, who will not tell it but who wish others to know that they have it. I am not in the least surprised that at different times and in different cultures cats have been worshipped; it is quite possible that the secret they guard so effortlessly is the secret of the universe, and although I think it would be going too far to say that cats are divine, they could easily be messengers from whatever is.

But I do not worship cats; I love them. My feeling for them is a very sensual one; it is not just the pleasure of stroking a sleek coat, for I do not take great pleasure in doing so, and rarely stroke a cat except to allay its suspicions of me (though I knew a Russian Blue which I would always stroke when I met it, because its close-packed fur, the badge of all its tribe, made it feel like a Chinese carpet), but I find the whole creature – its litheness, softness, warmth, facial shape – physically attractive. When a cat puts its paws down on a surface it is not quite sure of, the pad of the paw bends at right angles to the leg, very slowly, an action which seems to sum up the appealing quality of the beasts, perhaps even more than that gesture which a cat will only do for someone it knows very well and trusts absolutely, the infinitely gentle pat on the cheek from a paw. Sometimes I pick up a cat without making quite clear that I mean no harm, and it will bring out its claws; I love to provide the assurance the cat wants, perhaps by tickling it beneath the chin, and to feel those fearsome weapons slide back into their sheaths. That tickling under the chin is clearly something very powerfully pleasurable for cats, for they will stretch and wriggle, to experience it, in an almost overtly sexual manner, though I never heard tell that a cat's chin is a feline erogenous zone.

I can watch a cat for hours, even if it is sleeping. There is no doubt, incidentally, that cats dream; often I have seen them twitch and stir in their sleep, and even cry out, though the imagination which could guess at the nature of a cat's dreams would be vivid indeed. They are not necessarily carnivores, despite their greater relatives; I have known vegetarian cats. But I have never known a boring cat, though practically all dogs are bores and few other animals are positively interesting; the monkey's depths of character have been vastly exaggerated, probably out of self-protection by human beings who know its consanguinity and feel uneasily that we had better stick together.

I love the feel of cats, from the firm skull between the firm ears to the undulating tail with its amazing strength and versatility. I love their freedom from treachery; a creature which makes clear that it will pledge no permanent loyalty cannot be accused of breaking its vows, and there is nothing in the history of cats to match those dogs which, after years of fidelity, without warning turn and rend their owners. I love their intelligence and their waywardness, their persistence and their willingness to abandon it if it should prove fruitless (who ever heard of an obstinate cat?). I love their eyes, the most beautiful eyes in the animal kingdom, with their rainbow of flecks among the colour, and the extraordinary expanding iris, their agility (it is nothing for a cat to high-jump a distance five times its length), even their voice, thought not, I own, raised in sexual ecstasy on a nearby roof. But above all, perhaps, I love the detachment of cats, their willingness to be loved but not to respond beyond a certain very clearly defined point; no cat ever gave its entire heart to any human being. There is no danger in loving cats, even in loving one particular cat.

I suppose we all tend to remember only the happiness from our childhood, as a sundial refuses to tell the time except in fine weather; the subconscious banishing of entire years would then be only an extension of this practice. Later, of course, we are more likely to recall those episodes of our adult lives so well described by James Thurber as 'the kind of thing that makes us pull the bedclothes up over our heads at three o'clock in the morning and *scream*'; but perhaps all children, through some protective evolutionary process, filter out the bad times. However that may be, when I get, in my conjured visions of that unpeopled room, to the armchair and the reading I did in it, my memory is suffused with pleasure alone.

Of the children's books I must have read, indeed from which I must have learned to read, I can remember only those which remained on the shelves, as Onjie in the toy cupboard, past their time. There was a book, for instance, about a bird called the Nutatall, whose cry was 'Oh, Nutatall' (I didn't see the joke); there were Hugh Lofting's colourfully imaginative tales of Dr Dolittle; there was a series about a little bear called Mary Plane, who was much given to telling strangers that she came from the bear pits of Bern; the first time I travelled abroad, at the age of eighteen, I went to Switzerland, with my sister, and startled the tour guide by demanding to be shown the bear pits. (He said they were too far from the centre of the city; perhaps they only existed in the books, and the guide wanted a convenient answer to an impossible question.) Beatrix Potter I had never so much as heard of before I was in my twenties, and even then I got her inextricably confused with Beatrice Webb (née Potter) and was convinced that that gaunt and dreadful virago (whom today I have a tendency to confuse with Virginia Woolf) was given in her spare time to composing the gentle and beautiful stories that I discovered only when, weekending in the country, I faced the peremptory demands of my friends' children to read them a bedtime story.

I became an Arkub early. The only newspaper in my home was the *News Chronicle*, which had a strip cartoon about a Mr and Mrs Noah and their family; young readers were invited to join a kind of fan club, receiving a badge, which I think said 'I am an Arkub', and a codebook, by the use of which it was possible to communicate with fellow Arkubs in messages unintelligible to those not in the secret. But the Noah family became dear and intimate friends; I spent countless happy hours in their company (there was a Christmas annual of their further adventures every year), and can call the roll to this day. They had, naturally, three sons, called Ham, Shem and Japhet, though only Japhet played any significant part, his allotted role being much the same as that of Richmal Crompton's William – the infant scapegrace who is always precipitating disaster, sometimes innocently, sometimes less so. There was also a daughter, Selina, and a variety of animals, including a bear called Happy, a tortoise called Oswald, and a creature rather like a giant squirrel which was supposed to be a ring-tailed malagazook, and answered to the name of Muriel. The whole family, animals and all, would go on holiday to an African country, Andamalumbo, where the ruler was a friend of theirs, and where the staple fruit was the colobosh, which grew, naturally enough, on the colobosh tree.

When I went away to school, at the age of eleven, my contemporaries were all reading Arthur Ransome. I tried *Swallows and Amazons*, but could make nothing of it at all; the milieu was more foreign to me than the colobosh groves of Andamalumbo. The very props and scenery meant nothing to me; I had never before set eyes on a boat, a blackberry or a sheep, or for that matter a horse that was not between the shafts. But by that time I was deep in other worlds of my own. I was reading Baroness Orczy (identifying with Chauvelin, not Sir Percy) and Stanley J. Weyman ('Who touches my brother touches Tavannes!'), *The Three Musketeers* and its sequels (I invariably appointed myself Aramis), *Treasure Island*, *Jock of the Bushveldt* and *Black Beauty*, Harrison Ainsworth's *The Tower of London* (my favourite character was Xit, the dwarf), and a dreadful thing by W. J. Locke called *The Joyous Adventures of Aristide Pujol*. Not that I knew it was dreadful then, but years later I found it again in the sixpenny tray outside a second-hand bookseller's, and bore it home to help me to conjure up my youth. I read a few chapters with growing horror before flinging it aside, appalled at what must have been the sickening sentimentality of my early taste.

We all know the disappointment, one of the most piercing that life holds (a considerable claim, now I come to think of it), of these renewed encounters with the past, whether remembering a childhood scene as beautiful and romantic, only to find that the distance of time has lent a spurious enchantment to the view, or in the even more familiar form of a huge house that has shrunk to a tiny cottage; my own most striking memory of this particular phenomenon concerns the tea shop in the town near my school, to which I would repair on half-holidays. It was called The Copper Kettle, and the tea room was on the first floor; I would sit in the window and look down on the scene in the street below. But not so far below as I thought; years, many years, after leaving the school I found myself in the town, and sought out The Copper Kettle, only to find that standing on the pavement outside I could easily touch the very window that had been my lofty vantage-point.

Of all these ghosts, the worst for me is the book that turns out to be nothing like the masterpiece I thought it. Why should I find this common and trivial experience so desolating? It cannot be only that I am made uneasy by the revelation of my faulty judgment, for I have no such unease at finding I have come to despise music, or even people, I once admired. I can only conclude that because I relied on books to provide an immovable signpost, a chair that would never be pulled away from me as I sat down, I found it unbearable, and still do, to discover that a book has betrayed me. ('Panic and emptiness! Panic and emptiness! Even the flaming ramparts of the world might fall.')

The worst of these experiences was my rereading of *The Story of San Michele*. It is very much a book for adolescents, and it was as an adolescent that I read it and was transfixed. The appalling false romanticism of it escaped me, so hungry was I for romanticism in any form, as did (though this was less culpable) the obvious implausibility of most of it. So did the fact that it is covered deep in clichés, of thought and attitude as well as of language. All I could see was the dazzling sophistication, the exciting adventures, the gentle, noble character that Munthe took pains to give himself, the beautiful women, the medical lore, the names carefully dropped, the invocation of St Francis and the Emperor Tiberius, the love of animals and birds, which was his version of the search for a love that could never be betrayed.

I read *The Story of San Michele* until it fell to pieces in my hands, and until I knew great chunks of it by heart. Then, growing up, I stopped reading it, and did not return to it for nearly twenty years, when I had a shock from which I feared I would never recover; certainly it was a long time before I dared to pick up any other book that I had enjoyed and been deeply stirred by many years before.

When I did, I was reassured, for it was *The Man Who Was Thursday*. (I have always believed that Chesterton thought of that title suddenly one day, *à propos* nothing at all, and then devised a plot that would enable him to use it.) Chesterton was also for adolescents – he clearly never ceased being one himself – but the romanticism of his novels, particularly *The Napoleon of Notting Hill*, is of the true kind, and it can safely be approached by a reader who has outgrown not only adolescence but romanticism itself. I read huge quantities of Chesterton, and Belloc too, as an adolescent; Kipling also, though the poetry rather than the prose, and Peacock, without realizing that most of his characters are portraits of real people; Karel Čapek; *The Good Soldier Schweik*; M. R. James (another hideous disappointment later, for although the plots remain powerful and the horror consequently likewise, the style is flat, worn and tired), the Kai Lung stories of Ernest Bramah, of which I committed whole volumes to memory, *Don Quixote*, Max Beerbohm, Shakespeare and Dickens.

All nourishing fare for a growing boy; but who provided the bridge between such real writers and the blood and thunder of my earlier childhood? What was my *first* adult reading?

I can remember the author; I can remember the book; I can remember the effect on me of its famous first sentence, which is not altogether surprising, because the effect was that of

31

what I supposed electrocution would feel like, and I knew, instantly and without doubt, that I had finished with *The Hotspur* for ever.

'Call me Ishmael.' I know of no novel in English with a more arresting first sentence; any reader with an imagination capable of being caught at all is at once harpooned. I have no idea what prompted me to pick it up; certainly it was not love of the sea. Indeed, I had hardly seen waves in my life; there was an occasional holiday at Southend, and an experience so horrible that to this day I am by no means certain that it was not a nightmare. If it happened, the scene was a convalescent home, I think at Worthing, to which I had been sent after a childhood illness of more than usual severity; it was the only serious illness of my childhood, and almost the only one of my entire life. The weather was bitterly cold, the beach of pebbles, not sand, the people in charge remote as monsters, the other children terrifying in their differentness, the purpose of my being thus thrust from my home utterly incomprehensible to me. (To this day, I have no liking for any seashore, and when I find myself on one the only thing I wish to do is hurl pebbles at the sea, perhaps in some unassuageable yearning for revenge.)

I knew nothing, then, of the sea, and although I must have known what a whale was, I certainly did not know that they were fished for, like plaice. Nor did I know who Ishmael was; I found out only much later where Melville had found the name, and why he used it, though I am sure that if I had known when I first read it I would have identified with the narrator even more closely than I did. And I had no idea that I would come to believe that I had in my hands the greatest novel written in English in the nineteenth century, outtopping Dickens, Jane Austen, the Brontës, *Middlemarch* itself. Least of all did I know that I had stumbled upon one of the most powerful and lasting enthusiasms of my life. No, two; for *Moby-Dick* not only established itself, within half a dozen chapters, as a book destined to be close to my heart ever afterwards, but also fixed – 'fixed' in the photographic sense, as an image that would otherwise fade is made permanent – the love of reading that had first stirred in me, in the armchair of my childhood home, as a search for something permanent in a world of quicksand.

To the literate, illiteracy is one of the strangest conditions imaginable; to me, since I obviously cannot remember a time before I could read fluently, it is so strange that it induces something very like fear. My grandmother never learnt to read or write in any language, and my grandfather read English only with the greatest difficulty, and could hardly write it at all; their condition struck me, and still does in recollection, as a kind of deformity, with the disturbing feeling that deformity always gives us at first. I used to read to them.

Much more shocking was an experience from my adolescence; I was walking along the street when a man, quite young and looking in no way odd, stepped out from behind a telephone box and said abruptly, 'Can you read?' I assumed that he was being sarcastic, and that I must have walked past a sign saying 'Private', but when I told him cautiously that I could read, he said that he couldn't; then he pulled a letter from his pocket and asked me to read it to him.

The episode was already bizarre enough, but it now became much more so, because the letter was from a man who was accusing the recipient, in exceptionally direct and vivid terms, of making free with his wife. Every few lines I stopped and asked whether he was sure he wanted me to continue, so intimately personal was the message he was thus confiding to a stranger, but each time he insisted that I press on; possibly he thought that someone casually met, and young, would be a less embarrassing confidant than a friend or neighbour. So disturbing did I find this experience that when I had finished and walked on, I felt the necessity of devising a fantasy to rob it of its unpleasant quality; I decided that the man could read perfectly well, but that he was afraid that the letter writer was going to murder him, and that my evidence would at any rate help to convict his killer. A friend to whom I told this story not long ago suggested that the man may have been not illiterate but dyslexic, at that time a condition virtually unknown. But by then the incident had sunk so deeply into me in the form I have described that I was unable to readjust it in the light of this persuasive explanation, and the effect it had had on me was only secondarily due to the nature of the letter; much stronger was the realization that here was a grown man, not mad or blind or foreign, who *could not read*.

'Call me Ishmael'; still it echoes in my head. *I* could read, and still can, and I cannot imagine any deprivation – of music, health, freedom – more terrible than not being able to. The eighteenth century spent much time debating whether a man blind from birth, who had learned to distinguish among a cube, a sphere and a pyramid by touch alone, could, if his sight were miraculously restored, tell the difference by the use of his new-found eyes alone. Then the thing happened; a man who had been blind from birth did gain his sight, and the answer was no. But the point of the story, for me, is that in the article in which I read of the matter, the author stated that a good deal more is now known about the subject, and scientists have been able to study a considerable number of cases in which people blind from birth have later acquired the ability to see; of these, none who remained blind until fully adult has ever learned to read afterwards. There is an irony and cruelty here that would have shocked de Maupassant even as he embarked on a short story incorporating it.

'Call me Ishmael'; there it goes again, like a great gong beating to signal the start of some mighty enterprise. For me it was a mighty enterprise indeed, and I bless the mighty whale who began it. Well I might, too, for the enterprise was my love of reading, and the pleasure I take in it. The pleasures of reading are innocent, inexhaustible, incomparable, incorruptible, incalculable and infinite, and no one who can read at all is shut out from enjoying them. Age, frailty, poverty, ignorance, isolation, pain, fear – these will inhibit almost any pleasure in time, and immediately place an insurmountable barrier before some of them. But the pleasures of reading are not to be denied by any or all of these handicaps and hamperings; and even for the blind there is Braille. (Of all the complaints I have ever had from my readers about the excessive length of my sentences, only one has caused me to wonder whether I could, by an effort of will, change my style, and whether, if I could, I should. It was from a man whose wife was blind, and to whom he would read my articles. It was impossible, he said, to speak one of my very long sentences, as opposed to taking it in through the eye, without the sense of the beginning being lost before the end.)

Some years ago, a Glasgow man was convicted of terrible crimes of violence, including murder; when the case was over, and sentence passed, there were the usual articles in the newspapers about his life and background. One episode in it haunts me still. He was the youngest of several brothers; the others, along with most of the rest of the family, were all criminals already, but there was a spark in him that would not be quenched, and he had determined somehow that he would be educated and drag himself clear of the mire of his surroundings. One night, his brothers came home from some criminal enterprise and found him doing his school homework. They simply threw his books on the fire, and from that day forth his fate was certain. I sometimes think that was the wickedest action I have ever heard of, and not only because they made him a criminal.

There are societies for the prevention of cruelty to children, and to animals. There ought also to be a society dedicated to stamping out cruelty to books. 'The burning of the books'; that phrase surely sounds knells in any civilized ear. The Nazis burned the works of Jews and other authors of whom they ideologically disapproved, but even more dreadful, it seems to me, was the action of the Khmer Rouge in Cambodia, at the start of their insane destruction of their country (including, in the end, the physical destruction of something like one-seventh of the entire population); in the

35

sack of Phnom Penh which marked the beginning of their holocaust they burned every example of the printed word that they could lay their hands on, from ancient Buddhist scriptures to hospital record-cards. It is much worse to burn a human being than to burn a book, but the Nazis and the Communists burned both extensively, for one who will burn the former has already dehumanized himself sufficiently to make burning the latter possible. Even the destruction of the great library at Alexandria, which was fired by accident, casts a chill.

I do not find any of this surprising. My own love of books begins long before I start to read them. First of all, I am an incurable book-sniffer; when I open a new book I at once savour its scent, and I have had some odd looks from bookshop assistants in consequence, particularly since the next thing I do is to run my fingertips over the pages, for the sensuous pleasure to be had from touching fine book-paper is not to be underestimated. There is pleasure also to be derived from crackling a crisp page between finger and thumb; the Nonesuch Dickens, without doubt the most beautiful edition of his works ever published, has the additional advantage of being printed on paper that gives this satisfaction most intensely, and so does its baby sister, the four-volume Nonesuch Shakespeare (postwar successor to the even nobler seven-volume set), which is printed on a lovely yellow-tinged India paper.

Books, though, must never be objects, and I say that with an emphasis added from a time when to me they were the most important living beings. I cannot remember ever having bought a book for any reason other than a desire to acquaint myself with its contents; I am quite unable to understand what motivates those who collect bindings, or fore-edge paintings, or – oddest of all – first editions; such book-buyers can scarcely be said to understand what a book is. There was a book in the strongroom of the *Titanic*, made to the specifications of an American millionaire; its binding was 'thick inlaid with patines of bright gold', and studded with rubies and other precious stones. It was said to have been valued at a million dollars, which in 1912 must have been a stupendous fortune. If it turned out that God had struck down the ship for such an act of *lèse-livre*, I would not be at all surprised. In the beginning *was* the word.

'Call me Ishmael.' Conrad, asked to write an introduction to *Moby-Dick* for a World's Classics edition, would have none of it, calling the book 'a rather strained rhapsody with whaling for a subject and not a single sincere line in the three volumes of it'. I am quite unable to read Conrad; I cannot keep my attention from wandering for more than three pages (even with Proust I have often reached page 70 of the first volume before deciding that a brisk walk round the block would do me no end of good, though it is true that I have never resumed the book on returning). But at least I admit that the fault is in me, not in Conrad. I also admit, however, that I see his point about *Moby-Dick* before rejecting it.

In the first place, you do not have to be a particularly penetrating literary critic to notice that the style is steeped, soaked, *pickled* in the influence of Carlyle. I don't think anybody reads Carlyle today – I would not be at all surprised to learn that not even *The French Revolution* is in print – and most people never could, though him, too, I lapped up when I was young (at first I thought *he* must have got his style from Melville), starting with *Sartor Resartus*. But this passage, fully characteristic of *Moby-Dick*, though the influence of Carlyle is obvious, is without doubt by a man who is his own master, and owes nothing of his genius to anyone else:

> If, then, to meanest mariners, and renegades and cast-aways, I shall hereafter ascribe high qualities, though dark; weave round them tragic graces; if even the most mournful, perchance the most abased, among them all, shall at times lift himself to the exalted mounts; if I shall touch that workman's arm with some ethereal light; if I shall spread a rainbow over his disastrous set of sun; then against all mortal critics bear me out in it, thou just Spirit of Equality,

which has spread one royal mantle of humanity over all my kind! Bear me out in it, thou great democratic God! who did not refuse to the swart convict, Bunyan, the pale, poetic pearl; Thou who didst clothe with doubly hammered leaves of fine gold, the stumped and paupered arm of old Cervantes; Thou who didst pick up Andrew Jackson from the pebbles; who didst hurl him upon a war-horse; who didst thunder him higher than a throne! Thou who, in all Thy mighty, earthly marchings, ever cullest Thy selectest champions from the kingly commons; bear me out in it, O God!

There is a great, noble pity in that paragraph, for all its luridness. Indeed, there is the same feeling throughout *Moby-Dick*; Ishmael pities everyone and everything in the book, and Melville pities him. There is pity for Ahab and his mad, implacable hatred, pursued by the whale even as he is pursuing it (for surely the Leviathan represents for Melville what the Hound of Heaven – 'Lo, all things fly thee, for thou fliest Me!' – meant to Francis Thompson); pity for the leg that the whale tore from Ahab's body; pity for the *Rachel*'s captain and his lost children (it is the *Rachel*, remember, which picks up the sole survivor of Ahab's ruin, though Ahab refused all pity and succour for her captain and his castaways); pity for the whales themselves, a pity which rises to the full height of love even as the hunters close in for the kill; for the ship, as doomed as its mariners; for poor Pip, who loses his senses when he thinks he has been left to drown; for the one figure who hardly needs it, Queequeg ('better a sober cannibal than a drunken Christian'), the gentle black savage who is to die in the savage quest of a white man for a white whale; for Moby-Dick, who rejects it; pity at last for Ishmael himself, the only figure who escapes a disaster as incomprehensible as the Flood.

Was that what I responded to, adrift at the age of twelve or thereabouts on an ocean as unintelligible as the one through which Moby-Dick voyages eternally? Not the pity, perhaps, so much as the eternal voyage; again and again, I have found throughout my life that the books I love best are the ones which wander for ever through strange seas, seas of thought and feeling, of impulses followed and digressions encouraged, of conclusions postponed and certainties doubted, of a sense that possibilities are limitless, of a belief that though happiness is unattainable, it is not illusory. Why else do I love Montaigne above all other authors in any language, if not because he breathes this spirit with every word he speaks to me?

Emerson said that Montaigne makes you feel that you must have known him, or even *been* him, in a previous existence. It is so; the extraordinary question he provokes in the reader, again and again, is: how does he know so much about me? This is the other side of the Shakespearean coin; with Shakespeare, we are amazed that we already know so much about his characters even before they walk on to the stage. But Montaigne, who has the quietest voice in all genius, not only knows us, but knows us so well that he tells us things about ourselves that we did not know before. How does he do it?

He does it by telling us about himself; in his preface, he warns us that his book is about nothing else, and concludes 'there is no reason why you should spend your leisure on so frivolous and vain a subject'. And in a sense, he is right; there is no *reason* for us to do so, and it could be said that reading him is, literally, a waste of time. But I think that there has never been, in all human history, such a garden of a mind to walk in when the eve is cool, a garden of flowers familiar and exotic, of arbours and grottoes and hedges topiarized into friendly beasts, paths that wander with aimless certainty, fountains turning drops of water to gleaming jewels in the sun. It has been argued that Shakespeare based Hamlet on him after reading the John Florio translation of the *Essays* (but it has been argued, and very recently, too, that Florio wrote the entire works of Shakespeare), and the claim makes some sense (the Hamlet claim, that is, not the authorship one), because the reflective, self-doubting side of Hamlet does suggest much of Montaigne's incomparable self-portrait.

Surely the reason we keep meeting ourselves in the garden of Montaigne's mind is that he is the most human of authors, with a candour about himself that reminds us of Pepys without the private parts or Rousseau without the nastiness and megalomania; he shows us all his foibles, weaknesses, fears, hesitations, and lo! they resemble our own. He also shows us all his courage, tolerance, wisdom, understanding, goodness, and lo! although these do not resemble our qualities at all, we conclude that if he has got half of us right, he must have got the other half right, too; it is a curious fact, which every lover of Montaigne will confirm, that the reader invariably finishes his book not just thinking better of himself but quite genuinely determined to *be* better. Nor is it difficult to explain that, either; Montaigne's humanity is so complete that – unlike, say, Socrates, whom we can only admire, not hope to emulate – we feel that if he, with all his weaknesses, can encompass such strengths, then we who share the weaknesses can in time come to manage the strengths.

Besides, he wanders, and I will trust an author who wanders much more readily than one who keeps to the point. I think I fell irrevocably in love with Montaigne when I found him pausing in one of the wisest and most profound discussions of death any mortal has ever carried on to reveal that sometimes, though not invariably, radishes give him indigestion.

We do not know Montaigne's last words, but I will wager that they did not take the form of an epitaph or a lapidary inscription. He was never sententious in his life, and he would not have treated death with any more respect than was due to it. How could he? Did he not say, 'We must always have our boots on, and be ready to leave'? Assuredly, he at least was always ready to leave, and if, in leaving, he had looked back, it would have been without vain regrets for the years denied him, but with an amused gratitude for the years he had been given. (He died at fifty-nine, seven years older than Shakespeare. Everybody knows, incidentally, that Shakespeare died on his own birthday, but in doing so he played another trick, almost as neat; April 23rd, 1616, was also the day of Cervantes' death.) Anyway, Montaigne had already announced how he wanted Death to find him; planting cabbages and not being terribly interested in the task. Surely Death would not have been so churlish as to refuse so modest a request?

I have dwelt upon Montaigne because it seems to me that in him the pleasure of reading is not only at its most intense but at its most characteristic. Every page of him we turn makes us want to turn two more; we drink him in – drink, not eat, lest we think of chewing, and Montaigne slips down like the smoothest of old wine – because he is so *readable*. The source of pleasure in reading – the readability, that is, of an author – is to be found in certain qualities of which Montaigne has more than any other writer, and the surest clue to these qualities is the feeling we get when we meet such a writer, dead for centuries perhaps, and recognize him at once as a friend. But how do we recognize a friend? By seeing before us an open heart, and by trusting him, and ourselves, enough to enter into it. There are writers with closed hearts; this does not mean that we cannot read them, or derive profit from them – their books, after all, may teach us something we are glad to learn, may make us laugh or cry, may inspire us to faith or noble deeds – but I think it means that they cannot give us the highest pleasure of reading, for they do not offer us the love of a friend.

A fanatic cannot offer us that love; nor can a cynic or a judge, a formalist or a poseur, a maker of systems, a dogmatist, a codifier. Whatever else they may offer, who could derive *pleasure* from reading Calvin or Hegel, an Act of Parliament or Gray's *Anatomy*, Lenin or an advertisement, Hooker's *Ecclesiastical Polity* or Chesterfield's *Letters*? (The only thing anybody today knows about Chesterfield's book is that Johnson said of it that it taught the manners of a dancing-master and the morals of a whore, and it must be a century since anybody read it to find out whether Johnson was right.)

The authors from whom I derive most pleasure incline in temperament to the Montaignesque end of the spectrum; no two men will have the same list of loves among authors, for no two men are the same man (show me your library, and I will undertake to tell your character then and there, without further acquaintance), but I find it difficult to believe that a reader who derived no pleasure from *any* of the writers on my list could take pleasure in reading at all, or in anything else for that matter.

I love Herodotus more than Thucydides, Donne more than Keats; Pepys more than Clarendon, Aubrey's *Brief Lives* more than Foxe's *Book of Martyrs*; Molière rather than Racine (anyone, even Corneille, rather than Racine); Erasmus before Luther, the Shaw of *Arms and the Man* and *You Never Can Tell* before the Shaw of *Man and Superman* and *The Doctor's Dilemma*; Chekhov, not Ibsen, Pliny and Gilbert White, not Newton or Buffon; Ben Jonson, not Congreve, Parson Kilvert, not Parson Woodforde, Balzac, not Flaubert, Disraeli, not Thackeray; Hazlitt's *Essays* and Cobbett's *Rural Rides*; Pushkin, Cervantes, Xenophon, Dostoievsky, the King James Bible, the Goncourts, Ovid, Catullus, Thomas Mann, Gibbon, Aristophanes, Rebecca West, Pascal, Defoe, Homer, Lucretius, Villon, Schiller, O'Casey, Plutarch, Rabelais, Rabelais and again Rabelais ('I have nothing, I owe much, the rest I leave to the poor'), Burns, Bunyan, Hermann Hesse, Joyce Cary, E. M. Forster and Tolkien; poor mad Corvo, poor mad Clare, poor sane Swift; James Boswell, Charles Dickens, William Shakespeare; and the *Oxford English Dictionary* – the big one – supplements and all.

Why? Well, the patient wisdom in Herodotus, and his willingness to be frivolous, appeal to me more than the cold, moral genius of Thucydides; the gossip of Aubrey and Pepys, and the unashamed carnality of Donne, are human in

42

a way that some who have seen more deeply are not; when I read Molière (alas, he is almost never well staged) I can enter into his characters and laugh innocently at their absurd misfortunes, which is a great deal more than anybody has ever been able to claim for Racine; the sparkle of Shaw the real playwright is worth ten times the quantity of Shaw the hectoring teacher; the rich satire of Jonson has real blood in it, unlike the mordant wit of the Restoration; I once read the *Decline and Fall* while crossing the Atlantic – both ways – on the *Queen Mary*, and the weird unreality of living for ten days in a world that had come to an end a quarter of a century earlier added an extra piquancy to those rolling and scandalous periods; Forster in his essays I love for his refusal to allow historical relativism to determine morality, and in his novels because – even more important – he understands the complexity of love as well as its glory; Xenophon is the most unassuming of heroes; Villon and Catullus, for their ability to find eternity in a grain of sand and so express it that we can find it too, are the greatest of poets after Shakespeare; Aristophanes and Rabelais are splendidly coarse in a way mercifully different from what passes for realism today; Cobbett's passion for justice shines as bright now as when he was alive, and is no less necessary; *Don Quixote* is the noblest affirmation of man's mixture of divinity and absurdity yet written; every one of my best-loved authors I love for reasons that I could, if put to it, state clearly, which I believe to be an essential and unerring test of love for any writer by any reader.

But what do my favourites have in common? I think that what appeals to me most is that they are, on the whole, the great serendipitists of the written word and of the thought it enshrines, the collectors of pebbles from the seashore which, in their hands, turn into gold and jewels and endure for ever; the great roamers through the infinite jungle of the human heart and mind, image and concept, anecdote and reflection, philosophy and self-portraiture, mirror and doorway, joy and pain, truth and love, friendship and remembrance,

steadiness and eccentricity, faith and doubt, riddle and·
answer, cap and bells, folly and understanding.

And for me they have something else in common, something quite different from their visible and describable qualities, which anyone can grasp and take pleasure in. But here I must return to my childhood.

When I was a boy, the equivalent of today's 'O' levels was the standard attained in an examination called School Certificate; 'A' levels took the form of a more advanced test, called Higher Certificate, involving a good deal of work which the student could – indeed, was obliged to – do in his own time. By that stage in my school career I was, like everyone else, 'streamed', and although I had no gift for languages I was – since I had to be in *some* stream, and had even less aptitude for science – in the Modern Languages department.

Each stream, at the Higher Certificate level, had a miniature common-room, in which the private study was undertaken. That, at any rate, was the idea, but in the Modern Languages hideaway the reality was somewhat different. We turned the room into a Utopian city called Wheelburg, and gave it a good deal more than a local habitation and a name. We produced a weekly newspaper, the *Wheelburg Gazette*, founded a bank, the Bank of Wheelburg, which was largely used to finance the enormous bribes paid at election time when the choice of Wheelburg City Councillors was before us (cheques for 5,000,000 *wheels* – the unit of currency in our state – would change hands in a most profligate manner, and we must have come close, without realizing it, to understanding the theory of inflation long before it became a serious national problem), and presented the Freedom of Wheelburg, the token of which was a huge key, cut out of cardboard, covered in gold paper and resting on a purple cushion, to our favourite teacher of French.

The Constitution and laws of Wheelburg inclined more to Athens than Sparta, and perhaps more to the indulgent rule of the Abbey of Thélèma than either (not that, even in the

44

class of the popular French teacher and Freeman of the City of Wheelburg, we were ever introduced to the indecorous delights of Rabelais); no citizen was obliged to take part in the Republic's civic affairs, and many private activities flourished under the benevolent rule of the City Fathers. Two of my peers, for instance, passionate musicians both, wished to spend their time practising, but since even in the whirling anarchy of that room they could hardly lug a piano in and play it, they solemnly chalked out an entire keyboard on one of the tables, and sat happily playing silent duets for hours on end.

This was all very enjoyable; but it was not greatly conducive to the pursuit of the private study of French and German for Higher Certificate. The problem was solved by each of us in his own way. Some fled the room; some studied at weekends; some failed the exams. My own solution depended upon the fact that I needed then, as I need now, only a very few hours of sleep, and I got into the habit, during the summer term which concluded with the examinations, of waking at first light and, sitting up in bed in the silent dormitory, getting on with the work.

Two of the 'set books' I know practically by heart to this day: Hebbel's *Herodes und Mariamne* for the German paper, and *Richard II* (everyone, in whatever stream, included English Literature in the syllabus) for the Shakespeare. But I can recall even more vividly the conscious pleasure – this was the first time it had become conscious – of reading. The texts had to be read closely; questions about style and verbal usages abounded in the examination papers, and it was dangerous to pass over even a single phrase without being sure of its meaning. Not only, therefore, did I discover that the magnificent speech of the Bishop of Carlisle in Act Four –

. . . Peace shall go sleep with Turks and infidels,
And in this seat of peace tumultuous wars
Shall kin with kin and kind with kind confound . . .

45

referred to the Wars of the Roses; I also found out what 'The field of Golgotha and dead men's skulls' meant, and I even worked out for myself that the line contains a tautology.

As for the German play, Hebbel is not exactly another Shakespeare, and I had made somewhat earlier the pleasant but initially shocking discovery that famous foreigners could write tosh, when, as the equivalent set book for the German paper in the preliminary School Certificate, I had had to plough through Lessing's *Minna von Barnhelm*,★ but the powerful melodrama of the Roman tyrant and his faithful wife who dies because she scorns to prove herself true to him took hold from the start, and I emitted a yelp of delight when I came upon an absurd tongue-twister: '*Irr'ich mich nicht, so wachte ich dich selbst*,' and thus realized that famous foreigners could write carelessly, too.

I have never forgotten the mornings of that term. Solitude, at a large public school, is almost impossible to achieve, and it was solitude that I clearly craved, without knowing I sought it, let alone knowing why. To be awake, bathed in the golden light of the risen sun, when all around me were still asleep, provided a solitude the more dear for its precarious nature, when an unstifled sneeze might wake my neighbours and end my solitary vigil. To be *using* the purity of the dawn, not just living through it, redoubled the pleasure; to be using it in the pursuit of reading, of the study of language and of how it works, of words and their weight and colour – and in two languages, on top of everything else – redoubled it yet again, and in doing so fixed the time and its quality in my mind and feelings for ever. Is it too fanciful to suppose that something far below consciousness determined at that time that I would earn my living by the use of language, that I would – and the double-edged phrase cuts deep as I write it now and realize what it has really meant to me – *make words my life*?

★ This was said – still is, I think – to be the funniest comedy in the German language. A solemn thought.

Is that what I have done? Do I remember those still, silent mornings with such an intensity of pleasure because they were peopled only with words, 'that give delight, and hurt not'? Words have an existence of their own, they are not ours to command altogether freely; but without us they cannot come to life, and although we may read into them more, or other, than is there, and even write a meaning into them that we do not intend, that remains true. It is not true of other human beings who, even if they are harmlessly asleep, may wake at any moment.

Perhaps I make too much of one youthful experience; still, I have remembered it so fully and so deeply, and so long, that it is difficult to believe that it carries no vital meaning for me. I can see much more clearly the meaning of another such experience, a little earlier, when one of my English teachers, himself afire with enthusiasm for books and reading, would abandon rules, grammar, influences, forms, subtexts and the rest of the bones, and go straight to the flesh, talking about books and authors as though they were his friends and ours, and illustrating his love of them by reading us passages chosen to make us want to read more for ourselves. This wise man even taught us the 'facts of life' by the same method; he read us, from Richard Llewellyn's *How Green Was My Valley*, the chapter in which the boy who tells the story has these mysteries explained to him by his father. (Many years later, talking to a friend with a son of the relevant age, I mentioned my own experience, and wondered whether it would still work. It did.)

We are made and shaped by people, by events and experiences, by love and hate, by heredity, by what we eat and whether we hunger, by the things we understand and the things we fail to understand, by pain and joy, by accident and design, by whatever it is that gives us a life and the duty to make what we can of it. But we are also shaped by what we read. That comforting loneliness at dawn each day came at a time when, not surprisingly, I was beginning to discover what I believed, or at any rate what I thought I believed.

At the age of sixteen or thereabouts I went through the inevitable 'primitive communism' phase, when 'From each according to his ability, to each according to his needs' seemed an entire way of life; by the time I got to the university, or very soon thereafter, I had discovered that things were not quite so simple.

Karl Popper's *The Open Society and its Enemies*,★ published the year before I became an undergraduate at the London School of Economics, hit me like a wave, or perhaps a spear, from the first words of the Preface:

> If in this book harsh words are spoken about some of the greatest among the intellectual leaders of mankind, my motive is not, I hope, the wish to belittle them. It springs rather from my conviction that, if our civilization is to survive, we must break with the habit of deference to great men. Great men may make great mistakes; and as the book tries to show, some of the greatest leaders of the past supported the perennial attack on freedom and reason. Their influence, too rarely challenged, continues to mislead those on whose defence civilization depends, and to divide them. The responsibility for this tragic and possibly fatal division becomes ours if we hesitate to be outspoken in our criticism of what admittedly is a part of our intellectual heritage. By our reluctance to criticize some of it, we may help to destroy it all.

With that bugle call, he launched himself into the assault on Plato, Hegel and Marx – the three 'great men' whose influence, if deferred to, may 'help to destroy it all'. But the book could not have had such an effect on me if the ground had not been prepared, and it must have been prepared by the writers, in my catalogue given above, whom I had already discovered. I have never kept a register of books I have read; my memory has made me lazy in that respect. But no

★ Routledge, 1945

memory, however comprehensive, could marshal those authors in the order in which I read them, and I am therefore unable to chart the chronological progress of literary and philosophical influence on my mind and feelings. But I do know that I discovered Montaigne and Erasmus as a schoolboy, in addition to Shakespeare and Dickens, together with Cervantes, Swift, E. M. Forster and Carlyle, and whether they sowed seeds or reaped harvests, or both, I know that they have all been among the most crucial influences of my life. If you put no more than those eight writers together and stir (Carlyle, I suppose, provides the bitter herbs that remind us, even as they flavour the feast, of what hidden dangers can lurk within even the most innocent pot), the resultant mixture *cannot* be baked into a pie that tastes of anything but a liberal philosophy, and I can only conclude that Popper's masterpiece had its transfixing and transformative power over me because it provided a detailed analytical structure for the body of beliefs I had by then already, instinctively, acquired.

I did not, however, read those authors in order to assume the mantle of their beliefs; I read them for pleasure. There are books we are obliged to read; for examinations, for professional reasons, to provide us with necessary or useful information, as a favour to a friend, to strengthen or counter an argument. But that is the *profit* of reading; we pick up a book, and enjoy it, for pleasure alone, and whatever of power and glory, solace and truth, it may contain, it will work no effect on us if it does not provide us with pleasure in its reading. I will take this argument as far as words will reach; I believe that it is true even of the Gospels, which is why for me the *New English Bible*, that dead thing which purports to convey the truth of the greatest of live things, comes alarmingly close to persuading me that there are books which really ought to be burnt, and when the fit is strong upon me I even begin to think that there are some authors who should be burnt on a pyre of their works.

That white whale, then, had more of an effect on me than I

realized at the time. It must have been some years later that I first read *Job*, and saw in its context Melville's own question, the question that runs beneath the surface of the waves throughout the 220,000 words of his masterpiece: 'Canst thou draw out Leviathan upon an hook? Or his tongue with a cord that thou lettest down?' Literary symbols meant little to me at first, and mean not very much even now. But not even a schoolboy discovering adult literature can fail to notice that *Moby-Dick* is more than an adventure story, and the whale considerably more than a whale.

Already, perhaps, I had sensed unconsciously some of the reasons for the deep pleasure of reading, and that of all those reasons one of the very greatest is derived from the way in which a writer of genius offers us his meaning not directly but obliquely, so that we take it in, and understand it, without understanding that we have taken it in, and without taking in that we have understood it. One of my more morbid fantasies takes the form of wondering what I would have become if I had never learned to read. The truth, obviously, is that I would have become someone who *would* have learned to read. And perhaps it is just as absurd to speculate on what would have happened to me if I had never opened *Moby-Dick* until my mind and literary tastes were more strongly formed. All the same, it *was* the first fully adult book I read, and even if there are a thousand books that would have done the same for me – that is, made me realize that the pleasure of reading was going to become one of the richest and most sustaining joys of my life – as it turned out it was *Moby-Dick* that kicked loose the first stone of the avalanche.

When J. M. Dent launched the Everyman Library, that great, noble ship of theirs, a *Pequod* of literature hunting the white whale of pleasure (what household that buys and reads books at all has not got at least a score of those volumes on its shelves?), they chose for an epigraph a couplet from the ancient English morality play that also gave the Dent series its name:

Everyman, I will go with thee, and be thy guide,
In thy most need to go by thy side.

That is a handsome promise, but books have kept it for me, letter and spirit, all my life. And they can be with us in the greatest need of all. I have read that when Father Ronald Knox learned that he was dying, he planned the reading he would do in the days that remained to him. Most of it, naturally, was scriptural, theological, spiritual. But he included the works of one author, and one only, who had nothing to do with religion, and put aside all other secular writers for ever. All else was designed to equip him more fully for his journey to God; but P. G. Wodehouse he read for pleasure.

St Athanasius would not have read P. G. Wodehouse; indeed, the holy horror refused to read anything at all, or even talk about it, unless it concerned his religion. I prefer Ronald Knox's attitude, and so, I dare say, does God.

Three

I cannot remember when and how I began to look at pictures. This in itself strikes me as odd. I can remember very clearly my first steps into music, including the false ones, just as I can recall the details of my early reading, and of my first responses to landscape (though that last is easy, because my first *sight* of landscape, let alone response to it, was so late) and the theatre. But peer as I may into the darkness, I can see no clue – who, what, where – to the awakening of an interest in the visual arts.

This suggests that it must have taken place before I was nine, before the amnesiac curtain rises, but that cannot be true; there was no one in my home with any knowledge of pictures, no one, indeed, who would so much as have heard of the National Gallery. Nor was there anything I can remember on the walls of my childhood home that had anything to do with art, with the exception of a curiously ugly silk-embroidered picture in the Chinese manner.

What the walls bore was a series of huge and gloomy family photographs, studio portraits, all of which I can see most clearly. Chief among them was one of my maternal grandparents, to which there was a mystery attached, with a comic explanation. The mystery lay in the fact that on one side of the couple the photograph merged into a smudgy *drawing* of an aspidistra, and on the other into an equally unconvincing pillar. The explanation was that my grandparents had posed with their two eldest children, my mother and one of her brothers, but that they had made faces at the camera and had to be expunged in disgrace. My most vivid memory of the explanation lies in the shock I had (I can still feel it) at the discovery that my mother had been naughty; I found it impossible to attach the concept to her, or indeed to envisage her as a child at all.

My grandfather had been a handsome man; when I first knew him he looked a little like Stalin, and something of the resemblance lasted, but in that picture there was nothing either patriarchal or authoritative, just a gentle paterfamilias with a wife who already bore the sign of the shrew in the line between her brows. Still, she also bore one of the world's most beautiful names: Bathsheba.

The next photograph was of my mother, grown up now and no longer making faces at the camera. Oddly, the picture as I remember it made her look bigger than reality, for she was a diminutive woman throughout her life. She looked rather like her mother in the photograph, but the resemblance must have faded quickly, because I could never see it even as a child, though they were both always before me for comparison. My three uncles followed, one of whom, Mark, I never knew, for he had been killed in the Great War, long before I was born. There was a curious phrase attached to mention of him and his death, the meaning of which I did not discover till decades later: Lord Derby's Scheme. (It was a form of enlistment somewhere between volunteering and conscription.) My mother told me many years later that my grandparents had journeyed after the war to see his grave in Flanders, the only time either of them had left Britain since they arrived here from the Pale at the turn of the century (nor did they ever leave again); they found his headstone marked with a cross, and got it changed to a Star of David. Mention of Uncle Mark in my grandparents' presence was forbidden, as it would inevitably produce tears; the same was true, much more intensely, after my mother's only sister, youngest of the family, whose photograph completed the set, died soon after I went away to school. She suffered from asthma, and the house was often full of the curious sweet smell of the patent medicinal joss-sticks that were supposed to give her relief.

It was much more likely, though I did not realize it at the time, that she was suffering from the same sort of malady as that which afflicted Elizabeth Barrett – boredom and a feeling of aimlessness – but with no Robert Browning to pluck her from the chaise-longue. (I have only just realized, in the course of writing this paragraph, that my grandparents must have had a lucky escape after the Second World War; they were never naturalized, and could easily have been among those Russians who had been settled in Britain since long before the Soviet Union existed, but were nevertheless enthusiastically sent to Russia by the Foreign Office to be exterminated in Stalin's death-camps.)

In a home with different origins and customs the aunt on the chaise-longue would have sketched or painted, and I would have discovered that such things could be; as it was, the only point at which art impinged on my consciousness at all was the weekly hour under that heading in the curriculum of my elementary school, which revives memories so dreadful that I begin to sweat at the recollection as I write.

Art came in only two forms: clay modelling and water-colour painting. The clay took on, for me, the aspect of a science-fiction horror film. In the first place, it was kept in a bin, rather like those on the pavements of cities which contain grit for the roads in icy weather, and the bin stank horribly, for the same clay was used over and over, simply being pounded back into a mass and watered. Into this mess we plunged our hands and brought up a hunk of dripping clay; the extraction of my load of this glutinous mess, which immediately got under my fingernails (a sensation I have always detested), was bad enough, but much worse was the attempt to shape it into something – *anything* – recognizable. Here I first discovered, without consciously realizing it, that I am devoid, so completely that it seems as though there must quite literally be a part of my brain missing, of even the slightest capacity for artistic expression through my hands. I could not make the clay, whether I watered it to make it more elastic or squeezed the water out to make it friable, go

54

into any shape at all, not so much as a ball or a brick. Around me others were making recognizable pots, dishes, figures, heads, while I squelched myself filthy and tearful in the wholly vain effort to bend the clay to some artistic purpose. To this day I cannot touch clay without discomfort.

Nor can I hold a paintbrush, for if clay weeks were a bad dream, painting weeks (the hour alternated between the two) were hideous nightmare. Not only was my lack of artistic ability equally pronounced in the other medium, but the mess I made trying to paint was actually worse than the mess I made as a would-be sculptor. We used water-colours on thin cartridge paper, painting at easels, and every time without exception the same thing happened to me; the subject would be stated and I would start to daub shapes that could not possibly have been taken, even by someone who knew what I was supposed to be painting, for anything in the real world. That was merely my artistic incompetence; the real horror lay in the fact that I could never work out how to get the paint on to the brush without excess water, so that the paint from every brush-stroke began to drip down the paper as soon as it was applied. And it was worse than that, for it never even occurred to me that if I started at the bottom this particular problem would at any rate not become apparent for some time; I invariably started with the sky or the top of the house, and within seconds my paper was covered in watery trickles of feeble colours which ran into one another and, thus combined, into other trickles and combinations of trickles and combinations of combinations. Whatever the subject, whatever the colours in which I tried to depict it, the result was always the same; a mess of blotches slowly turning into a uniform filthy grey.

At my boarding school there were no compulsory art lessons (I think my discovery of that fact was the most joyful single instant of my life up to that point, and few have surpassed it since), but there was, instead, compulsory carpentry. It was in those classes that it was borne in upon me that my failure as an artist was not due simply to a lack of any artistic creativity; it was, and is, plainly part of something wider, for 'I discovered that if my efforts with clay and water-colours suggested a gap in my brain, my attempts to do *anything* constructive with my hands in the carpentry shop came close to imbecility. I could not learn to saw, to chisel, to plane, to use a gimlet, a bradawl, a mallet; it would not surprise me in the least to be told that the anniversary of the day I attempted to make a dovetail joint is still celebrated at my school with music, feasting and the recitation of epic poems, so memorably ludicrous was the result.

The woodwork teacher was a kindly soul. In what proved to be my last lesson in his class I was attempting to make a simple office filing-tray. I had cut one of the long sides, and it had turned out rather better than my usual efforts; or so it seemed to me, but in fact I had on that occasion surpassed myself in incompetence, for I had sawn the wood straight *across* the grain. When the teacher, making his rounds of the class, got to my bench be picked up the rectangle of wood and looked at it for a minute in silence, turning it this way and that in his hands, as if he could not believe the evidence of his eyes, as perhaps he really couldn't. Then he turned to me and, apparently in a spirit of genuine inquiry, asked, 'Is this a joke?' I assured him it was not, realizing a moment later that it might have been better if I had insisted that it was.

He nodded gravely, then took the slab between finger and thumb at both ends, snapped it in half, threw it into the rubbish bin and bade me follow him to his dais at the end of the room, where he intimated to me, in the most courteous terms, that he doubted if I would ever make a success of carpentry, a conclusion I had already come to on my own behalf. I awaited news of my fate; I was not to know that what lay before me were perhaps a hundred of the happiest and most satisfying hours of my entire life; indeed, so piercing was the happiness those hours gave me, that even now, as I conjure it up forty years later, I can feel it in all its power, and restrain the tears with difficulty.

In addition to a carpentry shop, the school had a forge; the

56

passer-by would hear the roaring of the furnace and the bellows, the clang of iron, and see, whenever the door was opened, a Stygian gloom lit by the fires of hell. Or so memory portrays it, and certainly the decision to transfer me from the comparative safety of the woodwork class to the unimaginable perils of the forge struck me speechless with terror. But the forge was an alternative to carpentry; one or the other was obligatory, and the woodwork teacher doubtless felt that I could not be more hopeless with iron than I had shown myself to be with wood, and that at least he would be rid of me. The next week, I reported to the forge; an enveloping leather apron was draped over me, I was shown how to operate the mechanical bellows and the simpler tools, and given instruction in safety procedures. Then, under careful guidance (possibly the woodwork teacher had passed the word along to his colleague in the smithy), I heated a bar of metal red hot, laid it upon the anvil, and hammered it flat.

The most suitable way for this story to continue would be, I suppose, in the form of a revelation that I turned out to be a metalworker of genius, culminating in a shy confession that it was I who made the iron chandelier, forty feet in diameter and most elaborately chased, with a thousand fantastically decorated candleholders, which hangs to this day in the nave of East Grinstead Cathedral. It is not so; I was quite as hopeless with my hands in the forge as I had been at the carpenter's bench, and all I had to show at the end of all my hours among the sparks and the furnace, my efforts twixt hammer and anvil, was a toasting-fork of extremely irregular design. But I had stumbled upon one of the great, holy, all-consuming loves of my life: fire.

I suppose I have wandered from the point; fire can hardly be said, even using the most elastic definitions, to be one of the visual arts, though it is certainly visual and for me an art. True, Turner painted the fire that destroyed the Houses of Parliament in 1834, Thomas Wyck painted the Great Fire of London in 1666, and Paris Bordone (among others) painted Vulcan's Smithy, but it will be some time yet, I imagine, before fire-painting is officially part of the curriculum at the Slade, and even longer, before fire-raisers are obliged by statute to consult the Royal Fine Arts Commission before putting a building more than a century old to the torch. Once, at dinner among friends, our host asked what crime we would each commit if all legal, though not moral, sanctions against it were abolished, and after my fellow guests had decorously limited themselves to such sins as embezzlement, smuggling and cat burglary, I robustly declared that my choice was arson, and that I was from time to time troubled by a powerful suspicion that I might not wait for the laws against it to be repealed, whereat a thoughtful silence fell upon the company.

I was first conscious of fire and the ease with which it can be kindled, together with its mysterious and beckoning beauty, in the form of the candles which are lit in Jewish households at the onset of the Sabbath – that is, Friday at dusk. My home followed hardly any Jewish observances; certainly I never heard any mention, except as the subject of my grandfather's ribald stories, of the Jewish or any other religion, and even the dietary laws were largely ignored. I went to Sunday school, though that was almost entirely a matter of learning Hebrew (at which I proved a singularly poor scholar), and there was a general assumption that I would at the appropriate time go through the ceremony of *Bar mitzvah*, though in fact I never did.

The Friday night candles, however, constituted a ritual that was invariably observed, and even though they were lit without the prayers that accompany the ceremony in Orthodox households, some sense that this was in its essence a religious act did make itself felt; the upshot was that I came to regard a candle as a holy as well as a beautiful object, and I still cannot repress a shudder, not do I wish to, when I see someone light a cigarette at one. I suppose, though, that somewhere in that belief there is, perhaps was from the start, a much deeper and older instinct; the feeling that fire itself is sacred, and a fit object for veneration.

Like everyone else, I love to sit beside a fire in a grate and stare into the flames; unlike everyone else, I see no pictures there, but only fire. I am not so far gone in pyromania as to rejoice at the sight of a building in flames if there may be people in it, but to see a derelict house afire, or better still a row of houses due for demolition and fired to make the wreckers' task easier, is one of the deepest (and, I suppose, most savage) pleasures of my life, and though my ignorance of farming is such that I cannot even make a guess at where right lies in the controversy over the burning of stubble, I get only pleasure from seeing it happen, and the clang of a fire engine's bell (now, alas, reduced to a siren) stirs my blood with the desire to see the flames mounting into the sky, and to bow down in worship as I do so. Staying years ago with friends in Provence, I arrived amid raging forest fires; my host was something of a stargazer, and had a fairly powerful telescope on his roof, through which I watched the burning fiery furnace on the other side of the valley, almost hypno-tized as I was drawn into the heart of it, and convinced that the telescope was magnifying sound as well as sight, so that I could hear the roaring of the flames.

Until that first day in the forge at school I knew nothing of this strand in my character, and did not really understand it until long afterwards, if indeed I really understand even now. All I knew was that I was happy, and that the happiness came from my proximity to, and use of, fire. When supervision slackened, I would take a bar of metal and experience the thrill of making it glow red and soft, then cool it instantly in the water trough (I had not seen *Siegfried* then, but from the first time I did I have always subjected the forging-scene in Act One to the keen scrutiny of one who knows how it should be done), with no further aim in mind than to do it again immediately, and then again, and again . . . I do not think that I would have produced much more than that toasting-fork even if I had proved to have some skill as a smith.

★

There was a picture in the dining-hall at school, filling the entire length of one wall, which means that it must have been fully forty yards long, and even so what was hung was only three-fifths of the original. I remember that it was by Antonio Verrio, but I took so little interest in it that I could not for the life of me say now what it depicted; the only use it had for any of us was as the basis for a game, the object of which was to see how many times the player could recite, in a single breath, the whole of the inscription beneath the picture, which gave its provenance. Verrio's monster mural was the only painting I can recall looking at, accidentally or deliberately, throughout my childhood, and I begin to be conscious of going to art galleries and exhibitions only when I had been a university student for some time.

What set me off, then, I cannot remember at all; certainly not the art classes at school, nor the forge, nor Verrio. But I know without doubt what painter first took hold of my imagination, nor is his identity surprising, any more than there is anything strange in a young music-lover giving his first allegiance to Beethoven. And that is hardly even an analogy, for Beethoven and Rembrandt rightly go insepar-ably together in the imagination of Europe, for all that the composer was born a century after the painter died, as two of the three pillars (Shakespeare died ten years after Rembrandt was born) on which Europe's cultural identity rests. They have nothing to do with the Renaissance, but they could not have existed without it, and it would lack meaning without them. More to my present point, Rembrandt overwhelmed me in exactly the same way as, a little earlier, Beethoven had, and obviously for the same reason; both, in being utterly subjective, became universal, and the young man, respon-ding to their fiery subjectivity, sensed, without knowing it, their transcendent universality.

To this day I am far more at home, by which I suppose I mean far happier, with Dutch, Flemish and German painting than with Italian, let alone Spanish. The list of Italian masters who leave me enthralled but unmoved includes Tintoretto,

Giovanni Bellini, Raphael, Michelangelo (except the Ronda-nini *Pietà* in Milan), most of Titian, most of Leonardo. I warm to Giorgione and Mantegna, more to Donatello and Caravaggio (the latter is the most Rembrandtesque of Italian artists), more still to Botticelli, Carpaccio and Veronese. But I am fired by Rembrandt, van Eyck, the Brueghels and Cranachs, van Leyden, Bosch, Grünewald, Dürer, Vermeer, de Hooch, van Ostade, Jan Steen, Holbein, indeed almost every artist from north-central Europe except Rubens, whose colours would make me feel sick even if his shapes didn't, and Franz Hals, in whom I have never been able to see anything but a proto-Munnings or an ur-Annigoni.

I am not at all sure what all this says about me, though there are one or two clues: there is a humanity about these Dutchmen and their neighbours that I can rarely find south of the Alps or the Pyrenees, where they are too close to God, or perhaps I mean too conscious of that inspiring but dangerous proximity. A much more obvious divide runs along the trenches of the Reformation; clearly I am more at home in Protestant than in Catholic Europe. On the other hand, though I love Erasmus as a wise, gentle brother, I would not like to meet Martin Luther on a dark night, even if he didn't know I was a Jew, and I revel – emphatically the right word – in the Baroque; I would exchange any dozen Gothic cathedrals for the Wieskirche, and the Ghiberti doors on the Baptistery in Florence for the interior of the seventeenth-century Opera House in Bayreuth (which Wagner originally thought of taking for his Festival, though the entire building would fit comfortably on to the stage of the one he finally built himself instead). If it comes to that, I would give you St Peter's for any Hawksmoor, and Milan Cathedral for nothing.

But all this measuring came later; there was no time for such speculations when I was haunting the art galleries by day as I haunted the theatres, the opera houses and the concert halls by night.

My early enthusiasm for Rembrandt, to which I shall

return, at once raised a mystery. Why was it that in the late sixteenth century and much of the seventeenth England produced playwrights from an apparently inexhaustible well, but no painters to speak of (Van Dyck was a Fleming, to rub in the irony, and Lely a Dutchman, and as for Holbein . . .), while just across the North Sea, which is hardly the other side of the world, there were no playwrights but a stupendous outpouring of genius in the visual arts? That is the kind of puzzle that can never be solved, though no doubt some idiot 'structuralist' or parlour-Marxist is at this very moment solving it by pointing to the different modes of exploitation and oppression adopted by the respective ruling classes. But even as a young man I could see another mystery in the visual arts which demanded an answer in the confidence that there was one, though I am still by no means certain what the answer is.

The question may be put thus: in one of the most important aspects of art, and certainly its most obvious – its subject matter – painting is showing us what we can perfectly well see for ourselves, without making an expedition to an art gallery. We cannot hear the Jupiter Symphony until Mozart has written it, nor read *The Brothers Karamazov* before Dostoievsky has invented the characters and given them a history and a life, together with a plot to move in. But we do not have to wait for Cézanne before we can look at the Mont Sainte-Victoire, or for Fantin-Latour before we can arrange a vase of flowers, or for Van Gogh before we can sit on a kitchen chair and admire the view of a wheatfield through the window. Why, then, do we allow the visual artist, and him alone, to insist that we look at his pictures when they are only an imitation of an already familiar reality?

There must be an answer to that question, or the world would be an even odder place than we know it to be. And for my part, I rather think that in the answer there lies the explanation of why the pleasure that painting gives me is so intense that sometimes it is almost more powerful than the pleasure I derive from music.

I first visited Amsterdam in 1956. That year marked the 350th anniversary of the birth of Rembrandt, and the Dutch authorities had summoned from all over the world the greatest collection of his work ever to be seen anywhere at one time. It was also, though no one then knew it, the greatest collection of Rembrandt that ever would be gathered together, for it was only a few years later that the financial and other difficulties of mounting a truly comprehensive international exhibition of *any* old master's work began to grow, as did the unwillingness of owners to lend their most priceless treasures (of which, in gallery after gallery and private collection after private collection, the Rembrandts were increasingly pre-eminent), until, in 1969, the 300th anniversary of Rembrandt's death, the Royal Academy, after struggling to put together an exhibition of his painting that would be worthy of the occasion, had to confess that it could not be done, and cancelled the show.

The Dutch tribute was so enormous that it could not all be housed in the same city, let alone the same gallery. So the paintings and the etchings were in the Rijksmuseum (there had long been a complete set of the etchings in the Rembrandthuis in Amsterdam), and the drawings in the Boymans Museum in Rotterdam. I heard about the exhibition from a friend, and since I was shortly setting off for a holiday in Germany, it did not seem as though it would be difficult, and did seem as though it would be worth while, to spend a few days in the Netherlands on the way. This I did; the holiday was a walking tour, and I was travelling only with a rucksack, which meant that I had to carry all the exhibition catalogues on my back on the march, and they were bulky. But it also meant that when I was weary, I could sit down on a milestone, pluck them forth and turn their pages, and refresh myself, body and spirit, with the reminder of the glories I had just seen and would never forget.

The exhibition achieved something that, even if Rembrandt gatherings-in on this scale had not now become impossible, would still have been, and would always remain, unique, for the centrepiece of the show was 'The Night Watch', which is far too big and too precious to be allowed to travel, and thus never seen anywhere at the heart of any international selection of his work other than one in his adopted city. The title it has acquired must have led countless unwary visitors to the understandable conclusion that what the picture portrays is a convocation of nightwatchmen, or possibly a detachment of the Amsterdam police force; neither theory would have pleased Captain Frans Banning Cocq, whose socially distinguished militia troop is in fact the subject of the painting, though the shambles of unmilitary attitudes we see – the fruits of Rembrandt's determination to get away from the stiffly posed and largely lifeless group portraits fashionable at the time – is no great tribute to the company's notions of discipline or the Captain's powers of leadership.

It is widely regarded as Rembrandt's supreme masterpiece; certainly it is the most popular picture in the Rijksmuseum – there is always a crowd before it throughout the day – but I have never been able to see in it the quality of 'The Syndics of the Cloth Guild', or 'Jeremiah Lamenting the Destruction of Jerusalem', both of which hang near it, or the 'Portrait of a Rabbi' in our own National Gallery, or any of the later self-portraits. 'The Night Watch' is not a lovable picture; though Rembrandt certainly succeeded in getting movement into the group, it is still obviously posed. We can never believe that these people were caught unawares, as the best portraits, whether of groups or individuals, invariably imply. And then, a visitor approaching it with a view to learning something about the Captain and his men will sooner or later be seized with a decided feeling that they were a lot of pompous asses, starting with the Captain himself, who is staring out of the canvas with a look of such astonishment on his face that it seems he could never before have set eyes on a paintbrush, much less an artist. And there is a clue in the picture to what Rembrandt thought of them.

Right at the back, between a man in a hat and another in a

helmet, there is a glimpse – nothing more than a right eye and the bridge of a nose – of a man whose presence in the picture is puzzling; the members of Captain Banning Cocq's outfit do get in each other's way, and some of them, it is true, are only half visible, but this man has been almost entirely excluded, and since the officers paid for the picture on a co-operative basis (the devil's own job Rembrandt had to get the money out of them, but that is another story), he would have had good reason to refuse to pay a single guilder towards it – and there is no record of any such financial fracas. Then who is this man, and what is he doing in the picture? I have always believed that the glimpse of him is Rembrandt's joke, that the eye belongs to the artist himself, and that he put it in as Alfred Hitchcock used to put a fleeting shot of himself into his films, as a kind of visual trademark or signature. If so, we should not feel too badly about our failure to take the men in the painting too seriously, because Rembrandt himself didn't: *the eye is laughing fit to bust.*

There is another strange quality in painting, another quality that does not seem to apply in the other arts. It would be absurd for any of us to say that we have 'a' favourite book, piece of music, play; there cannot be hierarchies in our minds so rigid that they will throw up a single work as to be preferred among all others, and even if there could be, the identity of the favourite would change constantly – with our moods, our condition, the context, our attitude to the art in question. The work itself does not stay the same, it changes in our feelings as we change, if we are capable of changing at all. Yet somehow, this obvious truth does not seem to apply to the visual arts; you will find many lovers of painting and sculpture who would not dream of claiming a single symphony or poem as their favourite but who are nevertheless willing to choose one picture and swear eternal allegiance, *primus inter pares*, to that and that alone. I, too, feel this contradictory impulse, and however absurd I know it to be, it does not *feel* absurd for me to say that I do have a favourite picture, even though I have a dozen favourite operas, and two dozen favourite novels, and three dozen pictures which are always tugging at my sleeve to insist that I transfer my allegiance to them, and giving me good reason to do so.

There is Holbein's 'Portrait of Sir Thomas More', for instance, in the Frick Collection in New York. That remarkable gallery is the town house of Henry Clay Frick, one of America's nineteenth-century robber barons; it was built to house his collection, and goes some way – though perhaps not quite all the way – towards justifying his appalling financial hornswogglings in the steel business, from which he made enough money to buy the pictures and fill the house with them.

They were a strange lot, those American rogues; some of them had real artistic taste and judgment, and most of those who did not had enough sense to let Duveen – in some ways a bigger rogue than all his clients put together – advise them. But the extraordinary thing about so many of them – not only Frick but Mellon, Carnegie, Morgan and many others – is that they seemed to make their money only to give it away; their passion was for making the money, not for having it, and their gifts, bequests and Foundations were on a stupendous scale. Only the first Rockefeller seems to have been a miser, and only the first Henry Ford and William Randolph Hearst seem to have been real swine. And Carnegie himself summed up the strange, twisted philosophy of all those who made huge fortunes and art collections and gave them, or lent them in perpetuity, to the public, when he said, 'A man who dies rich dies disgraced.'

Well, Frick died rich, though he made handsome amends after his death with this collection, which must be unique among the world's public galleries in that almost literally every item in it is a masterpiece; there are no rooms, no corners even, that we hurry past on the way to more appealing items. The Frick houses two of Rembrandt's noblest pictures; that late self-portrait, perhaps the very last, and the enigmatic 'Polish Rider', who is certainly a rider but almost as certainly not Polish. The Frick also offers Titian's noble portrait of Aretino, if 'noble' is not too incongruous a word to use in any connection with that engaging but appalling scoundrel, who wrote pornography with one hand and blackmailed his friends with the other, and died, it is said, of laughing at a rude joke. There is a Goya portrait, too, of choice quality, though not choice enough, unfortunately, to throw light on my curious blindness for Goya, and another of those haunting, candlelit pictures by Georges de la Tour, this one being 'The Education of the Virgin'. Every few years, some expert announces that half the world's supply of pictures attributed to him are fakes; fortunately, no two of these iconoclasts can ever agree on the contents of the list of the inauthentic ones, so I cannot say whether the Frick's de la Tour is at present supposed to be genuine or not, though I *can* say that it breathes authenticity as naturally as it breathes beauty, power and serenity.

The Frick encourages digression, like good encyclopaedias; but here at last is More. At first, all we can see is the luscious velvet gown, the sleeves catching the light in a score of folds and crinkles, the golden chain of office, the cap. But Holbein was no Sargent, and presently, after we have gazed our fill at the outer man, the artist nudges us very gently, and our eyes are drawn to the face.

If we did not recognize him, if we had never heard of him, we could be in no doubt that this was one of the finest intellects and most elevated characters of history; the firm set of the mouth, the level gaze of the eyes, the hint of worlds invisible to the rest of us yet seen by the sitter – all this, and what it means, Holbein has caught, and he had even caught, along with these qualities, the playfulness and the humanity of this man, the friend and mentor of Erasmus of Rotterdam.

Perhaps I should stop here and declare that this is my favourite among all the pictures of the earth, but what should I then do when I am back in London and feel impelled to have another look at 'Arnolfini's Wedding' in the National Gallery, though it is the hardest picture in the town to get to without being waylaid, by Titian's 'Bacchus and Ariadne' or Dürer's portrait of his father, or both.

The Van Eyck is an amazing thing; it seems almost impossible that it could have been painted at the beginning of the fifteenth century, so far has the artist moved towards a Rembrandtian view of humanity. Never mind the scandalous imputation that Mrs Arnolfini is about eight months gone on her wedding day; never mind the feeble counter-argument that it is only the way her dress hangs (who ever heard of a bustle at the front?); never mind the fact that the marriage, if it lasts at all, will have very little sunshine in it, for that dry old stick is far too narrow-looking for his soft and radiant bride. Mind only that these questions arise as we gaze at the picture, and that it is one of the very earliest paintings that impels us to ask them, that makes us yearn to break through into the looking-glass world beyond the surface of the canvas.

Come to Colmar. You can eat very well in the vicinity – Haeberlin himself is just up the road – but there is plenty of time to get to lunch, and we must first look in at the little museum, which houses yet another of my candidates for favourite picture, the astounding ninefold altarpiece of Matthias Grünewald, with the Crucifixion on three of the folds and the 'Temptation of St Antony' on three more. It is St Antony and the hideous demons that give this work its greatest force; the Saint, with a huge white beard, is beset by evil so real that it is capable of frightening a spectator in a daylit room so crowded that he has to jostle to see the picture at all. But St Antony breathes a certainty in his faith that recalls the martyrdom of St Lawrence, roasted on a gridiron, who called out to his persecutors to turn him over, as he was already well done on one side. Looking at St Antony, unafraid in the very teeth of hell, there tolls in the mind the great bell of that line from the *Chanson de Roland*:

Chrétiens ont droit, et paiens ont tort.

What if it were true!

There are three paintings in the Uffizi that clamour to be my favourites, all of them quite justifiably, and to all of them I swear undivided allegiance, hoping that they will not get together and compare notes until I am out of Florence and on my way to Venice, where there are a score more. If nothing else at all had happened to make the historical epoch we call the Renaissance, 'The Birth of Venus' would alone justify the era and its name; it speaks of an awakening new world even more directly and clearly than its companion on the wall to its right, the 'Primavera'. Just by the door of the same room there is Dürer's 'Portrait of a Young Man', who will surely come to no good, but will have an enjoyable time going to the bad, and somewhere in the building, though it moves too frequently and too fast to be confidently assigned a position after a visit, is Leonardo's Annunciation, with the most human and tender of all Virgins, even more so than the one by Giovanni Bellini in Venice, the one with the Babe in her arms.

In Venice, the choice is unbearable; almost every picture in the city is my favourite, though the Venetian authorities make my dilemma less painful by ensuring that at least half of the Accademia is usually closed, and quite often all of it. But even outside it there is Titian's 'Virgin of the Assumption' in the Church of the Frari, where it is possible for a visitor to stand on the exact spot where Wagner stood marvelling at this airy miracle, though it is not possible for the visitor to rush away, as Wagner did, to write *The Mastersingers* (he can, however, walk a few paces to his right and see Donatello's wooden sculpture of John the Baptist, which I sometimes think I would exchange for *The Mastersingers* itself if I couldn't have both), and the Carpaccios of the Life of St Jerome in the Scuola di San Giorgio degli Schiavoni (where the opening times have lately become as untrustworthy as those of the Accademia), with the Saint in his study in the last picture, the little white dog at his feet.

Inside the Accademia, *absit omen*, there is another roomful of Carpaccios demanding exclusive rights in a visitor's love.

These are the ones that tell the implausible but confident story of St Ursula and her eleven thousand virgins in colours so wonderfully bright and shapes so wonderfully swirling that the story deserves to be true for inspiring such rich and assured genius; there is, not far away, that strange and inexplicable thing by Giorgione, 'La Tempesta', which looks, with its apparently unrelated elements, like a dream, and is so powerful that it can get into your own; and, filling the entire end wall of Room IX, Veronese's 'Last Supper', which he had hastily to rename 'Supper at the House of Levi' when the Inquisition hauled him up before them and accused him of impiety for making the scene of that tremendous climax of the Christian religion so intimate, personal and free. You can see the Inquisition's point; there is a man who has just been punched in the face, in the course of a quarrel, who is holding a handkerchief to his bleeding nose, and – even worse – there is a dog in the picture, in the foreground, peering under the table at a cat. Suppose the dog should take it into its head to attack the cat, which is clearly ready for such an assault; there would be a mêlée under the table, and the Apostles, and even Christ, might be scratched or even bitten. For my part, I do not think Christ would mind very much, but the Inquisition certainly seemed to mind on Christ's behalf.

But now, still searching for my favourite picture, I must return to Amsterdam, where I started the search, and, after paying my respects once more to 'The Night Watch', and winking back at Rembrandt's laughing eye, seek a little further. It is difficult enough to get *to* 'The Night Watch', let alone past it; who could hurry by the slightest of the genre paintings of Jan Steen, with his peasants looking so happily drunk, and even quarrelling and fighting without ceasing to be happy, or for that matter ceasing to be drunk? Who would not be caught and held by the winter scenes of Hendrick Avercamp, or that almost pointillist work, 'The River in a Valley', by Hercules Seghers, who so powerfully influenced Rembrandt? (Rembrandt paid him the compliment of reworking one of his etchings in the original plate.) And who would not wish to stop and call at those wonderful little houses, quivering with the life and warmth within, of Pieter de Hooch?

But here is 'The Night Watch' again, at last. There was a flock in front of it last time we came round, listening attentively but lifelessly to a lecturing expert whose technique makes certain that none of the willing sheep will be able to see this or any other picture on their tour with feelings sufficiently open and natural to enable them to respond to the artist's vision and what he was trying to tell them with it; that flock has gone, but a new flock has taken its place, with a new shepherd anaesthetizing them. They, however, are not our concern, and nor, for the moment, is 'The Night Watch'. We turn right round; in the far corner of the room, to our right, there is a short flight of steps leading to an archway.

Beyond the archway there is a little room, housing only little pictures, and not many of those. One of them, indeed, measures only 45½ centimetres by 41, which is roughly one-eightieth of the area of 'The Night Watch'. There is no flock in front of it, with or without a shepherd; during most of the hours I have spent looking at it over the years, I have had it, and the room, entirely to myself. And I think that it really is my favourite picture in all the world. It is 'The Servant Pouring Milk', by Jan Vermeer of Delft.

It shows a scene in a kitchen, to be precise one aspect of a kitchen. In the bottom left-hand corner there is a table. It is covered in a grey-blue cloth, with a darker blue cloth lying on it and hanging down over the side. The corner of this cloth is anchored beneath a bread-basket, full of golden, crusty bread and one darker hunk; more pieces of the lighter kind lie on the table itself, in the corner opposite the basket. Behind the basket stands a blue jug, with a simple white decoration. Beside it stands a shallow earthenware bowl; into this the servant is steadily pouring a thin stream of milk. She is pouring it from another jug, identical to those still used for the breakfast buffet in any old-fashioned Dutch hotel and a million Dutch households; plain, reddish earthenware.

The kitchen maid stands almost exactly in the middle of the picture, an erect column, leaning slightly away from her work so that the picture's diagonal flows through the table, the bread and the bowl, up her forearms and into her head and left shoulder. She is a marvellous creature; serene, intent, pure, even beautiful. Her eyes, cast down upon what she is doing, look closed from where we stand; her left hand supports the jug and her right holds its handle. She wears a yellow bodice, stretched tight over her ample bosom; the sleeves are pushed up, revealing strong, sinewy arms, used to labour. Her skirt is red, with a blue overskirt or pinafore; a white bib-collar, and a white cap in the shape of a sou'-wester, complete the portrait.

In the left-hand wall there is a hinged window, shut; in the corner beyond it a basket and lantern are hanging. Behind the servant, on the floor, is a puzzling object, which experts insist is a footstool doing duty also as a cupboard, with pans showing inside it. (The first time I saw this picture in the flesh, I thought it was a kind of cage, and the contents a chicken waiting to be plucked.) Round the wainscot there are blue Delft tiles. A couple of nails have been knocked into the whitewashed walls, doubtless to hang utensils on.

That is all; but if you stand in silence before 'The Servant Pouring Milk', I swear that you can *hear* the milk trickling into the bowl.

This is not to say that the picture is realistic, though of course it is. I take no pleasure in photography at all (and very little in the cinema, probably for the same reason), and the literalness of many paintings repels rather than attracts me. But what this picture has, what leaps from the wall to warm the heart and the soul, is something vastly more important: veracity. And *there*, surely, the mystery of painting and the pleasure it gives is explained. The artist – the real artist – is not painting a milk jug, or sunflowers, or the Crucifixion.

He is painting truth, and it is the truth in light and shade, in inanimate objects, in fruit, in dogs and cats, in landscape, in human beings, in the gods themselves, that produces the pleasure we feel before the artist's work.

This is not a matter, in the case of the Vermeer, of telling us what the servant girl is thinking, though a glance at that determined chin and those set lips is enough to tell us that she is not, like the Mona Lisa, dwelling upon vanities. But in all things there is an essence, an ultimate reality that cannot be reduced to any lower terms. If we could split that final atom of inner meaning, we would know what the universe is made of, and even why. We can sense that meaning through the arts; I am convinced that that is what art is for. But only in the pictorial arts is there an attempt to make us *see* the meaning, and see it plain. As I stood before 'The Servant Pouring Milk', as I stand when I am among the Tate's best Turners, as I stand before the Leonardo 'Last Supper' in Milan, restoration and all, as I stand before Géricault's 'Raft of the Medusa' in the Louvre, or Velasquez's 'Maids of Honour' in the Prado, or for that matter the tiny pen-and-ink head of a child by Stefano della Bella that hangs at one side of the head of my bed or the Lucas van Leyden etching of 'The Standard-Bearer' that hangs at the other, that meaning emerges, if only for a moment, like a sight glimpsed from the corner of the eye.

And the extraordinary fact about its emergence is that the subject, and the artist's approach, do not have to be grand, solemn, or in any way consciously didactic; the pleasure, and even its intensity, is the same if our reaction to the first sight of a picture is nothing but an innocently happy smile. I mentioned Jan Steen, and might have added Adrien van Ostade; their brawling peasants and topers with clay pipes and carbuncled noses are just as much channels for the truth and pleasure of art as the most piercing of Tintoretto's studies in Christ's Passion. Of course the scale is different, and of course Tintoretto offers other qualities besides; but that pleasure, which comes directly from our understanding that what the artist is telling us is true, and that his truth matters, and matters most profoundly and awfully, is all of a piece, whoever the artist is, and whatever his subject matter.

There was a young artist, a real live one, in the Rijksmuseum last time I was there to call on the servant girl in her kitchen. Unfortunately, he was far too good to be true; no doubt he was an art student, but what he looked like was an actor auditioning for the part of an art student, and over-doing it most frightfully. His shirt was carefully loosened, the scarf at his throat was just casually enough knotted, his thumb projected through the hole in his palette at the approved angle, the palette itself was adorned with ten carefully arranged blobs of paint, of exactly equal size.

I wish him well in his career, but somehow I think he is not destined to eclipse the glory of Vermeer. In art, as in everything else, truth comes from within, and the artistic finery of the young blade, handsome though it was, will no more help him to discover the truth of art within himself and drag it forth into the light than Vermeer's poverty was any bar to his doing so.

I would like to be able to talk to the kitchen maid. I want to know exactly what she is doing, and why. Perhaps the broken bits of bread on the tablecloth are for steeping in the milk; perhaps, therefore, the servant is preparing supper for the youngest child of the house. But even as I come to that conclusion I know that it would explain nothing. In the end we have to fall back on the simplest of all the explanations of the mystery – the simplest and the best. 'Beauty is truth, truth beauty'; it must be somewhere in that famous equation, as in the explosion of hydrogen and oxygen atoms that produces water, that the pleasure of painting is generated.

Four

I am a child of the city. I was born in one, but that alone is not enough to make a man want, even need, to live and die in one, not even if the city of his birth is London, as mine is. Millions are born in cities and flee them, London included; other millions go on living in them and become more and more unhappy. I think I can understand what moves those who cannot endure city life, but that is largely because the things they cannot abide are the very things that made cities so attractive to me in the first place. I live, and always have lived, by the rigidity of the streets and the solidity of the buildings, the blotting-out of the ominous, all-seeing sky, the blind stare of the houses with doors for mouths and windows for eyes (surely Magritte must have painted a house as a face or a face as a house?), the lack of silence and the absence of darkness, the anonymous crowds in a hurry (too much of a hurry, at any rate, to stop and identify themselves), the chimneys signalling life beneath the roofs (all true Londoners deplore the passing of the Clean Air Act), the horses and the horse troughs, the cry of the cat's-meat man, the rag-a-bone man and the newsboy, the fog, the barrel organ, the British Union of Fascists, the Whoopees, the coalman with his curious sack-hat at the open coal hole, the trams, the Bank Holiday fair on Hampstead Heath, the voice of Neville Chamberlain on September 3rd, 1939, announcing the end of the world, and with it the end of the city of my childhood; and the barrage balloons, the air-raid sirens, the anti-aircraft guns on Primrose Hill, just behind my wartime home, and the bombs.

It will be apparent that in the course of that paragraph I have moved from an attempt to define the qualities that I respond to in cities to the easier task of reminiscence. But for a native Londoner of my age, and perhaps of my background also, there is really no difference. I do not know whether I would love cities as I do if I had been born in Newcastle upon Tyne or Birmingham; it seems unlikely to me, but the natives of those cities may think it the most natural thing in the world, or at least may have thought so once, for those are the two cities of England most comprehensively, vilely and irrevocably ruined by the postwar property developers and the corruption they found and battened on or created and used. Yet I am not just a Londoner; I am a lover of cities the world over, and indeed I have the feeling in the extreme form common to all the most passionate city-lovers, who would rather be in an ugly city than a beautiful field, amid the skyscrapered canyons of New York in preference to the natural canyons of New Mexico, the unrelieved hideousness of modern Athens rather than the slopes of Mount Olympus.

It is true that most of my favourite cities are beautiful ones: Edinburgh, Venice, San Francisco, Amsterdam, New York, Cambridge, Salzburg, Vancouver, Vienna, Rome. But I love West Berlin, too, which could not be described as beautiful by even its most infatuated admirer, something that could also be said of Marseilles and Basel, and even more strongly of Bombay, yet I love these no less. No city-lover is entirely indiscriminate, of course; I do not love Moscow, though many Muscovites clearly do, nor Liverpool, a harder test for its inhabitants, nor – a harder still – Tokyo (surely The Bullet, Japan's – and for a long time the world's – fastest train, which plies between Tokyo and its anagrammatic cousin, Kyoto, was developed so that the inhabitants of the capital could get from a week in the Tokyo maelstrom to a weekend in the peace and beauty at the other end of the line in time to catch their tottering sanity before it fell?). But however far I extend my list of cities that I love, it is not the length of the list, but the depth of the love, that marks me as a lifelong townee.

I was not conscious of it for a long time; I think these characteristics that we inherit or acquire or grow into are not fully understood until something extraneous draws them inescapably to our attention, any more than those living through a particular historical era are aware of the fact; I do not suppose that Cosimo de' Medici, when filling in forms, gave his occupation as 'Renaissance Man', though I did once see a historical play about Shakespeare in which the characters referred to the monarch throughout as Queen Elizabeth the First. But I can remember exactly when and where I first understood properly what cities mean to me.

In 1960 I visited Moscow; I had never been to the Soviet Union before, and have never been since (nor, it has been made plain to me, would I get a visa for a return visit if I wanted one); I think, though, that it was on that sole visit that I first understood properly not only what cities mean to me but what liberty is, and even what it means to those who lack it.

I had been in Moscow for two or three weeks, and in that time I had seen enough misery, cruelty, poverty and ugliness to last me the rest of my life and a bit over; one image that sums up all four of those aspects of life in a totalitarian society remains in my mind, and always will, as vividly as when I saw it. My visit was in winter, and it was the coldest winter Moscow had experienced for many years. The traffic guard-rails around Bolshoi Square were being painted, apparently with some rust-proofing material, and as I went in and out of my hotel I could see the progress of the work. It was being done by old women; most of them were coatless, and had nothing but a shawl over their dresses to protect them from temperatures of twenty degrees below freezing-point (Centigrade, not Fahrenheit), and nothing but mittens to protect their fingers from frostbite. They held pots of paint in one hand and paintbrushes in the other, but the paintbrushes hardly existed, the bristles had been worn away long since, in a semicircle, so that the 'brushes' consisted of little more than a bit of wood with a few hairs at either end.

This pitiful object the old women dipped into the paint, which they then smeared on to the metal as best they could. They were hunched against the cold as they worked, but I could see their faces, and on those faces there was a look of hopelessness, pain, exhaustion and pointless suffering pointlessly endured that I had never seen before, and hope fervently never to see again, on any human being.

I did not have to go to Moscow, even in 1960, to know that the people of the Soviet Union are brutally poor and brutally unfree. But seeing it close up, all round and every day made the knowledge hideously real, and it began to eat away at my control. No amount of telling myself that the pain for me was only something to observe and remember, but for the Soviet citizen something that had to be borne, and in silence, too, would lessen its effect on me, and I presently realized that I was approaching breakdown.

I teetered on the very edge of it in Leningrad; in, of all unlikely places, the Hermitage. In one room, as I went round, there was a crocodile of young schoolchildren, with their grey jackets and trousers or skirts, and their triangular red junior Komsomol scarves; they were being conducted round the pictures by a schoolteacher. The scene was innocent enough, but an idle fancy entered my head as I watched it; suppose some science-fiction event should take place, and I should find myself in consequence exchanging bodies, but only bodies, with one of the children, so that I would be trapped for ever in a life of nightmare. The crocodile moved dutifully around the walls of the gallery, as the teacher commented on the pictures, and I tried to get a grip on my absurd fantasy; to my horror I found that I could not, and that the more I tried to put it from me the more insistent it became. Eventually, I could bear it no longer, and ran from the room, indeed from the building itself, into the street.

It was in that condition that I left the Soviet Union, a condition that led me, as soon as I had finished the work that had taken me there, to demand a ticket for the first plane going anywhere on the western side of the Iron Curtain.

This, it turned out, was Copenhagen; an hour after I landed there it was added to my list of favourite cities, and an hour later I had realized how deep in me is city-love, whereupon I began to think about the origins of that love, and what it meant for me.

I walked about all night, soothing my shaking nerves with great draughts of the freezing warm air of liberty and civilization. I spent hours staring into shop windows; I had never known until then that ordinary manufactured objects with no great quality in their design – plain kitchen knives, briefcases, plates, scarves, wooden furniture, blankets, type-writers, bottles, electric razors – could be so beautiful, after the hopeless shoddiness of everything in Moscow and Lenin-grad. The very advertising signs, in familiar neon, took on an elegance I had not noticed before, and I knew that my nightmare was lifting; before dawn, it had fled entirely, as nightmares do at first light, when I was seized by, and gladly succumbed to, an urgent desire to make a pile of snowballs and throw them at a statue.

Next day, at lunch, I spotted something on the dessert section of the menu called 'Ice-cream surprise'. I asked the waiter what it was, but he said, reasonably enough, that if he told me it would no longer be a surprise. So I ordered it; it was an attractively presented vanilla ice; a circle of sparklers was embedded in it, and in the centre, sticking out of the top, was a thicker metal rod. The waiter lit the sparklers, which duly blazed briefly and prettily, and as they died out there was a click, and a tiny Danish flag emerged from a cave in the igloo, ran up the metal mast in the middle of the roof, and fluttered proudly at the top. The very last remaining trace of my crisis flared up; I burst into tears. But they were tears of innocence and happiness, provoked by the realization that what I had missed most in the Soviet Union was just such purposeless absurdity, the true mark of civilization and one of the qualities, along with laughter itself, that divide man-kind from the brutes. But by then I was thinking also about cities, and my life.

The first house I can remember living in, though it was not the first I did live in, was in Camden Town. When I first went there the address was King Street, but the name was changed a few years later to Plender Street. I went about telling my schoolfellows that 'Plender' was Latin for 'King'; since neither they nor I knew what Latin was, except presumably a foreign language, the theory took rapid hold, and for all I know there may be middle-aged men and women today who never had my further educational advantages and who therefore believe it still.

But the confusions of childhood are uncountable. My school was called the Richard Cobden School, and a statue of the great reformer stood in Camden High Street, a few hundred yards away. None of us had ever heard of him, let alone of the Anti-Corn-Law League; for that matter few of us had ever heard of corn, and fewer still set eyes on it. When I first read *Winnie-the-Pooh* and came upon the passage in which Piglet insists that TRESPASSERS W on the broken board next to his house was his grandfather's name, being short for Trespassers Will, itself short for Trespassers William, I believed it literally, because the famous interdiction is an exclusively rural affair, towns contenting themselves with 'No Entry'. (If it comes to that, a figure in a top hat is still 'a funerman' to me, as that object was inseparably associated by me with funeral processions, and I had no idea that it had any other use.) Anyway, we believed that Cobden was a victorious general in the First World War. I once asked a teacher 'if we beat Germany, why isn't Germany red on the map?' I am still not quite sure that I know the answer.

Plender Steet, in my memory, is a wide thoroughfare, but this must be another example of the child's magnifying eye, for there were no wide streets in those parts, except the High Street itself. Looking out of the front window to the right, I could see a huge red-brick building; this was the furniture repository of Maples, a store which at that time, and in that milieu, was synonymous with the very farthest extreme of luxury, advanced design and unimaginable expensiveness.

Looking up the street the other way, I could see the market barrows; these were pressed into service as barricades when Mosley and his Fascists were on the march ('The Yids, the Yids, we gotta get rid of the Yids'). I cannot now imagine what they were doing so far from their breeding swamps in the East End, for there were very few Jews in the area to hate, and even fewer Jewish shops to have their windows broken by the weedy *Herrenvolk*.

Almost outside our front door, there was a stone horse trough, and, more often than not, a horse drinking at it. On its side – and this seemed to be the rule for horse troughs everywhere – was a strange couplet, the origin of which I have never been able to discover, any more than I have ever learned who ordered it to be carved in such an odd place:

> New days, new ways,
> Pass by. Love stays.

No longer are our streets marked by that haunting – and surely true – rubric, for the horse troughs have vanished along with the horses, and no longer is it sport, as it was for us, to run behind a cart, then leap, catch the backboard, and swing from it, while – it was the corollary of our fun, and I never remember resenting it – others, themselves no stranger to the game, would call out to the driver, in a curious musical chant which I can sing to this day, 'Whip behind, guv'nor', to tell him that his cart was being used for purposes other than conveying his merchandise. As I recall, few drivers did in fact flick us off; live and let live was the rule.

These, however, were the full-sized carts, the equivalent of a modern lorry; the ice cart, bearing a most unhygienic open load of blocks that dripped steadily, was smaller, and the rag-a-bone man's smaller still, drawn by a pony rather than any of the broadfooted workhorses that pulled the drays. The cat's-meat man's cart was smaller still, and he pushed it himself; I suppose it was horse meat, though I cannot remember ever inquiring.

Once a month, from the High Street end, a colourful troupe poured down Plender Street, pushing a barrel organ and doing cartwheels in the middle of the road. These were the Whoopees, though whether that is what they called themselves, or merely their nickname in my home, I do not know; whatever their name, the pavements on both sides of the street were crowded when the Whoopees came dancing, juggling and making music, and I recall a rain of pennies, at the end of the performance, from the windows that provided a perfect view of the show. Another form of street entertainment, at much the same frequency, was provided by two elderly men, said to be unemployed Welsh miners, who sang gloomy duets so badly that they might have been the originals of the chestnut about the busker who made his money from being paid to go and sing in the next street; they invariably included 'All through the night' in their selection, and finished with 'Trees', a mournful enough tune even when sung well:

> Poems are made by fools like me,
> But only God can make a tree.

The Welshmen's performance, for some reason, always inspired my mother to song, in very much the same idiom; there was a ballad about Thora, and another (possibly the same one) in which a gentleman laments his lost love:

> I loved thee in life too little,
> I love thee in death too much.

Of professional entertainment of any kind I can remember nothing. The Bedford Music Hall was just round the corner, in the High Street, but I was never taken to it, and entered it for the first time many years later when Donald Wolfit put on a Shakespeare season there. Even then I had never heard of Sickert, and by the time I discovered him the Bedford was closed and derelict, though it was not torn down until much later still.

Early visits to the cinema constituted perhaps the strangest experience of my childhood; I had heard much about the wonders and delights of the moving pictures, and yearned to see for myself. So, eventually, I did, after a fashion, for what neither I nor my mother knew was that I had very poor sight; at that time it was not customary for children's eyes to be tested without special reason, and I did not discover my deficiency until I went to my public school, where an eye test was a standard part of a standard medical examination, and for me ('But this child is half-blind,' cried the examining optician) led instantly to a prescription for spectacles. '

At the time of my first visits to the cinema, however, I assumed, as is the trusting way of children, that the strange mist in which I spent my life (and which may provide the reason that I am so unobservant, never having learned to use my eyes because there was nothing to see with them) was the real world; I had instinctively solved the obvious school problem by making for the front row of desks, from which I could see the blackboard.

If, therefore, what I saw was what everybody saw, it followed that what I could see at the cinema was all there was to see. The cinema, then, was a long, dark room, in which the audience sat at one end, while at the other noises, including voices, emerged from a strange, flickering, shapeless light, grey in colour; patrons sat before this unintelligible and almost unimaginably boring spectacle for a couple of hours, and then went home.

And that was all; or rather, in my case, almost all. The one thing I could see on a cinema screen was the Censor's certificate at the beginning. At the top of the screen there appeared – I think still do appear – the words 'British Board of Film Censors'. These words were in type large enough for me to read them, as were, though smaller, the words immediately below them, which read 'This is to certify that – ', followed by the name of the film, on the next line. This, however, was in much smaller lettering, and moreover in cursive script; to me, it was only a grey smear, and the words below the title, in even smaller letters, which must have said, for an audience including children, 'has been passed for Universal Exhibition', were to me completely invisible. So the first two lines of the certificate, being all I could make out, were for me the whole of it; it never occurred to me that the text continued but that I could not see it, and I simply concluded that the cinema was not only pointless and boring, but run by people who were plainly mad, because every film began with an announcement, tautological to the point of lunacy, to the effect that (as I instinctively stressed it): '*This* is to certify *that*'. The shock, the amazement, the overwhelming and inexpressible delight, that I experienced when I finally donned my first pair of glasses and saw that there was a world around me the very existence of which I had not so much as suspected will remain with me for the rest of my life; at the first film I saw thereafter, when I discovered that not only the cinema, but the very classification certificate, made sense after all, my surprise and delight were hardly less.

Further up the street, past the barrows, was the dairy, where I first saw the terrible sign, perhaps the most powerful monument ever erected to meanness of spirit: 'Please do not ask for credit, as a refusal often offends.' But the dairy provided another, gentler, memory; of an institution now as irrecoverably extinct as the muffin man with his tray and his bell. It sometimes chanced that there was no milk in the house at a time when the dairy was shut; late-night super-markets, indeed supermarkets themselves, were then unknown. But there was an alternative solution; I was dispatched, with a penny and a jug, to the dairy, in the door of which was embedded a bronze tap, with a slot above it. The penny was inserted in the slot, and the jug held underneath the tap; when the penny dropped, the milk began to flow, the supply drying up as soon as a penn'orth (which I suppose would have been a pint) had been delivered. This was the Iron Cow, and was certainly the only cow I had ever seen.

The dairy also, of course, sold butter, of a deep yellow hue, but so urban was the world I lived in, and so difficult was it for me to understand that there was another, very different world, that there was no connection in my mind between the dairy's butter and the dairy's milk, and even more strange would have been the news that they both came out of an animal; I suppose I must have thought, if I thought of the matter at all, that such things were made in factories, just as everything else was. I do not expect to be believed, and hardly dare to admit it, when I say that I did not even know that there was a connection between a chicken and an egg, and when I first heard the riddle I was quite unable to make any sense of it at all.

There was grass a couple of streets away, a miserable enclave called 'the gardens', presumably a miniature park, but it was hardly bigger than a swimming-bath. (There were public baths – washrooms, that is – only a few doors along the street from my home, but though the only bath we had was a tin one that sat upon the floor and was laboriously filled from kettles and saucepans by my mother, 'the baths' were spoken of only in tones of fear and contempt, being thought a repository of countless diseases and a means of keeping clean resorted to only by those who had fallen so low as to have lost all sense of decency and shame.) 'The gardens' were laid out in the dreariest style, with benches in railway-station green, probably the most depressing colour ever invented.

Sometimes there was an expedition to Waterlow Park, and occasionally a visit to Hampstead Heath or Parliament Hill Fields, the latter being fixed in my memory because it held the only tree I have ever managed to climb. Once a year, though, there was a special visit to Hampstead Heath, on Bank Holiday when the Fair was in spate, and my grandfather would take me on what must have been the very last open-topped bus. The walk up to the Fair proper from where the bus stopped is more vivid in my mind than the roundabouts and sideshows themselves; both sides of the avenue were lined with vendors of sweets, toys, favours, comic hats, rattles, whistles, liquorice sticks, monkey nuts, ribbons, streamers and an object the name of which I cannot recall, if it even had one: it was, in effect, a paper cat-o'-nine-tails, with a slim cardboard tube for handle and a colourful bunch of strips of paper attached to it. Once, having preserved one of these past Fairday, I was playing with it in the room where my grandfather plied his trade as a tailor, and where there was a gas ring on which he would heat the iron; I waved the toy about like a semaphore flag, and inevitably went too near the flame. Only the providential entrance of one of my uncles at that point prevented the blaze from spreading; he snatched it from my terrified grasp, flung it to the ground and trampled on it.

One of the chief consequences of this life, though I imagine it was not inevitable, was that I grew up, and remain, ignorant of country matters to an extent which now seems almost incredible; even an oak I know only by its acorns. (I suppose I half know a chestnut – half, because I know it only if, in due season, it is surrounded by fallen 'conkers'.) Perhaps I love cities in sheer self-defence, because I would be so helpless in the country; in addition to my ignorance of nature, I am night-blind, and any place without street lamps is therefore for me *terra incognita* in a very special sense.

Of course it is more than that. There is a quality about a city that only a city has, and it is that quality that sets the string of life vibrating in me.

Cities deteriorate; all of them, I think. So does the country, but the country deteriorates by becoming uncountrified, by taking on the aspect of the town; motorways and picnic areas and 'amenities' destroy and cover the land, and the Forestry Commission covers with its carpet-bombing whatever is left showing through the concrete. Cities deteriorate while remaining fully citified, and therein lies their tragedy, and the pain it gives city-lovers. Cities run down because their inhabitants cease to care about how they should be treated, and hardly know that the question arises, and visitors, at least those from other cities, seem to go out of their way to treat them badly.

This inexorably downward course can be seen in the history of pedestrian precincts, one of those promising ideas (like high-rise blocks of flats) with a catch in them. The idea of a pedestrian thoroughfare is soundly based; it recognizes that a city needs somewhere in which people can stroll or saunter, without having to be ever watchful for the traffic. The catch, however, is that the pedestrian streets begin to cater, by some horrible kind of Gresham's Law, for the worst in the strollers and saunterers, and these, encouraged to linger, bear out in full measure the ancient adage that Satan finds work for idle hands to do.

If people are not in a hurry they can be sold things; thus, the reasoning of the shopkeepers in the pedestrian thorough-fares. So far, so good; but then Satan rears his head. If the pedestrians are not going anywhere, it is likely that they have nowhere in particular they wish or need to go to. They must therefore, runs the reasoning, be shiftless, idle folk, on whom good quality products would be wasted. It would be better, therefore, to stock our premises with cheap rubbish: food-rubbish, drink-rubbish, clothes-rubbish, jewellery-rubbish, pop-music cassette-rubbish. Moreover, though we want them to stop long enough to buy our rubbish, we do not want them to linger over doing so and thus deter others from buying in their turn. So we shall put the racks of rubbish-clothes on the pavement, and dispense the rubbish-food and rubbish-drink from hatches, to be taken away, not at tables, to be consumed on the premises, and we shall put the rubbish-music on players in our shops, and amplify the noise to the street.

Then the strollers and saunterers are let loose. Sold beer and soft drinks in cans, and fried chicken or hamburgers in cardboard containers, they throw cans and containers alike on to the ground. Spending the day drinking, it is only natural that they should pass the evening fighting. Gazing, empty-headed and aimless, at the same stretch of blank wall for an hour, they break the monotony, of their lives as well as of the wall, by spray-painting *graffiti*. (Has anyone ever pointed out what a huge proportion of *graffiti* in modern cities consist of the names of the *graffitinieri* and their friends? It is as though they are desperate to prove to themselves, as publicly and stridently as possible, the one thing that, with good reason, they doubt: that they exist.)

That describes Carnaby Street; but few cities elsewhere have the right to jeer. On my first visit to Copenhagen it did not have its pedestrian precinct, the Strøget; my Retreat from Moscow was therefore untouched by such speculations. More, I had nothing from the past to compare with the present when I revisited it twenty years later, so the wretchedness and dirt of the Strøget held no greater poignancy for me than was provided by the wretchedness and dirt themselves. But the first time I went to Amsterdam, in the 1950s, its pedestrian precinct, the Kalvesstraat, was already in existence, a gentle and gracious concourse, with shops of high quality and window displays sensitively arranged, beneath facias of fine and elegant design; over the years, I have watched it take on the same aspect as the others, ugly, cheap and defiled.

Le mieux est l'ennemi du bien; would that that were all. Unfortunately, *le pire est l'ennemi du bien* also, and a far more deadly and powerful foe. Within a hundred paces, on my anniversary return to Copenhagen, I saw McDonaldburgers, Skyburgers, Tastyburgers, Mackayburgers, Burger King Burgers; in half a mile I saw only one little restaurant catering for diners who were willing to take their time. As for cafés, they seemed hardly to exist at all; where the devil is a visitor to Copenhagen supposed to eat a Danish pastry?

In Amsterdam, as in London, whole city blocks have been taken over by the pornography industry, and the property developers lie awake at night wondering what further beautiful old buildings they can pull down. In London, as in many other British cities, there are enormous and obtrusive rubbish bins on the pavements, put there by the municipal authorities or civic-minded shopkeepers and businessmen, but they are painted in such vile colours, and bestrewn with municipal or commercial advertising in such ugly typefaces, that the result is to make the streets worse than if the bins were not there and the litter was thrown upon the ground, which it usually is anyway. And everywhere, sooner or later, the fountains, one of the greatest glories of any city for centuries, run dry, and those with eyes to see and hearts to feel realize that the barbarians have taken over.

Yet even a dying city is still a city, and still works its magic for me. And that magic, though it is much greater than the sum of its parts, is not entirely inexplicable, springing from nowhere into my heart. There are qualities in a city that I know I respond to, and these can be defined. First of them, surely, is water, and few great cities are without it. They could hardly be, because most cities were not built arbitrarily or overnight (though a few were – Jaipur, St Petersburg and Brasilia most notable among them); they grew up at points convenient for survival, security and trade, and no city could ensure any of these, let alone all of them, unless it had ready access to the rest of the world. The power and prosperity of cities are writ in water, and a city does not have to be Venice or Amsterdam to recognize the fact.

I go so far as to feel uneasy in a city without water, or without enough to make the point; that absurd trickle called the Spree, for instance, in Berlin, does not deserve the name of river, and although I have been repeatedly assured that there is a river in Manchester, and even told its name – the Irwell – I have never been able to find it, though a real city river calls attention to itself. Not surprisingly; rivers are more alive than any other natural phenomenon, more so even than the sea, and not just because they are in constant motion, or even because they bring life to the city and contain life in the form of their fish. A river is invariably *going somewhere*; it therefore has a destination, and a purpose, something that only living creatures can claim.

Rivers have been personalized (Old Father Thames), fantasized (Anna Livia Plurabelle), sung to (Ol' Man River), regarded as sacred (Ganges, Alph), invented to symbolize the inevitability of death (Styx), remembered because they mark turning points in human history (Rubicon). If it were not for the winding Maiandros we would not meander; without the Rhine literature and music would be the poorer by the loss of countless legends; Christ was baptized in the Jordan. And when river and city meet, the human race puts down the roots of civilization; it is my consciousness of that truth that makes it impossible for me to get used to the idea of invisible rivers, those streams that have been covered over as cities spread, but continue to flow silently and unseen beneath the streets. One day, I believe, the Fleet and the Cranbourn will rise from the grave, burst through the pavements and take a watery revenge on London.

The water of a city does not, of course, have to be that of a river, though even in those cities which have water in other forms it seems to aspire to the condition of a river; the Grand Canal itself is more like a river than most rivers I know, and I defy any but the most knowledgeable citizen of Amsterdam to distinguish between the Amstel River and the canals. Copenhagen has no river, though it has a handsome little canal; but it has the noblest water of all, nobler even than a river, for the very sea flows around and through it, in the form of various creeks and sounds and fiords. Brasilia, which was simply carved out of the jungle, has no river, and it would have had no water at all if the men who designed it had not divined that even an artificial city must be able to get its feet wet, and therefore incorporated a huge artificial lake into the plans. There are other lakeside cities which thus dispense with water thoroughfares; Geneva, for instance, with its *jets d'eau* leaping high into the air in the harbour, and Constance, where the lake is fed from the source of the Rhine, and feeds the growing river in turn as it leaves the lake at the other end. And there is Buffalo, which is surely excused rivers, canals, lakes, nay duckponds and kitchen taps, for the city of Niagara hardly needs to draw attention to its water.

Almost all city rivers are slow; you can sometimes stare down at the Thames for an hour without being quite certain that it is moving at all, and the rivers of New York, crawling lazily beneath the bridges sagging beneath their load of rushing cars, are a permanent reproach to the hurry of the citizens. So, even more, is the Jumna, which washes the feet of the Taj Mahal; or it would be if the citizens of Agra were ever in a hurry. But they are not so foolish.

The motto of a city river is *Tout lasse, tout casse, tout passe*, but cities themselves generally reject this calming philosophy, and some are determined to show that they will have none of it. So the citizens, not only of New York, fight back by scratching their initials on the sky to prove that they passed this way. The skyscrapers of Manhattan reject the calm wisdom of its rivers, which have seen the years come and go, and know that nothing ever really changes; angry stone fingers point presumptuously at the heavens in unconvincing denial.

Spires, whether of twentieth-century skyscrapers or twelfth-century cathedrals, provide the second essential for a city. Some of the world's cities seem to be made of nothing else. Oxford, for instance, has a river, though the people of the city have to call it the Isis to remind themselves that it exists, for all that it is nothing but the Thames; yet Oxford will go down to history – has already gone down to history – as the City of Dreaming Spires, for it is spires that make a skyline, that provide landmarks for the approaching traveller or enemy, that pin the city to the ground even as they tether the sky above it.

I think of some of these searchlights, these jabbing forefingers, in the cities I love. The Campanile in Venice, dominating even the city's thousand church towers; the homely Scott Monument in Edinburgh; the spire of St Stephan's in Vienna; the two most beautiful crowns of Copenhagen – the barley-sugar spire on the old Stock Exchange building and the golden staircase twisting round the spire of the Church of Our Saviour; even the strange bent spire of Chesterfield, of which coarse locals say that it leaned over in astonishment when it saw a virgin go past, and will lean back straight again when it sees another. And then, in my native London, Westminster Cathedral (an ugly building but an impressive tower); St Martin-in-the-Fields; the ridiculous but lovable Senate House, a parody of a skyscraper; the television mast at Crystal Palace, our secular version of those Gothic supplications to God in stone; and Big Ben. I saw none of these as a child, and as for the spires and towers of the English cathedrals that I have come to love – Salisbury, Durham with its attendant fortress (spirit and substance allied against the world), Peterborough, Gloucester, Canterbury, Lincoln, York – I did not so much as suspect their existence.

Nor, for that matter, have I any childhood image at all from the centre of London. Did I see Piccadilly Circus, St Paul's, Buckingham Palace? Memory is silent; I have the faintest recollection of Tower Bridge, but that is all. Not even Trafalgar Square? No, but I have a much later remembrance of that noble plain, which will have to suffice, for to this day I start with shame when I recall it, though it must have been much more than twenty years ago now. Some friends who lived on the south coast asked me to meet two children, son and daughter of Danish friends of theirs, at Liverpool Street Station. They were coming to spend a holiday with my friends, and I was to meet them at the boat-train which they would be taking from Harwich after a sea voyage from Copenhagen, and put them on the Eastbourne train at Victoria, from which they would be plucked by their hosts.

The children – a boy of twelve and a girl of ten – were almost like a caricature of what Danish children are supposed to look like; beautiful, fair-haired and blue-eyed, and the girl actually curtseyed when we met. Also, they spoke English almost faultlessly. There was time in hand before their train to Sussex was due to leave; I thought I would show them – it was their first visit to Britain – some of the famous buildings and sights that they must have heard about and seen photographs of.

Tower Bridge, St Paul's, the Embankment, the Houses of

Parliament; Westminster Abbey, Buckingham Palace, Piccadilly Circus; the children's eyes grew ever rounder, their cries of delight and astonishment more unrestrained. Then we came to Trafalgar Square. 'There,' said their guide, very pleased with the effect his city was having on the visitors, 'that's Nelson's Column – and there's Nelson on the top.' There was silence from the children. 'Nelson,' I said, 'Nelson – you know, he put the telescope to his blind eye and said "Fight on". Surely you've heard of *Nelson?*' The silence deepened; fancy, I thought, they've heard of Queen Victoria, and even Christopher Wren, but they've never heard of Nelson.

It was time to go. I delivered them to their train at Victoria, equipped with instructions and toffee-apples (another curtsey from the girl), watched it pull out, and rang my friends to tell them that the children were on their way. I left the station; I had crossed the forecourt with its bus lanes, and was just stepping up on to the pavement on the other side, when I was struck paralysed in mid-stride. I had at last remembered what Nelson had been doing when he put his telescope to his blind eye and ignored the signal to withdraw.

A city needs, as its third necessity, a heart; if I did not, as a child, know that my own city had a most splendid one, I certainly understood later. Some cities have been planned from the start, or look as though they have, round a central square. The Plaza Mayor in Salamanca is a miracle of harmony and proportion, and pours out serenity like balm upon the traveller; surely the square was built first, and the city obliged to tiptoe round it to avoid disturbing its peace? I do not know whether the Grand-Place in Brussels is truly the centre of the city, but that extraordinary gallery of noble frontages draws the traveller to it as though some unseen but irresistible centripetal force is at work. Paris is more cunning; from the Arc de Triomphe to the Tuileries, via the Champs Elysées, the Rond-Point and the Place de la Concorde, it looks as though it was planned and built as one mighty, marching vista of perfectly fitted segments, though of course it was not. But it gives that beautiful, heartless city, in which I have never spent an entirely happy day, and only one entirely happy night, an axis on which to turn that is as strong and fixed as any square or rotunda, even that mighty sea of marble outside St Peter's, with its famous conjuring trick of the vanishing columns.

I cannot remember seeing Trafalgar Square before I was at least fourteen. In those days, the Old Vic Theatre Company, bombed out of its home south of the river, was installed in St Martin's Lane, at the New Theatre, now called the Albery. In those days, too, theatres still had galleries, and even pits, and the seats for both, in the case of the Old Vic at the New, were sold only on the day of the performance, lest those theatre-goers not quite quick enough, or quick enough but unlucky, should go to their graves still failing to buy tickets from among those bookable in advance, which were inevitably all sold out as soon as the box office opened.

The demand was easily explained; those were the days when a single play, let alone a season, could contain Olivier, Richardson, Guinness, Sybil Thorndike and Lewis Casson, Margaret Leighton and Joyce Redman. In the school holidays, therefore, I would rise before dawn and catch the first Underground train to Trafalgar Square, then walk up to the theatre and queue until the tickets were sold at 10 a.m. The precious slip of paper obtained, I would go and have a cup of tea – at, if I was in funds and feeling dashing, the Lyons Corner House in Coventry Street. Those dawns, too, which must have been around the time of my dormitory vigil at school, remain in my memory, not just because of the riches of the theatre that they led me to in the evenings (Olivier as Hotspur, Sergius, Oedipus, Astrov, the Button-Moulder, Richardson as Vanya, Peer Gynt, Falstaff, Bluntschli, Cyrano, Guinness as Abel Drugger and the Comte de Guise), but because they gave me a satisfying feeling of independence which I can savour still. I woke myself, travelled by myself, bought my ticket by myself, even breakfasted by myself; the first blood of adolescence, clearly, was flowing through my veins. It was from that time, also, that I have my first recollections of Piccadilly Circus, then, as now, a mess, but a mess with character, life and a heart, not the filthy, hopeless squalor that now dominates it. Considering how we boast still that Piccadilly Circus is the hub of the world, it is astonishing that for decades on end we have permitted it to deteriorate in this fashion, a decline mitigated not at all by the constant succession of official plans put forward for its rebuilding, none of them ever started, much less finished.

Piccadilly Circus, in my youth, had a shabby elegance as well as spirit, and Coventry Street, though it is impossible to believe as much today, was a thoroughfare of high quality, with a very distinguished restaurant in Scott's and the old-fashioned middle-class charm and respectability of the Corner House. It also had a newspaper seller, just by the entrance to the Underground, who terrified me, and even now I cannot entirely repress a shudder when I think of him. He was there for years, and what gave me nightmares was that his nose was gradually but inexorably disappearing; month by month, something seemed to be eating it away, and eventually he had no nose left at all, only a leather patch where it had been. At that age, I had never even heard of syphilis, which was presumably the agent of this strange disintegration, and I could not understand what was happening to him.

Gradually, my conscious feeling for the city took hold. I had dreamed of Cambridge as the university I would go to; I had never seen it, but I had read *The Longest Journey*, and been fired by Forster's love of it, and the way he showed his characters growing and blossoming, under its benign, unhurried influence, into complete human beings. I, too, would go to Cambridge and talk the night away, discussing whether the cow was really in the meadow, whether the meadow itself was really there. A violent youthful infatuation with politics, set off by, of all forgotten authors, Douglas Reed, put paid to that, and I made instead for the

London School of Economics; I blush now for the naivety that made me want to be a politician, and a deeper scarlet for the notion that the L.S.E. was a good place to go for those who wanted to become one. (A good many of my fellow students did, though; Sydney Irving became a Labour M.P. and would probably have become Speaker in time, had he not lost his seat and failed to get back into the House; John Stonehouse became Postmaster-General; and Errol Barrow, who could have had a career in Labour politics in Britain, decided to return instead to his native Barbados, and was rewarded for his loyalty by becoming, and remaining for many years, prime minister of that tiny but most friendly of the Caribbean nations.)

It is strange, at least I find it so, to reflect that my life, crowded, apart from my career, with disappointment and failure, contains only one absolutely unassuageable yearning for a second chance, only one vain regret that I cannot shake off: my desire to have been a student at Cambridge. It became one of my favourite cities later, and when I visit it now, and wander into those courts with their grass shining in the sun, as bright as a sword, I never leave without having to fight back the tears. What makes it worse is that if I had been a little older, even by a single year, I would have had the best of both worlds, for L.S.E. was evacuated to Cambridge during the war, and housed in Clare College; the year I went up, 1946, was L.S.E.'s first year back in London. Oxford I have never learned to love as much.

When I began to travel, the city took hold even more strongly; not for many years did I make for any kind of countryside, and I have never willingly spent as much as a day by the sea or an hour on the beach. Salzburg and Edinburgh were two of my earliest loves among cities, both visited for their Festivals. Both, of course, are liberally strewn with the remains of the eighteenth century, though they experienced that extraordinary epoch in very different ways, and reflect it very differently now. But both gave me, and continue to give, a lightening of the heart from the

96

moment I set foot in them, and I know few sights more refreshing to the spirit than the noble lantern spire of St Giles in the Royal Mile, a fitting crown for the Queen of Scotland, and Fischer von Erlach's Holy Trinity Church in the Marktplatz, standing guard over Salzburg's two best hotels, the *gemütlich*, old-world Bristol, and the suave, bustling Österreichischer Hof.

I was late to Italy, and much later still to Venice. I had spent a lot of time in Austria and Bavaria, and was familiar with the sophistication of Munich, which is still a handsome and fruitful city, before I had set eyes on Milan, or even Florence. And I had met the ghost of Vienna, where only the *Schlamperei* (together with the *Tafelspitz* and Demel's) is still what it was, before I knew where Siena or Assisi were, let alone why I should visit them.

In Vienna, of course, before finally crossing the Alps, I haunted the opera, but my most vivid memory of the city is of my first sight of the salt cellar that Benvenuto Cellini made for Francis I, in the Kunsthistorisches Museum, from which I concluded that Francis must have been uncommonly fond of salt, for he could have had a bath in it. I also saw there the two Dürer drawings, of the hare and the supplicating hands, that are among the chief glories of that gallery. Nowadays, they are no longer on show, and the visitor sees only copies; but I have seen the originals, and have not forgotten them.

Nor my first sight of Venice. It was winter, and I was staying at the Danieli, which puts the date back a long way, for I would not have dreamed, these fifteen years and more, of setting foot in the place either to sleep or to eat.

I dropped my bags at the hotel and hurried out to San Marco; I had arrived late, and it was already dark. It was also snowing. It does not snow much in Venice, and what little does fall comes but rarely; I have never seen snow there again, though I go only in the winter now, but one experience is enough to fix such a sight in the mind for ever. As I stood in the deserted Piazza at the Basilica end, and looked up at the fine snow drifting diagonally down, gleaming in the lights above the pavement, I thought I had never seen any sight so beautiful in my life. Nor have I since wished to revise that opinion, though Venice has never been as close to my heart as many other cities; it died too long ago, and is too obviously uninterested in resurrection, a Vienna without the music in the air, a Berlin without the determination.

It was in Venice that I discovered the fourth necessity of a city, and on my first visit, too. Not surprisingly, perhaps, for Venice is probably richer in courtyards than any other place on earth, indeed she is practically made of them, but there are few lovable cities in Europe without them, and they will save the soul of a city otherwise damned beyond redemption, even the horrible Palma. There is a lovely one in Copenhagen, called Brøste's, full of old shops and odd proportions, and many in The Hague, though of the two Dutch cities I prefer the more robust Amsterdam. Florence is liberally supplied with court-yards, too, and so is London, particularly east of Charing Cross. The rebuilt Munich lacks them, but they have been included in the rebuilt Nuremberg, where I went in 1971 for the colossal exhibition mounted for the quincentenary of Dürer's birth, and the new production of *The Mastersingers* that the Opera had staged as its contribution to the festivities; nor did I fail to dine at the Goldenes Posthorn, which was founded in the year Dürer was twenty-one; I like to think he had his coming-of-age party in that noble cellar.

American cities I got to know even later, and though I find almost all of them rife with that essentially American belief that any achievement is possible given sufficient hard work, few that I know are either beautiful or lovable, let alone both. There is San Francisco, but San Francisco is so self-conscious (and so European) that it is hard to take it seriously, for all the marvels of its setting and the use that has been made of it. It is a city in which the visitor, if he is to avoid disillusion, would be wise to remain on the surface, and there, certainly, the City by the Bay offers an invigorating combination of beauty, gaiety and creativeness; only the third of these is a false front, but it is the third that is the most important.

Still the first two are not to be dismissed too readily. Once, I found myself in San Francisco on the eve of the Chinese New Year, though I had had no idea in advance that my visit was to fall on a day of such celebration. (San Francisco's Chinese population is said to be the largest of any city in the Occident, and the New Year being ushered in on that occasion was the Year of the Dragon, a particularly auspicious period in the septennial revolution of the Chinese years.) In the evening, I was told, there would be a grand procession, which I should on no account miss; nor did I, nor was there any great difficulty in finding a vantage-point from which to see the parade, for the extraordinary hills of the city, which make some of the streets slope at an angle of thirty degrees, form natural grandstands, and since all traffic was banned from the central area of the city while the procession was on the march, the spectators simply sat in the road for a perfect view.

The dragon is a benign creature in Chinese mythology, not, as in the west, a hostile one (St George must be a puzzling figure in China), and any Chinese New Year would be attended by large quantities of them. But for the Year of the Dragon they were pressed into service from one end of the parade to the other. Phalanxes of cyclists, entirely enveloped in beautifully designed dragon canopies (so that all that could be seen was the bottom of the bicycles' wheels), led the procession, followed by every imaginable variation on the dragon theme, from individual dragon-costumed marchers to massive dragon 'floats'; on either side of the column, gaily-dressed children carried baskets from which they drew an apparently inexhaustible supply of fire crackers to throw beside the marching feet or the turning wheels, in an incessant series of explosions. And the parade, which must have been fully a mile long from fire-breathing nose to brandished tail, ended in the most magnificent dragon of all, a monster nearly a hundred yards long, its motive power supplied by sixty pairs of children inside its body, holding poles which also formed the beast's ribs; only their twinkling feet, showing beneath the dragon's silken skin, revealed that even dragons need human aid to come to life.

I arrived no less fortuitously in New Orleans once, to be greeted with the news that the following day was Mardi Gras, marked in that city with two huge parades, one white, one black (this was many years ago). The parades, which included giant lorries invisible under their coating of flowers and southern belles, were indeed impressive and enjoyable; even more so was the immense street party that filled the whole of the Vieux Carré, the original city, with its mixture of French and Spanish architecture, the most noticeable and attractive feature of which is the elaborate metal tracery that decorates the balconies of the old houses. By dint of criss-crossing the empty streets as soon as one of the processions had gone by, the spectator could arrive at a new vantage-point to watch it go by all over again. On one such journey, I found myself alone on a traffic island in the middle of a wide thoroughfare, and heard the band that led the black procession approaching; they were playing, for all the world as if they and I and the whole city were part of a sentimental film, 'When the Saints Go Marching In'. I stayed on my island, and the parade split to pass either side of it; surrounded by that most famous of all American Negro songs, I looked up from the heart of the parade at the street sign on the corner of the building opposite: I was in Basin Street.

Los Angeles is a problem that every city-lover must face sooner or later. By all reasonable tests it is beyond the farthest reaches of horror. It has streets thirty or forty or *fifty* miles long; giant motorways cutting through it like the handiwork of a berserk giant with a scythe, complete with interchanges like the knitting of a no less frenzied giantess; residential areas in which upstart Elizabethan half-timbering nestles uncoyly beside a patent Greek temple and a Babylonian palace stands cheek by jowl with a French château; it contains two dozen monster villages – Pasadena, Long Beach, Florence, Montebello, Santa Monica, Glendale, Burbank, Inglewood, Arcadia, Anaheim, South Whittier,

Beverly Hills, Garden Grove – jammed, vainly protesting their individual identity, into one uniform megalopolis with no central area anywhere; and the sign outside the Paul Getty Museum at Malibu is a knell for our world even if the oil never runs out: 'Pedestrians not admitted'.

Los Angeles also has Hollywood. Hollywood, they tell you before your suitcase has touched the floor, is not a geographical entity but a state of mind. The splendours are faded now, in some parts even seedy, and a certain air of living in the real world is to be detected where once upon a time there were only worlds of fantasy. And yet I defy anyone who has ever been a child not to feel the magic of the old Grauman's Chinese Theatre, where the forecourt is paved with the names of the stars, invited to step into the wet concrete, write their names in it, and then watch until the cement dried and gave immortality of a kind to the gods and goddesses of the most ephemeral of the arts.

I went once on the tour of Universal Studios, where in the course of a morning I shook hands with Dracula, was captured by spacemen and rescued after an epic battle with the forces of Galactica, encountered prehistoric monsters, narrowly escaped the snapping teeth of Jaws himself, drove through the Red Sea, which obligingly parted as I arrived and closed again behind me, survived a most impressive avalanche, and readily allowed myself to be photographed in a snowstorm, a stagecoach and the stocks. But as I wandered among whole streets and squares of houses and shops that were nothing but façades, the very bricks made of foam rubber, I could understand why Hollywood's magic-lantern show so entirely captured the imagination of the whole world, and has not quite let go yet.

This place ought to be unbearable, its population collectively insane and its visitors catatonic with shock. Well, it does have the melancholy distinction of the highest murder-rate in the western world. And yet when I apply the city-lover's most searching test – does the heart lift or does it sink? – Los Angeles, to my astonishment, comes out on the side of the angels it was named after. It is impossible and absurd, yet it is full of character, and even of beauty – I have never seen so many attractive private gardens so well kept, and for me at least it stimulates, charms and entertains like few other places I know. Surely it is no accident that it was in this bewitched, bewitching city that the dream factories of the cinema were built, and if you are seeking Baghdad-on-the-Pacific, where Sindbad's ship may be moored at the waterfront and Aladdin's Cave is round the next corner, it is in Los Angeles that you will find your heart's desire.

Even so, it is New York that seems to me to possess almost everything a city needs, apart from age. Every imaginable taste in every imaginable area of life can be satisfied in it, and I can never tire of those vast valleys which will so amaze the archaeologists of the thirtieth century (provided they have long enough shovels) when they come to excavate New York's remains. The American spirit of possibility is at its strongest here, made all the more visible by the sight of the penalty for failure, and the contrast with the inward-looking hopelessness of Britain, where nothing is believed possible any longer unless somebody else is willing to pay for it, is at its starkest.

I guessed, or was told, most of this before I first went to New York; what I did not guess, and what nobody told me, is that it is beautiful. Yet surely it is as lovely, in its way, as any ancient city of Europe with its layers of history and architecture; only because New York's way is so startlingly different is it difficult to think of it in terms of beauty. Few of those towering blocks, in every possible shade and texture of stone, concrete, steel and glass, are beautiful in themselves, and fewer still are particularly fitting or comfortable to live or work in. But if we think of downtown Manhattan as composed of huge sculptures rather than individual buildings, we must, if we have any imagination at all, find those sweeping panoramas as exciting, harmonious and heart-tearing as any combination elsewhere of time and genius.

India I began to visit even later, and I may yet acquire

another vain and unquenchable regret: that I did not start to visit that limitless land in my youth. It was in the cities of India that I had the living proof of something I have long believed but never before been able to prove; that nothing in the external circumstances of human beings determines their essential nature, which – for good or ill – is made inside them. I saw this truth demonstrated first in Jaipur (which really is a rose-red city, and looks – though it is not, for it goes back only to the late eighteenth century – half as old as time), when I was wandering down one of the lanes of hovels which are to be found in every Indian city, and beside which the most decayed and bug-ridden tenement of the Gorbals is as a Mogul Emperor's palace in the greatest days of the Mogul Empire. Peering, in my unthinking occidental manner, into a home made of cardboard, sacking and a few pieces of corrugated iron (these last making it a palace among palaces, and the showpiece of the street), I saw poverty as I had never seen it before, not even in the faces of the old ladies freezing in Bolshoi Square.

As my eyes grew accustomed to the darkness, I could make out the family, and its entire possessions; these were a couple of plates, a few spoons and knives, a tin mug, a bit of string. But the plates and the cutlery had been washed and scoured after use, and were arranged neatly on a cardboard box (the family's only furniture). The string ran across the hovel, bearing the family's entire wardrobe apart from what they were wearing at that moment; and those few rags, too, had been washed, and were now hanging up to dry.

In one form or another, I have seen such conditions in every Indian city I have visited, and worst of all in Calcutta, where the city was overwhelmed beyond saving, as what city would not be, by the flood of refugees into it at the time of the Bangladesh war; it was said that a million extra human beings poured into a city already intolerably and suicidally crowded, in *three months*. But what is so extraordinary – so remarkable, indeed, that after every visit to India I cease to

103

believe it, and hasten to check it again as soon as I return – is that the eyes which I see looking out as I look into their pitiful homes are almost invariably steady, level and serene, the eyes of unconquered people, uncrushed by their terrible circumstances, who know that what makes them human is inside them, and know also that if they become beasts it will be because what will make them beasts is inside them also.

There is a street in Jaipur, with rows of tiny shops and tinier booths, and still tinier pushcarts, where one trader, too poor for any of these premises, has spread out his wares on the pavement. He is selling food-grains, in round metal pans a yard across, and has arranged the dishes around him and his scales. The dishes are full of colourful miniature seas of the various grains: white, yellow, red, brown, purple. And he has taken the trouble to arrange the goods so that the array of colours makes a harmonious total picture, like the palette of a giant artist. I do not suppose that he sells an ounce more of his produce – all staple foods, after all – by reason of these careful juxtapositions, and I doubt if it has ever occurred to him that he might. Where did he find the necessity and the will to make more of his tiny store than the mere setting down of it would achieve? Inside him; as the hovel-dwellers found inside them the strength that filled their eyes. The Indian city is surely the most awful test the idea of a city has ever had to endure; it seems, however, that these teeming places pass it, for even in Calcutta the citizens do not suddenly go roaring mad and murder one another by the hundred thousand. Indian cities, terrible though they are and terrible though it is that human beings should have to live thus whatever the inner serenity they can command among the ruins, strengthen my faith in humanity and what humanity lives by. But – and although this is much less important, it is not entirely to be ignored – they also strengthen a city-loving visitor's faith in cities.

A city is a record of history, for most of them are old, some older than history itself. Any city which has existed for more than a few generations bears the traces of all the storms that have swept over it, and all the suns that have shone on it. A city, and not only an Indian one, is testimony to man's powers of endurance and adaptation, in a way which is not true of the countryside, where Nature is in charge and must be obeyed. And because that testimony cannot lie, we can read from it how the city has become what it is, and what sort of people made it, and what they did with it generation by generation.

My own love for cities comes ultimately from this layered richness, this slow accretion of the years and what it is capable of telling me. It comes also from the firmness of cities, the pavement beneath my feet which resists, rather than, like earth, yielding. There is too much sky in the country; I feel weightless there, and fear I may float away. But the sky in a city is tethered to the roofs and domes and spires and lamp-posts, and becomes a friendly canopy rather than an awful infinity.

Throughout history, it is cities that men have fought most tenaciously for: who ever heard of a meadow besieged? Bunyan's Pilgrim flees from the City of Destruction, but not to the land or the sea; his goal is the City Celestial. They call Cologne the City of the Three Kings, because it is said that the Magi are buried there; if the first three men to worship the newborn Christ were willing, their task accomplished, to die in a city, who am I to allow myself to be buried in a country churchyard? Rome is called the Eternal City not because she believes she will last for ever, but because she believes she holds an eternal truth in trust; no rolling plain, no lush green hill, would dare to make such a claim. And what did St Augustine call his most justly famous book? Why, St Paul, in the hour of his greatest danger, asserted his claim to appeal, face to face, to Caesar by reminding his captors that he came from no mean city.

And that was only Tarsus. For my part, though I hardly hope to enter the City of God, I can at least console myself with the thought that I am a native of 'the flower of cities all' (a title given to it, moreover, by a Scotsman), and I shall always offer thanks to whatever fate arranged for me to be born in London, not too far from Bow Bells.

Five

I did not acquire the habit of walking for pleasure as a child. It was a strictly utilitarian activity, done mostly under maternal supervision; I have a memory, second-hand but very powerful indeed, of crossing a busy road unsupervised, amid my mother's terror and reproaches, and another, which must be my own, of being narrowly missed by a speeding car, the driver of which tossed a cigarette end out of the window as he passed, hitting me on the cheek with it. My grandfather once snatched to safety a small child who had wandered off the kerb with the evident intention of going under the hooves of an approaching horse or the wheels of the cart it was pulling; there was some feeling in the family circle that he should have had a medal, accompanied by a sum of money, for this action, though he thought the idea absurd. But the episode reinforced the early conviction that walking was a necessary but dangerous activity. I must have walked to school, though I have no recollection of doing so, and I am sure I would not have been allowed to do so on my own. At my public school we *marched* everywhere – to chapel, to the dining-hall, even to the swimming-pool – and the resultant distaste for the collective practice of individual activities has, I am happy to say, lasted the rest of my life.

Nor did I embark upon a love of the country walk, though boarding school was my first experience of the country. As was the marching to purposeful walking, so was the 'run' to walking for exercise or pleasure. I think the institution of the run is peculiar to the English public school; I would certainly wish it no wider currency, and at the time heartily wished it a considerably narrower one. Led by a teacher or prefect, a herd of us would set out, in shorts and singlets, to run round a particular route – they varied widely in length and difficulty – but the pace (though I was inevitably one of the rearguard, and would often straggle in long after everybody else) was too hot to offer any chance of learning anything about nature. The Entomology Society, or the Bug-Hunters, as they were inevitably known, went on organized rambles looking for their miniature prey, but that held no interest for me at all, except for the day when the Bug-Hunters returned with the wonderful news that the mildly unpopular teacher who directed this activity had, while drawing the group's attention to some kind of marsh life, slipped and fallen into a pond, and had thereupon so far forgotten his duty to set an example to the young that he had sworn for some time without stopping, using expressions in the course of doing so that the Bug-Hunters claimed they did not even know.

In season, there were blackberries, which were at first very strange to me; I had the townee's customary belief that the hedges of the countryside were crammed with poisonous fruit, not to be distinguished, except by the most learned eye, from the innocent kind, and it was some time before I could swallow a blackberry without unease, provoked by my fear that I was in fact eating deadly nightshade or poison ivy. I survived, and in doing so conceived a passion for blackberries that I have retained, though of recent years it has been surpassed by my discovery of blueberries. No doubt they existed in the hedges of my youth, too, but I would not have risked them even after I had gained confidence in blackberries, and indeed I would hardly risk picking and eating anything else to this day – certainly not a mushroom, imbued as I am with the townee's even more firmly held conviction that they are all toadstools, one bite of which must inevitably prove fatal. There was one other exception, a fruit as strange to me as the blackberries: *fraises des bois*. When my schoolfellows introduced me to the wild strawberry, I thought for a long time that they were playing a trick on me, and that the tiny creature was unfit to eat, if not poisonous. If I knew one thing about nature, it was that everything starts small and unripe, and becomes large and ripe simultaneously; the wild strawberry is red, and therefore ripe, but it is small, and therefore unripe, and the only way I could solve the riddle was with the assumption that it was something nauseating disguised as something delicious and familiar, for the idea of different species within the same genus was quite foreign to me.

When I conquered my suspicion and acquired a taste for wild strawberries, a dilemma presented itself. We would wander off on a Saturday afternoon with jam-jars, determined to return bearing a vast treasure for tea. But the temptation to eat as we went, returning replete but treasureless, was strong for us all, and we could be divided into spenders and savers, the weak-willed and the strong. I was a saver; I do not think it is much of an exaggeration to say that most of the subsequent years have been spent learning, with great pain and effort but of course with resultant understanding and joy, to trust life sufficiently to eat my wild strawberries as I go. But I did learn the lesson, and would never take a jam-jar to the strawberry fields today.

If I did not acquire a love of walking as I moved down the lane with the blackberries, where did it come from? I have nothing of the explorer or pioneer in me at all; I am heartily glad that I was born long after the railway, the motor car and the aeroplane were invented, that there are means of rapid communication, together with comfortable hotels and adequate restaurants, in any country I am likely to want or need to visit, and that industrial specialization has progressed far enough for me to devote myself entirely, while travelling, to the purpose of the travel. I have never learned to drive a car, or even to ride a bicycle; I am altogether unwilling to trust myself to what Kai Lung called 'the uncertain apex of a trustworthy steed'; living in a log cabin in the wilds, hewing my own wood and drawing my own water, is a prospect that repels rather than attracts me.

We forget how recent are the circumstances that enable me to take this self-indulgent attitude. Metalled roads, the internal combustion engine, the growth and geographical spread of population, civil order – all these, measured on the time-scale of the world's history, are of the most immediately recent development, however prevalent and accessible they have become. I was struck by their novelty, and even more their fragility, a few years ago when motoring through Spain to stay with friends. We had the address and directions; the day of our arrival had been appointed; we were starting from, respectively, New York and Marseilles, to meet in Madrid and drive south. We were aware, though not very consciously, that something might go wrong; planes can be delayed or diverted, cars can break down. But we also knew that if any of these things took place, nothing very serious would have happened. Telephone calls would arrange another rendezvous, messages could be left at hotels, information could be acquired or relayed, if necessary, through our host's London office or mine, a replacement car could be hired from one of the ubiquitous rental agencies, two Spanishless travellers could always find an English-speaking villager, and in the unlikely event of real catastrophe, our friends could eventually get in touch with the authorities to set in action a network of activities by police, frontier officials or hospital staffs, to discover why we had neither arrived nor announced a delay in our arrival.

All of this, even the melodramatic part at the end, we felt was quite unremarkable; today, all of us who live in centralized, technologically advanced societies, think likewise. But our confidence, and the confidence of our friends, that we would appear when we were expected and that if we did not they would be warned in advance, is something that all mankind, until very recently, would have found very odd.

For almost the whole of mankind's existence the fastest means of progress was the horse, though even the domesticated horse is a comparative newcomer if we consider the whole span of man's history, and no form of drawn carriage existed for many centuries after the horse had been caught and tamed.

The earth, almost every square foot of it now, has been explored and opened up, mapped for travellers, criss-crossed with roads that wheels may safely run on. Erasmus of Rotterdam is one of the brightest luminaries of civilization, and was fully recognized as such in his own lifetime; he corresponded with all Europe, and all Europe invited him to come and stay. That was less than five hundred years ago, yet his letters are full of apologetic refusals of such invitations, explaining that he could not afford the powerful bodyguard which would be essential if he were to travel safely through the bandit-infested territory of the most advanced and civilized lands. Even stranger is the matter of his correspondence itself; all the letters he sent abroad, and received from his correspondents in other countries, were written on the assumption that they might take anything up to two years to arrive, depending on the travelling intentions and achievements of trustworthy friends or acquaintances, and many were the letters that Erasmus and his contemporaries dispatched to correspondents who were dead long before the letters were written, let alone delivered.

Go back only a few more centuries and move only a little way to the east, and you come to forests before which the hardiest explorer might well quail, with every yard of his progress through the pathless interior having to be hacked out with axes, and with no idea in the traveller's mind of the extent – whether one mile or five hundred – of the barrier that faced him.

Yet there have always been men to take the axe in hand and walk intrepidly into the forest. There was no river too turbulent, no mountain range too high, no desert too arid, for men to wonder what lay on the other side, and to go on wondering until their desire to know the answer would give them no peace, and they slaughtered their cattle and went to find out. A few, a very few, of the brave, those imbued with not only courage but a special kind of imagination, even

111

wondered whether there might not be something on the other side of the sea itself, and eventually set off to find out, amid the cries of those who knew that they were going to their certain doom, falling over the edge of the world.

Throughout history, men have been moved to explore the unknown, in the search for trade, or booty, or souls to save, or simply knowledge, and one by one the untravelled parts of the world have yielded up their secrets. Most of those pioneers have no more identity in the world of today than have the inventors of fire, the knife or the wheel; Columbus and stout Cortez, and Lewis and Clark, are exceptions.

I have, as I say, nothing of this in me; no doubt that is why I so admire and wonder at the pioneers who pushed on beyond the last settlement, the last camp, the last railhead. And I also admire and wonder at those whose endeavours and achievements may not have opened up a continent, mapped a country, discovered a civilization, but who embarked, from necessity or curiosity, on an epic journey. There are few categories of men whose minds are more remote from mine than mountaineers; the anthropophagi and men whose heads do grow beneath their shoulders are hardly more strange. But I would think myself a poor creature if I did not thrill to the story of the attempts to conquer Everest, the still-echoing mystery of Mallory and Irvine, the final triumph of Hillary and Tensing. And who is so mean of spirit as to be unimpressed by the magnificent absurdity of Thor Heyerdahl and the Kon-Tiki Expedition, or the fearful impiety of those who dared to pluck bright honour from the pale-faced moon with the words 'That's one small step for a man, one giant leap for mankind'?

Through the centuries, most of these explorers, these travellers, have gone slowly on foot, or at the fastest on horseback. My own hero among them is Xenophon, and has been since my boyhood. I had encountered the word *anabasis*, oddly enough, before I came upon Xenophon, for Jaroslav Hašek uses it of the epic journey to Budejovice undertaken by the Good Soldier Schweik, and Schweik had been an intimate companion ever since I was fourteen. Then I read Xenophon, and have never ceased to marvel at his achievement at the head of the Ten Thousand.

Consider: amid the ruins of Athenian power and beneath the risen shadow of Sparta, the ancient Persian enemy, routed by a united Hellas at Marathon and Salamis, was still strong and still hungry. Xenophon, who could see almost as clearly as Thucydides what had brought Athens down, looked to those who exhibited the Spartan virtues, and found them in Cyrus, son of Darius, the ancient enemy himself. When Cyrus summoned an army of mercenaries from all over Greece to follow him home and help him overthrow his brother Artaxerxes and seize the Persian throne for himself, Xenophon was part of an Athenian unit that marched from Sardis to an appointment with disaster at the Battle of Cunaxa.

By all accounts, the Greeks acquitted themselves well on that field, fighting in their almost invincible phalanx, and might well have succeeded in the object for which they had enlisted. But Cyrus himself was killed in the battle, and the Greeks suddenly realized that they no longer had any business being where they were. A thousand miles of implacable deserts, mighty rivers, hostile armies and tribes, lay between the Greek army and their homes; if they were not to perish, they needed a commander who would gather them up, inspire them, marshal them, and lead them safely home.

Xenophon was the man called forth in the hour of their need; the journey was his journey, the book his book. Through all the perils that beset them he brought the Greeks, in good heart; it is one of the greatest and bravest of all the endeavours of human history, and I think it worth quoting the famous passage which tells of the moment when the Greeks caught sight of the sea and knew that, though in distance they were still only halfway, their greatest dangers were now behind them:

They came to the mountain on the fifth day, the name of the mountain being Thekes. When the men in front

113

reached the summit and caught sight of the sea there was great shouting. Xenophon and the rearguard heard it and thought that there were some more enemies attacking in the front, since there were natives of the country they had ravaged following them up behind, and the rearguard had killed some of them and made prisoners of others in an ambush, and captured about twenty raw ox-hide shields, with the hair on. However, when the shouting got louder and drew nearer, and those who were constantly going forward started running towards the men in front who kept on shouting, and the more of them there were the more shouting there was, it looked then as though this was something of considerable importance. So Xenophon mounted his horse and, taking Lycus and the cavalry with him, rode forward to give support, and, quite soon, they heard the soldiers shouting 'The sea! The sea!' and passing the word down the column. Then certainly they all began to run, the rearguard and all, and drove on the baggage animals and the horses at full speed; and when they had all got to the top, the soldiers, with tears in their eyes, embraced each other and their generals and captains. In a moment, at somebody or other's suggestion, they collected stones and made a great pile of them. On top they put a lot of raw ox-hides and staves and the shields which they had captured.

Note that when he thought the vanguard was being attacked and set out to go to their aid with the cavalry, 'Xenophon mounted his horse'; until then, he had been, like his men, on foot (the Ten Thousand had only a tiny body of cavalry), thus demonstrating, as he did in almost everything, the quality of a commander who inspires his troops not by minimizing their hardships but by sharing them. That enduring image of the Greeks' first glimpse of the friendly sea and the salvation it promised them has brought me closer than anything else I have ever read to understanding, and envying, the spirit that throughout the ages has animated those who

114

have travelled further than their fellows, and that feeling of understanding and emulation led me gradually to an impossible dream: to retrace, in a journey of my own, the route of the Ten Thousand.

I was not proposing to do it on foot; even so, a glance at the map is enough to show why the dream was an impossible one. The route of Xenophon's journey lies today through some of the most horrible and unpredictable states of the modern world, most of them cruel tyrannies and some run by bloodthirsty maniacs; only one dream I have ever had was even more extravagantly unattainable, and that was my desire to visit Angkor Wat, a dream which possessed me just when the Khmer Rouge was about to embark on the homicidal frenzy which ultimately drowned Cambodia in a sea of blood.

I admire Xenophon, and dreamed of following him, not only because of the romance and heroism of the *Anabasis*, but also for another, far newer and more prosaic, reason. We live, certainly I do, in a largely sedentary world, deafened at our desks by incessant warnings from eminent physicians, to say nothing of the vendors of slimming aids, exercise manuals and diet sheets, to the effect that we are overweight and idle, and that unless we take more exercise we shall succumb to the heartache and the thousand unnatural shocks that modern flesh is heir to. From all quarters the message is the same, and differs only slightly from that given to the man sick of the palsy: get off your bed and walk. We must, they tell us, exercise or die; for generations we have been breeding a race susceptible, because of the way we live, to afflictions of the heart, the arteries, the blood and the respiratory system, to an extent which was never true of our ancestors, who until very recently, when they wanted to go anywhere, were obliged to walk, since no other means of locomotion existed. Nor does the message fall upon deaf ears; quite the contrary, for the sale of books recommending particular diets as the way to health and slimness continue to increase, one or more being found in the best-seller lists on both sides of the

Atlantic at almost any time, though most of the diets put forward are absurd, many of them fraudulent and some dangerous.

In *The Demi-Paradise*, a film comedy made in 1943, Laurence Olivier played a Russian engineer sent to Britain to engage in some technical co-operation in furtherance of the war effort. The character speaks English, but with a notably imperfect grasp of the idioms of our language, and when he sets out, early in the film, to find the offices of the company he is to do business with, he asks a passer-by for directions to the street he is seeking, only to be told, 'It's about two miles as the crow flies.' Olivier goes glassy-eyed with dismayed incomprehension. 'Pliss,' he asks plaintively, 'how far is it as ze legs walk?'

Xenophon walked a thousand miles to Cunaxa, and a thousand miles back. But he did not do it for fun. And the tragedy of our world is not that it takes too little exercise, but that it seems to go out of its way, in its search for a route round the supposed danger, to devise means that give no pleasure at all. It is worse than that: deeply embedded now in the mind of modern sedentary man is the hideous belief that *unless* the means devised for health are painful and unpleasant they *cannot* bring the improved health that is desired. This, of course, is the ancient puritan curse, the conviction that pain must be beneficial for no better reason than that it is pain, and pleasure concomitantly harmful for no better reason than that it is pleasure.

In that unspoken but tenaciously held belief there is a terrible fallacy; the belief ignores the vital and creative truth that mankind always seeks happiness and wholeness, however difficult the search may be and however disappointing the goal may prove when it is found, and that anything which strives to turn man's head in the opposite direction, and urges that suffering should be the aim, is denying man's nature, and thus harming him as surely as a gardener who puts an iron collar on a growing tree harms the tree.

It is certainly true that in this world pain is inevitable;

116

indeed, all the greatest joys are inseparably accompanied by it. But to blur the distinction between pain and joy, shadow and sunshine, and to maintain the heretical claim that pain is good and pleasure is bad, is to be on the side of death against life; which, alas, many are, mostly without knowing it.

The results of this doctrine can be seen all round us; the latest version of the belief that mortifying the flesh is good not only for the soul but for the flesh itself, is jogging. There are joggers now in every town in the west; in some places, like Los Angeles, they are so numerous that they hinder traffic and cause inconvenience to those going quietly about their lawful business. But their very ubiquity makes possible an obvious and I think conclusive experiment, which I have carried out on many occasions, achieving exactly the same result every time. All that is required is for the experimenter to get up early in the morning, when the joggers are to be seen in their greatest numbers, and observe them closely as they go by. Such observation will always, no matter how often it is repeated, record the same phenomenon: the expression on the joggers' faces is invariably one of revulsion, pain and hatred.

I do not jog. But I do walk, even if not as far as Xenophon. It is indeed the only form of human locomotion that I practise at all, for my inability to master the arts of driving, bicycling or horse-riding leaves me no choice in the matter. I do it, however, because I enjoy it. It may also do me good; if so, so much the better. But that is not why I do it; I do it for pleasure, and if it is beneficial the benefit comes from the pleasure, not the other way round.

It should therefore be clear that I have no wish to establish or break records, to walk farther or faster than others, to create or reinforce any theory or philosophy of walking. I do not admire the prodigious walkers of history merely for the distance they have traversed; if I did, I would be obliged to include in my Pantheon, alongside Xenophon, Mao Tse-tung. I do admire some great walkers, one of the most notable in our time being John Hillaby, who walked from

117

Land's End to John o' Groat's, and then from the North Sea to the Mediterranean, avoiding roads almost every step of the way; he wrote two fine books about these walks, *Journey Through Britain* and *Journey Through Europe*,* and they are full of enviable adventures and a zest for life itself as well as for walking through it. But John Hillaby stands – walks – on the other side of a gulf that divides all walkers into two groups: he is of those who carry their house upon their backs, and pitch their tent, at the end of the day's march, beneath the stars.

I have never been attracted to this aspect of walking, despite the increased freedom it gives the walker. Some – not Hillaby, who does it solely for the freedom – would advocate it on puritan grounds; a tent on uneven and stony soil, particularly in rainy weather, will mortify the flesh, which otherwise, warm, dry and comfortable in an inn, will remain culpably unmortified. Others would not go so far, but would advocate a tent not only for the Hillabian freedom, but for the satisfaction of being beholden to no one else, and perhaps also for the extra discipline and efficiency it requires of the walker, and even for the extra weight he must carry – though here the advocate has strayed on to the puritan's cold ground.

I am of the school which holds that it is perfectly possible to combine walking and comfort, but not walking and comfort and camping. Moreover, the tent-pitchers are liable to have their quarters invaded without invitation by animals, insects and even snakes, all of which fill me with apprehension; I never admired Hillaby more than when he writes that, wishing to find a dry patch for his tent on ground that was generally wet, he 'kicked a cow to its feet'. Besides, if the walker leaves the path altogether and strides across country he is obliged to navigate himself; it was when John Hillaby began to talk of taking 'back-bearings' (he might as well have taken ball-bearings for all I understood of the matter) that I decided not to emulate him.

* Constable, London, 1968 and 1973 respectively

Lewis Carroll once proposed the making of a map of England which would be the same size as England, so that the user would always know where he was, because he would be there. I have to say that whenever that image comes into my mind without careful preparation I am invariably unable at first to see the fallacy in it. This is because I lack a sense of direction, though 'lack' is surely too weak a word; the lack is so complete that I frequently have to open three or four doors in my own home before I can find the room I am seeking, and in a strange house I can only find my way by learning the route as a parrot learns to swear, by repetition. I have often attracted puzzled and even fearful glances from those who hear me muttering, 'Turn right at the Chinese vase, go up one flight and turn left, then through the white door on the right.' That is bad enough, but the alternative, which I have experienced on countless more or less embarrassing occasions, is to blunder into everything from the invalid's bedroom to the broom cupboard: it is a mercy that I have never been accused of trying to rape the *au pair*.

It follows, obviously, that my sense of direction out of doors is even worse. I can use a map, with some difficulty, though I can only do so if, when I have to consult it, I am facing the same way as it is; at a crossroads I am to be seen turning round and round until I am correctly oriented, and although I always take a compass with me when walking, it is of no use to me except as a toy. Once, after dining with friends in Chelsea and finding on emerging that the night was fine, I thought I would walk for a little before hailing a taxi. My hostess, knowing of my weakness, gave me careful directions for getting to the main thoroughfare leading towards the centre of London, which happened to be Fulham Road. I learned the instructions by heart, and eventually reached that familar avenue; my hostess, however, perhaps calculating that although I had no sense of direction I was not actually an imbecile, had failed to tell me which way I should turn along it. At this point my no less extreme lack of

119

observation (a man once dropped dead at the next table to mine in a restaurant, making – as I afterwards learned – a considerable noise and stir in doing so, without my noticing that anything out of the ordinary was happening) combined neatly with the absence in me of a sense of direction; and it was only when the buildings began to thin out, that I suspected the truth. ('But what did you do', inquired my hostess of that occasion when I later told her of my adventure, 'when you came to Putney Bridge?' I considered the matter for a moment. 'I think I crossed it,' I said.)

One who does not carry his own accommodation, and fears to leave the ordered path because he will instantly be lost, can hardly be ranked as a serious walker. But I am *not* a serious walker; I walk only for pleasure, not for glory or even exercise, and I am not at all averse, when I come to an uphill stretch of no particular beauty, to accepting a lift. But that takes me back to my youth.

I did a lot of hitch-hiking when I was young. For students of my generation it was the dominant mode of travel, which dates me almost exactly, because barely a decade after I stopped thumbing lifts round Britain and Europe the whole practice fell into disfavour, and in some countries was even banned as dangerous, after a growing number of attacks by hitch-hikers on motorists (and to some extent vice versa).

I covered immense distances sometimes, on one occasion getting from the Channel to Salzburg in four lifts, a record which I dare say still stands. But it is a day on the trip back from Salzburg that I remember best of all; I remember it in such detail that I can summon up any part of it at will, as though I had a film of it in my head and could stop it at any frame I choose. I returned alone; I can no longer remember why, though I know we hadn't quarrelled, for when I unpacked my rucksack at the end of the first day's travelling, I found a loving note tucked into my pyjama pocket. (Would we be better off if we had no memories, or if we had memories that could recall everything? Would *I* be better off if I could remember less, anyway? Best of all, no doubt, would be memories that enable us to remember what we want to keep and forget the rest, but this is a boon unlikely to be granted, and for a good reason, too: we can never know at the time what we shall later want to keep, which pains and sorrows most enable us to understand and to grow, and which thus become, though no less painful, precious in retrospect. *Nothing* is wasted entirely.)

I had spent the night just south of Karlsruhe; the day dawned fine, and I started early. I was on the Autobahn; even in those days it was illegal to hitch-hike on Autobahns, but the law was not very rigorously enforced – I even got a lift on one from a tank once – and the *Polizei* looked the other way when they saw the giglamped young student plying his thumb on the sacred macadam. I had not waited long when I was picked up by a Frenchman from Nancy, with an English wife; he was working in Düsseldorf, I did not gather at what, and I was aiming to make landfall for the night in Cologne. There was a moment of comic misunderstanding after the introductions; the wife asked me if I knew Nancy, but her accent was such that I thought she was asking whether I knew 'a Nazi', and I began to wonder what sort of company I was keeping.

The unending ribbon of road unwound before us, and eventually the Frenchman announced that he was sick of it: was I in a hurry? No, I said, I was in no hurry at all, as indeed I was not, for Cologne by dusk was now well within my reach. In that case, he said, would I mind if we left the Autobahn and made for the road along the river? I had never seen the river in question, except for the moment we had taken to cross it, at Basel, on the way out, but I had heard a lot about it, and was eager to know more. I should be delighted to take the low road, I told my kind driver.

We were just approaching Mainz, where the River Main makes a T-junction with the Rhine; we left the motorway near Wiesbaden, where some years later I lost a lot of money at the Casino and suffered – on the same night, too – the worst attack of indigestion I have ever experienced. There followed what still remains, after more than thirty years, the most magical day of my life.

From Wiesbaden to Bonn the old road follows the Rhine like a faithful dog, unwilling to let its master out of its sight for a moment. At times we seemed to be hanging right over the bank, and the countryside looked as it must have done five hundred years before. Conversation in the car was still brisk when we joined the river, but it died out in all three of us soon afterwards; for the Frenchman and the Englishwoman this territory was familiar, and to me it was unknown, but we were all three ravished by what we saw, and felt, without discussing it, that words could add nothing to what lay before us, so that we need do nothing but feast upon it with our eyes, our feelings and our souls.

The road wound as the river did; at every bend there was a change of view. The fields were golden, the villages, each with its whitewashed church, many of them onion-spired, slept in the sun as though determined not to awaken until Barbarossa's return; the castles, looking more like the sets for a production of *Tannhäuser* than any stage designer would dare to provide, were perched high on scraps of crag that would have given the very eagles vertigo; valleys and hills so gentle that between them they constituted little more than ripples in the earth undulated on either bank; terraced vineyards stepped gingerly down to the water's edge, as if to try the temperature with a toe.

Just past Oberwesel we saw the Lorelei, which I recognized from photographs; as the sun struck slantwise on the rock, it was not difficult to conjure up its resident, false but fair, and hear her lethal song come wafting across the water. I was not long out of school; those silent, golden dawns when I was studying French and German were only two or three years behind me, and I proceeded to break the silence in the car by reciting the whole of Heine's poem (it is by no means one of his best – Schubert never set it, though it was published in 1824 – and the familiar tune is dreadful), to the astonishment of my hosts and my own considerable satisfaction.

They dropped me in Cologne. The war was not long over and the city was a wilderness of rubble; walking along the corridor of my backstreet hotel, I found that the wall opposite my room was thin grey plasterboard, and assumed that it was a partition separating two sections of the hotel, but when I peered through a crack in it, I was speedily disabused, for it was all the bomb-damaged building had for an outer wall, and on the other side of it was the sky and a four-storey drop to the pavement. All the same, I could have happily slept on the pavement after the day I had just spent, and which I wore like a suit of armour. The sun had not long risen when I began my journey to the Rhine, and had nearly set when I thanked my hosts and left them. But in the hours between I had discovered, for the first time in my conscious life, the joy of landscape, which has ever since been one of the greatest joys of walking.

I sometimes think that if I did not want to read or look at pictures I could be the happiest blind man in the world, so little use do I make, for other purposes, of my eyes. It is not just that I fail to *notice* my surroundings; I hardly even *look* at them. Walking along a street, even in an unfamiliar town, even in a handsome unfamiliar town, it never occurs to me, unprompted, to glance at the buildings I am passing, to examine the turnings that open beside me, to look at the vista ahead. I do not walk with my eyes turned to the pavement, but I might just as well, because I simply do not see that which is in my vision; and if that is my situation in towns, where I feel at home, how much more blind am I in the country, where in any case I feel an alien unease.

The first landscape I saw, though I have no recollection at all of noticing it, was the area surrounding my boarding school. This was the landscape of Sussex, between the North and South Downs, and was very green and very gentle; there was a hill nearby, called Sharpenhurst, hardly more than a mound, and the River Arun was not far away (it figured on the route of many of the 'runs' we were obliged to go on, and I must have forded it countless times). But I took not the slightest interest in what lay before my eyes; the shapes and colours of some of the most beautiful and unspoilt country-side in Britain meant nothing to me, and the changing seasons had no effect on me at all, if I was even aware that they *were* changing. (I suppose I must have spotted the fact that the land tended to turn white in a hard winter, but I certainly did not notice that the leaves fell off the trees, even though we were regularly set to sweep them up in the autumn – not, I seem to remember, for the sake of tidiness but because they were used, or so we gathered, for some agricultural or even industrial purpose useful to the 'war effort' – another phrase which dates me as a child of the Second World War; we also had to collect huge quantities of 'conkers', the rumours as to their intended use being more specific – we believed that toothpaste was to be made from them. For all I know it was true.)

That was really all the landscape I ever set eyes on, let alone noticed, until the heavens opened that day by the Rhine. For most of the war my family lived in Bedford, where I would therefore spend the holidays from school, but I have no recollection of ever going outside it, though I remember the River Ouse that flowed through it, if only because I used to fish from its banks, occasionally landing a gudgeon but never anything larger. Nor did my early visits to the Edinburgh Festival, for all the hills that can be seen from the city, persuade me to venture into the Lowlands countryside. And I have no recollection at all of anything seen beyond the verges while hitch-hiking; once, travelling to Polperro, I managed to cross Dartmoor without noticing it, and even the outward journey to Salzburg left no trace on my mind's eye. (I can remember that we stopped to get out of the car at the top of the Arlberg Pass, but it was the zest of the air that struck me, and that I now recall; the scenery visible from 6,000 feet made no impression whatever on me, not even so much as to enable me to observe the extent of the view, let alone its beauty.)

The day by the Rhine, then, when for the first time I saw

how an ancient landscape was made out of hills and hedges, valleys and fields, sun and water, and how the composition, more innocent and more perfect than any painter could aspire to, produced an effect overwhelmingly greater than the sum of its parts, a revelation of something far more important than the fact that I had eyes and that they could tell me things I would be pleased to know. It is a curious fact that second-rate poets can write first-rate poems about landscape though they can only manage their usual lame stanzas when they try their hand at love, history or God, and much the same is true of the artists; how many times have you turned away without a second glance at a bad portrait in a junk shop, but lingered over a landscape with no greater artistic merits to commend it?

That would have been heresy to Ruskin, and by the time he has erected the stake and piled the faggots, we would have to agree, and not only to save our skins:

A man accustomed to the broad wild sea-shore, with its bright breakers, and free winds, and sounding rocks, and eternal sensation of tameless power, can scarcely but be angered when Claude bids him stand still on some paltry chipped and chiselled quay, with porters and wheelbarrows running against him, to watch a weak, rippling, bound and barriered water, that has not strength enough in one of its waves to upset the flowerpots on the wall, or even to fling one jet of spray over the confining stone. A man accustomed to the strength and glory of God's mountains, with their soaring and radiant pinnacles, and surging sweeps of measureless distance, kingdoms in their valleys, and climates upon their crests, can scarcely but be angered when Salvator bids him stand still under some contemptible fragment of splintery crag, which an Alpine snow-wreath would smother in its first swell, with a stunted bush or two growing out of it, and a volume of manufactory smoke for sky. A man accustomed to the grace and infinity of nature's foliage, with every vista a cathedral, and every bough a revelation, can scarcely but be angered when Poussin mocks him with a black round mass of impenetrable paint, diverging into feathers instead of leaves, and supported on a stick instead of a trunk. The fact is, there is one thing wanting in all the doings of these men, and that is the very tribute by which the work of human mind chiefly rises above that of the daguerreotype or calotype, or any other mechanical means that ever have been or may be invented, Love. There is no evidence of their ever having gone to nature with any thirst, or received from her such emotion as could make them, even for an instant, lose sight of themselves; there is in them neither earnestness nor humility; there is no simple or honest record of any single truth; none of the plain words or straight effects that men speak and make when they once feel.

But Ruskin was not content to leave the argument there, lest it should be thought, despite the fervour and the thrilling plea to paint nature in all her majesty, an aesthetic argument. For Ruskin it was no such thing, and the words in which he makes this plain must make us all stop and think why we love landscape. Not because it is beautiful; the love of landscape is given us for a higher purpose, and in condemning those who have ignored, denied or failed to live up to that purpose, Ruskin makes very clear what that purpose is:

No moral end has been answered, no permanent good effected, by any of their work. They may have aroused the intellect, or exercised the ingenuity, but they have never spoken to the heart. Landscape art has never taught us one deep and holy lesson . . . it has not prompted to devotion, nor touched with awe; its power to move or exalt the heart has been fatally abused, and perished in the abusing. That which ought to have been a witness to the omnipotence of God, has become an exhibition of the destiny of man.

Let us leave the omnipotence of God out of it for the moment, and consider whether Ruskin was right. I do not want to make my journey to the Rhine sound like a religious experience; I am sure it was not. None the less, it was more than the combination of the harmony and beauty in what I saw that day and the extraordinary awakening that I had, in a few hours, to something I had until then been quite unconscious of. Whatever Ruskin says of landscape painting he would obviously have said even more forcefully about the subject of it; if the landscape painters are to be condemned for failing to teach deep and holy lessons, prompt to devotion, touch with awe, speak to the heart, it must be that those duties are laid upon them for a purpose that encompasses them, their art and the landscape itself. If we do leave God out of it (and what fools Ruskin would have thought us for doing so!), are we left with nothing?

Not quite, I think. If we fear to go all the way to belief, we need only be still and silent in a landscape to understand that there is something to believe in. The most beautiful music ever composed by Mozart, the most lyrical lines of Shakespeare, and of course the loveliest landscape painting, even one which fully met Ruskin's test (as he believed – rightly – Turner's did), would be coarse and jarring if they accompanied the contemplation of a landscape. Mozart, Shakespeare, Turner are only men, wherever their inspiration came from and whatever it led to; they are mysterious enough, but a landscape is infinitely more mysterious. For although it must be true that music, poetry and painting are not made by man without help, it is quite certainly true that landscape is not made by man at all. That is why the peace and harmony of a landscape – even a turbulent one with a rushing river and scudding black clouds – are so powerful, and it is also why those feelings can be conjured up again so easily, as Wordsworth knew when he recollected in tranquillity the hills and water and green, green grass among which he lived.

More than thirty years after my Rhine journey I had

another such day of landscape, which induced the same feelings, and which I cannot but believe that I am destined to remember for the rest of my life, as I have remembered that earlier occasion with the sun on the enchanted river, the vineyards and castles on its banks, the peace in my heart. It was in Spain, a land I hardly know at all, country or town. The main road was narrow and dull, and a seemingly endless line of lorries stretched ahead of us. But we were in no hurry, any more than I had been when the Frenchman wanted to leave the Autobahn and follow the river, and we decided to turn off, strike across country, and find our way by side roads.

So we did, and were rewarded shortly afterwards for our intrepidity with a sight that transfixed us with amazement and happiness. We must have stumbled upon the principal sun-flower-growing area of Spain, because we found ourselves driving through a sea of them, a mighty ocean, stretching to the horizon, it seemed, in every direction. 'Ten thousand saw I at a glance', said Wordsworth of his daffodils, but here there must have been ten million, and they lit up the landscape until the sun itself was dimmed.

The road wound on through this flood of brilliant gold, and in some strange way it seemed to sum up my love and experience of landscape as completely as the Rhine had done, all those years before. Like the scenery of the Rhine, with its castles and villages, this picture was made by man as well as nature; someone had had to plant the sunflower seeds, after all, before the sun could draw them forth from the ground. But the flowers with their great round faces knew that they were temporary sojourners on the face of the earth, that although they might propagate themselves, generation by generation, the earth was older than they could ever be even if the line stretched out to the crack of doom; the terraces and churches had been painted on the landscape of the Rhine, and the sunflowers were painted on that of the Spanish plain, and the landscape of the former will still outlive the works of man's hands, even though it will take longer than the Spanish landscape will need to outlast the sunflowers.

That said, and experienced, I must add that I certainly began to walk in towns before the country. Perhaps my urban upbringing and character asserted themselves after I failed to acquire the walking habit at school; I do find the wholly urban walk a particularly satisfying one, and I have devised a number of London routes which I rank as comparable to those rural marches that take in even the most beautiful natural scenery. For one of these, I take train to Bushey, then walk into London, all the way to Marble Arch, down that almost Roman-straight diagonal that eventually becomes the homely Edgware Road. A similar walk begins in Epping Forest, taking me to central London via the City; another, and one of the most varied and entertaining, consists of following the Underground round all the stations of the Circle Line, a walk which provides a curious little extra satisfaction in that, again and again, the walker finds the ground trembling beneath his feet as the unseen trains rumble subterraneanly by.

If the country walk at home was too shaming in exposing my ignorance of nature in circumstances that meant others might discover it (once, struck by an overpoweringly beautiful scent while out in the Scottish countryside, I had to be told that what I was breathing in with so much pleasure was honeysuckle), it was not surprising that I soon began to take my country walks abroad, and the pleasure of rural walking only really took hold on my first holidays in Germany and Austria. At first, I would pick a centre in a beautiful and unspoilt area (some have been extensively spoilt since): the Taunus, the Black Forest, the Salzkammergut. From my hotel I would devise each day a circular tour, which would bring me back to base in the late afternoon. In the German-ophone countries this is easy, even for the direction-blind like me, for the German and Austrian touring clubs mark the forest paths, and in a particularly simple and effective manner; they cut a small patch, about four inches by one, in the bark of a tree, and paint the patch. All the walker has to do thereafter is to follow the colour of the route he has chosen; there is a marked tree every fifty yards or so, and always at a fork or crossroads, and the better walking-maps colour their tracks to correspond. (Fortunately, I do not add colour-blindness to my other deficiencies.) In the valley, where several walking routes start, there are usually boards with details of all the routes available for the walker to choose among, and these boards often provide a rough guide to the length of time the blue walk, the red walk or the yellow walk should take, though the walker realizes very early on that the timings are always overestimated, based as they are on the speed of the most corpulent or indolent of walkers, just as a convoy of ships goes at the speed of the slowest vessel.

The walker who sets up such a base-camp, and explores the countryside around it, will get to know the terrain better, but will eventually begin to chafe at the limitation the method puts on the variety of walking experience it provides. After a time, therefore, I decided that I would walk instead from place to place, like a mendicant friar, and although I remained resolved not to carry my lodging on my back, I would at any rate not go so far as to refuse to carry my luggage. So I went to Harrods and bought myself a luxurious rucksack, made of stout grey canvas with a light but sturdy metal frame and shoulder straps padded with foam rubber. Inside the flap that closed the rucksack after the drawstrings had been pulled tight was a zipped pocket, into which I folded an all-enveloping cycle cape with a hood, which has often enabled me to keep on walking even in the rain (a sensation which I enjoy provided I am well wrapped up), for it completely covered me and my rucksack, and would doubtless have covered my bicycle, too, if I had been on one.

A man who carries his own luggage, however softly his rucksack's shoulder straps are padded, speedily learns which items he can, and which he cannot, do without. In the course of my early voyages I discovered that drip-dry shirts which really need no ironing are far fewer than the advertisers claim; I also discovered an inflatable coat-hanger, a method of rolling a pair of trousers so that they do not become creased, and the fact that there is an even better way of reducing the weight of reading matter than by taking only paperbacks, which is to take only paperbacks and throw away the pages as they are read.

Thus equipped, I would set forth, always taking care to make landfall before dusk, in time to find a room for the night; occasionally I miscalculated and had to spend the night under the stars, and once I bedded down in the doorway of a border customs post, but generally there was no difficulty, and as anyone who has travelled off the beaten tourist track in Bavaria and Austria knows, the inns, with their gaily decorated fronts and bright wooden rooms and furniture, are among the most comfortable and pleasant of stopping places in all Europe, and although it is rarely possible to eat outstandingly well in them, it is almost impossible to eat badly.

All my love and knowledge of Baroque architecture was garnered on these journeys, and those years of my youth were *Wanderjahre* indeed, as I tramped from Banz to the Wieskirche or from Ottobeuren, with its stupendous ceiling which has more than once caused me to fall flat on my back while craning too far in order to take it all in, to Birnau on the shores of Lake Constance, marvelling all the while that ecclesiastical architecture could be so powerful yet so ungothic, and singing as I went.

The question of singing while walking is an important one, and more complicated than the non-walker or non-singer realizes. First, where the musical memory is concerned, *l'appétit vient en mangeant*; no one should fear to embark on, say, the Eroica without being sure how it goes on after that hair-raising E flat avalanche, for the more the walker sings, the more he finds he knows. Nor is the question of rhythm as important as it might be thought; true, it is not easy to walk to the *Rheingold* prelude, or to Ravel's 'Pavane for a Dead Infanta', or the slow movement of the Eroica itself. But that leaves a great deal before the walker is reduced to 'Marching Through Georgia', and it does not have to be music with a very marked rhythm, indeed in my experience it should not be, for then the impulse to fall into step with it becomes almost irresistible, and those who walk for pleasure alone should be bound by nothing, not even the tune they are singing.

Rossini is excellent; there are few subdivisions of the pleasure of walking comparable to coming round the last bend in the road before the overnight village and breaking into the gallop from the *William Tell* overture or Basilio's 'La calunnia' from the *Barber* or the 'Largo al factotum'. For more serious walking – say high in the hills early on a clear morning – Mozart comes into his own, clearing the head and the soul in preparation for the day. Strenuous uphill sections demand Beethoven's more triumphant passages, though unfortunately they demand more breath than an uphill progress normally leaves. Schubert is more tricky; though the Unfinished might have been designed to accompany walking, trying to keep up with *Rosamunde* or the C major Symphony can be exhausting, and if you fall back on the *Lieder* you will find that they overpower the walk altogether, and there is nothing for it but to sit down under a tree and abandon all thought of progress until you have sung your fill.

It is not necessary to sing well, or even in tune. I sing abominably, and in keys so remote from the original, or from anything else, that Berio and Xenakis would denounce me as an iconoclast, but even a bad singing voice can be an asset in an emergency; I once scared off a huge Alsatian – animals I detest and fear more than anything else that goes on legs – by bawling Siegfried's Forging Song in its horrible face.

Nowadays, the walker can have his music provided for him, in the form of those lightweight cassette-players with featherweight headphones; I do not at all despise these aids, and indeed have walked up a mountain in the Canadian Rockies with Bruckner's E minor Mass in my head, though I certainly could not have remembered enough of it to sing it myself, and if I had tried to it would have left me with less breath than the Beethoven Fifth. (The walker in Germany has the colour-coded *Wegweiser* to help him; in Alberta, he has signs telling him what to do if he should meet a grizzly bear. I did not meet a grizzly bear, which was just as well, for I was uneasily conscious of the stories I had heard about this most terrible of living creatures, aptly classified by the taxonomists as *Ursus horribilis*.)

A walking-stick is not necessary, but it is useful for acting out fantasies, and would have come in handy if the Alsatian which didn't like Wagner had stood its ground. I bought mine on one of my earliest Bavarian walks, in the village just below mad King Ludwig's maddest castle, Neuschwanstein, and have occasionally inspected it for signs of sprouting, in accordance with the miracle in *Tannhäuser*. It is a noble staff, tapering from a solid boss to a thumb's thickness, and could, reversed, be a club for seeing off not only Alsatians but bandits. Alas, times have changed; I am no longer allowed to take it on to aeroplanes, lest I should prove to be a bandit myself, and use it to hijack the aircraft. But that odd fact is a reminder of a much odder one, which is the extraordinarily recent origin of sky piracy; it began only in the early 1960s, though it had been possible ever since regular commercial flights between countries had existed, and certainly there has never been any shortage of sufficiently ruthless criminals, political and commercial. Why did no such malefactor make the simple imaginative leap for so long? The answer illuminates much more in our world than the practice of this modern form of piracy and the taking of hostages; there were until very recently a set of generally shared assumptions, held so strongly that they precluded such an invention altogether. In the past two decades or so, the pillars – of authority, of artistic form, of the relationship between sections of society, of restraint and self-restraint of all kinds – have been collapsing all round us. They will not be rebuilt in our time, and it is better for our peace of mind that we should not speculate on what fearsome shape they will take when they are.

Such speculations are not for walkers. True, the walker's motto is 'I walk, therefore I think'; when the singing is done for the moment, a reflective mood is almost invariable (I am speaking, of course, of the solitary walker, for the practice of walking in company is so entirely different that it would demand its own separate study), but I have found that the graver questions of the hour do not figure large in the thoughts that ebb and flow in the walker's mind. Indeed, a long walk is an excellent cure for the unhealthy dwelling upon the international situation, the balance of payments or the next election, which is so prevalent among the stationary. On the other hand, though word games and mental arithmetic are valuable aids to the walker, it is the greatest questions of all – the very ones that make political and economic discussion seem so temporal and petty – that return, again and again, to dominate the walker's thoughts. And here a most fascinating light is thrown upon the walker's state of mind.

I have almost invariably found – certainly far too often for the phenomenon to be the result of coincidence – that when the great questions arise, when the world and its meaning are considered, when the purpose and value of life are weighed, when success and failure are measured, when vain regrets tug at one sleeve and vain hopes at the other, when, in short, it is time to cast up accounts, the walker's thoughts are positive, life-filled, confident and serene, though such considerations are all too likely, when made at home, to lead to doubt, fear and negativity.

This must mean something. Perhaps the hills and fields, the sky and sun, remind the walker of the slow certainty of nature, of how extraordinarily unlikely it is that the universe is a random collection of atoms assembled haphazard, of the amazing truth about human beings, which is that there are far more good ones than bad (another nail in the coffin of the Manichee). Or perhaps the walker who is sufficiently conscious of being alone with himself and his heart can afford to be quite frank with himself, and admit that the perennial philosophy is true, and the materialist false – an admission so much harder to make while, getting and spending, we lay waste our power.

Walking, then, induces happiness, not just at the level of a pleasurable physical activity, but at the deepest level of all; even as I write about it, that spring sends up the water of life, and I feel the surge of quiet hope that fills me when I am on the march – so much so that I am impelled to leave my desk and go for a walk, in which case it had better be my most familiar, and favourite, London one. I think I may have invented it myself – certainly I have been doing it for years – though there is nothing particularly ingenious about it; it consists of walking back and forth across the Thames, crossing every pedestrian bridge from Tower to Hammersmith. (It can be done the other way, of course, but if the route is traversed westwards, and the walker starts on the northern side of Tower Bridge, he has the most beautiful section of the entire march – the southern shore between Putney and Hammersmith – to finish with.)

There are sixteen walkable bridges on the route: Tower, London, Southwark, Blackfriars, Waterloo, Hungerford, Westminster, Lambeth, Vauxhall, Chelsea, Albert, Battersea, Wandsworth, Fulham (a railway bridge, but, like Hungerford, with a pedestrian walkway stuck on the side), Putney and Hammersmith. There is no signboard, German fashion, on the northern approach to Tower Bridge, with an estimate of the time the walk will take; this will depend not only on the speed of the walker but on his policy regarding rests and refreshment. (The walker in Venice, where everybody is a walker, a fact which does not make walking in Venice any less pleasurable, has not only the routes but the refreshment stops laid out for him, provided he has the sense to take with him the best guidebook in the world, Mr J. G. Links's *Venice for Pleasure*,* which shows the traveller Venice in a series of comfortable strolls, and is so perceptive about

* Bodley Head, London, 1966

the stroller's feelings that just as the thought of a refreshing drink occurs to him, he turns the page and reads 'by now, you may feel like a drink', followed by directions to a nearby café with a fine view from its windows.)

Properly paced and with a serious pause for lunch the London bridges walk will take from mid-morning to tea-time, but the true walker – who walks, remember, for pleasure only – will stop whenever he feels like doing so, and never has to remind himself that he is not out to break records, though he will be conscious of the truth that one of the pleasures of a walk is its end, and not at all in the sense of the gentleman who insisted that he banged his head on the wall to enjoy the sensation of leaving off. The feeling of being tired has to be kept at bay while any walk is in progress, otherwise it will cease to be a pleasure, and the puritans and flesh-mortifiers will mark another victory; but the pleasure of physical exhaustion after physical exertion is not to be counted to the enemy, for it is a positive and enriching sensation, quite divorced from the evidence it provides, satisfying in itself, of achievement. The hot bath at the end of any long walk, rural or urban, is restorative and healing; but it is also the best way of surrendering to the pleasure of being tired for good reason, as the limbs and torso – and feelings – expand in the water and suffuse the soul itself with the agreeable sensation.

When going on this or any other serious walk, I don my walking shoes, and acknowledge every time a direct debt to John Hillaby. For many years I used to walk in frightful beetle-crushers, with rigid soles and unbending uppers; I felt as if I had a Churchill tank on each foot, and the only consolation (for they were also devilish heavy to lift) was that I could have dispatched a fully-grown grizzly bear, never mind an Alsatian, by fetching it a single kick between the eyes. Then John published *Journey Through Britain*, in which he described his shoes; the book had a picture of them on the very jacket. Inquiring of the author for the name of the supplier, I hurried off to Lillywhite's, and found I was by no means the first to ask for a pair of 'those shoes that John Hillaby walked in'. They are as soft as the gentlest bedroom slippers, but they must be impeccably constructed, for they have lasted, with only an occasional soling and heeling, and an even rarer stitching, for a dozen years so far, with no sign of their ever giving out. If I had met a grizzly on that walk in Canada, these shoes might not have been powerful enough to deal with it, but happily I met no bears, only a gentle Labrador. But here I am at Tower Bridge.

'Did Julius Caesar build that place, my lord?'

'He did, my gracious lord, begin that place,
Which, since, succeeding ages have re-edified.'

On the whole, singing, for obvious reasons, is confined to the rural walk, and would still be so even if I sang better than I do. But reciting, though it raises eyebrows, is a reasonable compromise, and a London walk is particularly rich in associations that bring passages of prose or poetry to mind – as, in the very first steps of my bridges walk, those lines from *Richard III* presented themselves. Not that associations are necessary; often I will simply recite my favourites with no more justification than that they *are* my favourites, which is surely justification enough, though the musical problem of rhythms inimical to walking comes up in the form of unsuitable metres; great care has to be taken with Shakespeare's pentameters, for instance, if they are not to sound, as the right foot comes to ground on a stress, like a carpenter who hates his work banging in nails. But there are also, as I have said, word games to be played; it was while walking that I discovered the curious fact that it is possible at every attempt to recall the names of 49 of the 50 United States, but never the 50th, *though the missing one is different every time.*

There is also the Gray's Elegy trick. The famous third line of the famous first stanza contains five significant parts, viz., The ploughman/homeward/plods/his weary/way. Now:

treating the pronoun and the article as spares or super-
numeraries, to be fitted in wherever the sense demands, one
can rearrange the five principal elements in all their possible
combinations, and make sense each time. Thus:

Homeward the ploughman plods his way weary.
His way homeward plods the weary ploughman.
Plods the ploughman weary homeward his way.
The weary ploughman plods his way homeward.
The ploughman his weary way homeward plods.

There being five elements, the number of possible combinations is what mathematicians call 'factorial five' – i.e.,
$5 \times 4 \times 3 \times 2 \times 1 = 120$. I do not think I have ever got all
120 on a walk, though I have never come across an arrange-
ment that does not make sense; even 'Plods weary his way
homeward the ploughman' is perfectly acceptable. (Some say
that this game should be played by those unable to get to
sleep, as an alternative to counting sheep, but a more
mischievous suggestion can hardly be imagined, as not only
would the unwillingly wideawake victim then spend an
entirely wideawake night; it is doubtful, once the thing had
taken hold, that he would ever sleep again.)

It is the bridges walk that brings me as close to using my
eyes as I am ever likely to get. I never cease to marvel, as I
begin, at the sheer absurdity of Tower Bridge; there can
hardly be another structure in all Europe with its proportions
so hopelessly wrong, yet which cuts so striking and
romantic a figure. I have not seen it open for many years
now, though I well remember the thrill of the sight. London
Bridge, next along, is dull. When the previous one was
replaced it was bought by an American in Arizona and
shipped home stone by stone to be reassembled in that arid
land; I believe he bought himself a Venetian gondola to go
with it, and now glides beneath its arches on the artificial
canal he had constructed. The old bridge had lasted since
1831, when it was rebuilt to replace the first one of all, which

was the first bridge over the Thames to be built in London, and had shops and houses on it; there was a brief campaign to persuade the authorities at County Hall to go back to something like the original, or at least to have little booths on it like the Rialto Bridge in Venice and the Ponte Vecchio in Florence, but it came to nothing.

The next stretch of shore is rich in Chaucerian associations, though there was no Southwark Bridge for the Pilgrims to cross, and there is the first good view of St Paul's from the next one, Blackfriars. Then comes the elegant span of Waterloo, and a mystery, for it is from here that the full ruin of London can be plainly seen. On one side a wilderness of concrete, and on the other a row of blind and lifeless tower blocks, hardly redeemed even by Somerset House, St Paul's, the sweep of County Hall and the weird battlements of Whitehall Court, happily described by Paul Jennings as 'looking as though it had been built by generations of mad aristocrats'.

The mystery, of course, is why? If it was necessary to demolish this part of London and replace it with new buildings, what madness got into those responsible, so that the new buildings were things like the Hayward Gallery and the Queen Elizabeth Hall? These objects are not merely hideous, they are actively and aggressively hideous, they are like drunks at closing time who are not content to reel home singing but must needs cross the pavement deliberately, to bump violently against a sober passer-by and shout obscenities at him. Why? What good purpose did anyone think such things might serve? Who persuaded whom, and with what arguments, that they ought to look as they do? Who wants them to?

Contemplation of this dreadful enigma will keep the bridge-walker occupied all the way to Battersea, via Westminster (where the riddle must be shelved to permit the walker to recite the Wordsworth sonnet), the marvellous broadside view of the Houses of Parliament from the Albert Embankment, and the curious fact that Lambeth Bridge has its name painted on its side, as though if it had not river mariners might think they were on the Trent, or even the Rhine. The Houses of Parliament give the lie to those who claim that the architectural ruin of London was inevitable, but it can be argued that such genius as that of Barry and Pugin is not available simply because it is wanted; no such argument can be sustained at Battersea, where the Power Station was built with nothing but talent, yet is still handsome, still dignified, still undated.

The bridges walk is some fourteen miles long, and the legs know it by the time they cross Hammersmith Bridge, with its mighty eightfold cables on which it is hung like washing on a line. Not quite Xenophon, I agree, but it is possible, looking downriver at the completion of the journey, to imagine something of what the Ten Thousand must have felt when they saw the sea and knew they were as good as home. Other walks I have done swim into mind now; round the walls of York, for instance, and those of Nuremberg; right round Lake Annecy in a day, a day broken by a very long pause for lunch at Père Bise in Talloires; from the sophistication of Munich to the innocence of Lindau; all these I have done on foot. The old folks used to say that if we had been meant to ride in motorcars we would have been born with wheels on, and the satisfaction that comes to the walker from his knowledge that he is doing it entirely out of the resources of his body, looking neither to other people nor to machines for assistance, will, if he is not careful, persuade him to feel smug and agree with them.

But that would bring the pleasure-walker dangerously close to the pain-walker. We who walk for pleasure alone must never allow ourselves to think teleologically; our pleasure is in the walking, and in that alone, and we have no need to seek outside the walking for any justification for it. The rhythm of our stride (I take some 30,000 paces on the bridges walk); the gradual tempering of our lungs and muscles to the effort; the thoughts that fill our minds; the peace that descends on us as the miles go by; the sights and sounds that accompany and divert us, whether we are in town or country or – as on the Hammersmith Embankment – *rus in urbe*; these are the happinesses of walking, and they are their own justification. As I lie in the bath and count the bridges, conjuring them up one by one, I am filled with the pleasure that they have given me, that any long walk gives me. I think I can allow myself one forbidden taste of smugness, one wisp of identification with those who walk because it does them good rather than because it does them pleasure, and I have succumbed to the lapse before stepping into the bath: the scales tell me that I have lost four pounds.

Six

It seems unlikely, but I believe that I knew nothing at all of Shakespeare before I went away to boarding school at the age of eleven. I must have heard of him, I suppose, but certainly I had seen none of his plays (an easy enough claim to make, as I had never been to a theatre at all), or read any, either. My mother, to my retrospective astonishment, knew one Shakespeare passage, and would occasionally, *à propos* nothing very much, recite it:

> A fool, a fool! I met a fool i' the forest
> A motley fool; a miserable world!
> As I do live by food, I met a fool;
> Who laid him down and bask'd him in the sun,
> And rail'd on Lady Fortune in good terms,
> In good set terms, and yet a motley fool.
> 'Good morrow, fool', quoth I. 'No, sir', quoth he,
> 'Call me not fool till heaven hath sent me fortune.'
> And then he drew a dial from his poke . . .

She never mentioned, however, that it was from Shakespeare, and may not have remembered, as she must have learned it at school, and would certainly never have seen it acted. I committed it to memory from her recitation alone, but I had no idea what it was about, and naturally took 'fool' to have its modern meaning; what motley was, or what 'sans intermission' meant, or who was the aristocratic Lady Fortune, I could not imagine, and as for

> My lungs began to crow like chanticleer

it might have been in a foreign language. But I can still hear the way she stressed 'goooood set terms', as I can hear the way she said my name. British usage puts the stress in 'Bernard' on the first syllable, American on the second; my mother is the only person I have ever known to make it a true spondee, stressing both evenly.

One of my uncles used to recite, in a very funny parody of an old-fashioned melodrama, Hubert's speech from the scene with Arthur in Act IV of *King John*:

> Heat me these irons hot; and look thou stand
> Within the arras: when I strike my foot
> Upon the bosom of the ground, rush forth,
> And bind the boy which you shall find with me
> Fast to the chair: be heedful. Hence, and watch.

'Heat me these irons hot' became a family catchphrase; but of its Shakespearean provenance I was likewise unaware until later. There was no copy of Shakespeare in my earliest home; indeed, the only books I can recall, apart from children's books and my grandfather's Hebrew bible, were some from a very motley uniform edition of long-forgotten authors who meant nothing to me, though I remember the look of the volumes, which had a disconcerting trick of falling to pieces, and their musty smell. I got my books from the local public library.

So presumably I first encountered Shakespeare at my boarding school, and as it chanced the first play I studied in class was *King John*; my delight and astonishment when we got to 'Heat me these irons hot' was greater even than what I felt when I later met Jaques in *As You Like It* and not only recognized my mother's recitation but found out what chanticleer meant. (Later still – much later, for the *Canterbury Tales* were considered grossly improper for my generation of public schoolboys, and we studied only the Prologue, and that cautiously – I came on Chanticleer himself in the Nun's Priest's Tale.)

Much indignant breath and print has been expended, over the years, about the practice of making children study Shakespeare line by line for examinations; it is said to kill any possibility of a spontaneous love for him, by removing the excitement that comes from reading him straight through, and better still from seeing him acted, or even acting him. Perhaps; though I find the argument rather like the claim that television has killed the art of conversation, as though the people who sit comatose before their sets every hour of every evening would, if it had never been invented ('No good will come of this device,' said C. P. Scott, 'the word is half Greek and half Latin'), spend their time scintillating at one another like so many SAINTE-Beuves or Dr Johnsons. I doubt it, as I doubt whether any child capable of responding to Shakespeare has been prevented from doing so by being obliged to understand him word by word and then to 'Write short notes on the characters of, a) Laertes, b) Rosencrantz and Guildenstern, c) Fortinbras'.

Anyway, when Sir Toby Belch declares that he 'would as lief be a Brownist as a politician' I discovered from such study not only what a Brownist was, but also that a politician was not what is now meant by the term (though the two meanings, as it happens, are today growing closer together again, which is a comment on the development of politics, not of language). And somewhere in the course of such study, I began to discover Shakespeare.

What was I responding to? I think it must have been the abrupt assault of emotion; more precisely of emotion I could feel in safety. Much later, when I discovered Wagner, the same thing happened, far more intensely, and it was not long before I realized consciously what was happening to me when I listened to *Tristan* or *The Ring* in the knowledge, simultaneously held and rejected, that this was not the real world but an opera house; for a few hours, no restraint on feeling was required, because for one thing it could be

144

reimposed as soon as the performance ended, and for another and much more important thing it was too dark in the auditorium for anyone to see.

I am sure, though I was too young to wonder about it, let alone understand it, that Shakespeare offered me the same release. Though *King John* was the first Shakespeare play I studied at school, the first of the canon that I read as a 'set book' for an examination was *Twelfth Night*, and its music opened windows on such vistas of poetry, beauty and emotion that to this day I can recapture in their full strength my feelings as I gazed out upon the new, moonlit landscape. *Twelfth Night* is not really for children; they can enjoy the comics, of course, and the gulling of Malvolio (though no doubt they are still, as I was, steered rapidly past the appalling obscenity concealed in the most innocent line of the Letter Scene, which I was not only steered past but never spotted for myself either, finally learning it a quarter of a century later from a friend in the Chichester Festival Theatre during the interval of *The Wild Duck*), but the delicacy of the emotional relationship is too fragile and subtle for a school-boy, and too often appears to him to be only 'soppy'.

I remember that some primitive instinct for self-preservation warned me to join in the jeering at Olivia and Viola, lest I should be thought as soppy as the play. But I *was* as soppy as the play; I had nothing to measure the feelings against, but when I got to

> Make me a willow cabin at your gate,
> And call upon my soul within the house;
> Write loyal cantons of contemned love,
> And sing them loud even in the dead of night . . .

I felt as though I was being drowned in a strange sea, the very existence of which I had not previously suspected, or which, if I had suspected it, I had instinctively denied.

This could not, I feel sure, have been the stirrings of adolescence; it was too early, and I was far too backward emotionally. I was vibrating to the sounds of a different music altogether, that of Shakespeare's unique ability to understand the human soul and its needs and powers, and to clothe that understanding in thoughts and words that enable his readers and listeners at least to glimpse what *he* sees in its entirety, which is what I mean when I say he allowed me to respond to the assaults of emotion. But that brings me to his understanding itself, and my discovery of it.

It is possible to learn a greal deal about Shakespeare by reading him, and taking steps to ensure that you understand what you are reading. But there is a dimension to him that can only be discovered through seeing him acted. That is true, of course, in a fairly mundane sense as well as in the innermost feeling of all; however many times I had seen *Richard III* I could still never remember the Who's Who of Act IV, scene iv:

> 'I had an Edward, till a Richard kill'd him;
> I had a Harry, till a Richard kill'd him;
> Thou hadst an Edward, till a Richard kill'd him;
> Thou hadst a Richard, till a Richard kill'd him.'

> 'I had a Richard too, and thou didst kill him;
> I had a Rutland too, thou holp'st to kill him.'

> '. . . Thy Edward he is dead, that kill'd my Edward;
> Thy other Edward dead, to quit my Edward . . .
> Thy Clarence he is dead that stabb'd my Edward . . .'

Then, in the 1960s, the Royal Shakespeare Company staged, under the title of *The Wars of the Roses*, an extraordinary conflation of the three parts of *Henry VI* together with *Richard III*, and at last the scene made perfect sense, since all the killings to which the tragic women were referring had taken place before my eyes only a few hours before, and the dynastic relationships, as well as the killers' motives, were fresh in my mind.

But that is not what I meant when I said that Shakespeare

has to be seen to be comprehended. The first productions I ever saw were also among the best I have ever seen, those magical performances in the Old Vic's days of glory in St Martin's Lane, and John Gielgud's last *Hamlet*, at the Haymarket Theatre in 1944, at the end of which I walked all the way home, a distance of some four miles, without being in any way conscious of my surroundings until I found myself, to my extreme astonishment, putting my key in the door. But Shakespeare was only one of the authors in the Old Vic's repertoire, and *Hamlet* was the only Shakespeare play in the Gielgud season, and of course this was many years before the Royal Shakespeare Company set up home in London as well as Stratford. So I had had no opportunity to see Shakespeare with any frequency or regularity, or to see more than a handful of the plays, or any of them more than once.

Not long after the war, however, Donald Wolfit took the old Bedford Music Hall, in Camden High Street, and announced an all-Shakespeare season of a month, with eight plays: *Hamlet, Othello, Lear, Macbeth, As You Like It, The Merchant of Venice, Twelfth Night* and *The Merry Wives of Windsor*. I went to more than twenty of the twenty-eight performances, and realized immediately that there was a very great deal more to Shakespeare than I had until then supposed, though exactly what it was I was unable to say. In a sense, my life ever since has been a quest for the meaning of Shakespeare, in which quest I am not by any means alone:

> Others abide our question. Thou art free.
> We ask and ask: Thou smilest, and art still
> Out-topping knowledge . . .

That, I suppose, is another way of drawing attention to Shakespeare's uniqueness, to the nature of which Emerson provides a useful clue:

> What point of morals, of manners, of economy, of philosophy, of religion, of taste, of the conduct of life, has

147

he not settled? What mystery has he not signified his knowledge of? What office, or function, or district of man's work, has he not remembered? What maiden has not found him finer than her delicacy? What sage has he not outseen?

The mystery of Shakespeare, the greatest and last of the mysteries that lie behind that lofty brow, is not that of his identity, for he was not Francis Bacon, or Christopher Marlowe, or the Earl of Oxford, though much more ingenuity and ink will be vainly spent, between now and the end of time, demonstrating that he was; nor is the mystery to be penetrated, the darkness significantly illuminated, by those who have sought to trace the origins of his learning or the roots of his philosophy; nor does it even lie in the astounding and undoubtedly unique breadth of his range, from Hamlet to Falstaff, from Iago to Prospero, from Imogen and Rosalind to Cressida and Lady Macbeth, from the Rialto to the walls of Troy, from the Forum to the Court of Navarre, from the sea coast of Bohemia to another part of the forest, from the death of King Lear to the birth of Queen Elizabeth, from Clarence's Dream to Bottom's Dream, from tennis to chess, from tinkers to tailors, from

> . . . this my hand will rather
> The multitudinous seas incarnadine

to

> Making the green one red.

What, then, is the secret, where is the key that will fit the lock – the lock that I discovered at the Bedford Music Hall, seeing Shakespeare horribly travestied (not that I realized that at the time) by Wolfit and his dreadful company? It was a strange period for me anyway, Shakespeare or no Shakespeare, for the brief weeks of the Wolfit season coin-

148

cided with the only period in my life after my buried infancy in which I had the direct acquaintance of my father, who then vanished entirely from my life; I possess no photograph of him, indeed no memento at all other than the inscription on the back of my watch, a handsome black-faced Movado with Arabic numerals (a rarity today), which he sent me (according to the inscription, though I have no recollection of his doing so) for my seventeenth birthday, and which still keeps perfect time. He and I went to one or two of the Wolfit productions together, though he had no knowledge of Shakespeare at all, except as the provider of plots for opera, about which he knew a little.

By then, I was a first-year undergraduate, and for several years had been a reader of eclectic tastes and almost insane voracity. I had read widely in the literature of eight languages beside my own (though very little of it, alas, in the original), and what I discovered – 'sensed' would be a better word – in the dusty interior of the Bedford Music Hall, watching the 'acting versions' used by Wolfit (he used to bring the curtain down on *Hamlet* at '. . . and flights of angels sing thee to thy rest', lest he should not hold the centre of the stage to the last) and his scratch crew, was that the genius unfolding before me, in all its glory despite the conditions, was of a beauty, vigour, humanity, wisdom, wit, imagination, maturity, grace, feeling, profundity, richness and understanding that embraced all the qualities of everything of all the authors I had ever read put together, and a very great deal more besides.

That extraordinary truth I worked out only slowly; but in what I actually experienced on those evenings just round the corner from my childhood home I had leaped the argument and the evidence, and had arrived, without really knowing it, at the right conclusion.

Such actor-managing could not survive today; Ronald Harwood's shrewd and entertaining play *The Dresser*, which is plainly based on the character and career of Wolfit (Harwood started theatrical life as Wolfit's dresser), gives an idea,

149

and a good one, of what his work was like, and T. C. Worsley's description of his curtain speech (reproduced almost verbatim, incidentally, in *The Dresser*), with the old megalomaniac, as he thanked the audience, indulging in 'the same exhausted clutch of the curtain whether he had been laying himself out with Lear or trotting through twenty minutes of Touchstone', will also serve to remind those who saw Wolfit's productions of their nature.

None of that mattered in the least to an eighteen-year-old experiencing total immersion, for the first time, in Shakespeare acted. I did not know that the productions were grotesque, designed as a frame for Wolfit's own performances; I could not compare his interpretations with those of other actors, because the only play he did that I had seen before was *Hamlet*; I did not realize that the costumes were such as might have come from the nursery dressing-up basket in the home of a family that had come down in the world; as a matter of fact I had never so much as heard of Donald Wolfit before I read of the season he was about to present, and I was certainly not going, night after night, to see him, let alone his company. I was going to see – to see, hear, feel, drink, gorge myself upon – Shakespeare. That I did; and although it is the fashion now to decry Wolfit in retrospect, a fashion which I have myself here adopted, and although everything said about the awfulness of his work is true, I remain none the less devoted to his memory for that score of performances which still live so vividly in mine.

One of the very few sensible things Swinburne ever said, possibly the *only* sensible thing he ever said, was that the name of Bowdler should, so far from being an object of execration and derision, be honoured among the generations, because he made it possible for untold thousands if not millions of children, for the best part of a century, to become acquainted with the works of Shakespeare, which in an unexpurgated edition would never have been allowed in their hands. That is very like what I feel about Wolfit, and I cannot be alone in my debt to him. (I must, incidentally, be one of the few people to own a complete set of Bowdler's Shakespeare, and it is difficult to see, looking through it, why the good doctor should still arouse such ire; does it really matter very much if Shylock speaks not of one 'who, when the bagpipe sings i' the nose, cannot contain his urine' but of a less gross figure who 'cannot contain his choler'? Mind you, when the reader gets to *Measure for Measure* it *is* a little difficult to tell from the bowdlerized version just what it is that Angelo wants from Isabella.)

Take that list of plays I saw in the Bedford Music Hall: the four principal tragedies, plus *The Merchant of Venice* (another thing I didn't then know about Wolfit was that he would never refer to Hamlet, Shylock, Macbeth or Othello – in his mouth they were always The Dane, The Jew, The Thane and The Moor); two of the greatest comedies; and the Falstaff farce. I can remember details from almost every one of the productions. In *The Merry Wives*, for instance, when the search is going on in Ford's house and before Falstaff gets into the laundry basket, he tries to hide behind a wall hanging, but it turns out to be a *pair* of wall hangings, and his stomach protrudes between them into the room; in *Twelfth Night*, after Malvolio's final exit ('I'll be revenged on the whole pack of you'), Wolfit used the Duke's line 'Pursue him, and entreat him to a peace' as the cue for a dumb-show in which Malvolio is led back and reconciled, with Olivia hanging his chain of office, which he had torn off and hurled at her feet, round his neck again; playing The Jew, Wolfit ended the trial scene lying on the floor, writhing and weeping, but dragged himself to his feet, stumbled to the door and, before he left the courtroom and the play, looked right round the entire cast of his enemies and comprehensively spat at them all.

Those scenes have remained in my memory for more than thirty-five years; not because of Wolfit, but because of Shakespeare. For, much more vividly than these scenes, I remember the excitement that swept me along as the plays unfolded, the stupendous prodigality of the verse that

151

flooded over me, the passion and the drama that seized me, the richness and variety of the gallery of characters that passed before me, the instinctive realization which told me that this man was a being unlike all other writers in history.

When that I was, and a little tiny boy . . . Later, at some point, I began to understand consciously what Shakespeare meant to me. There was no single moment, no flinging open of the doors of perception, though I have never felt so completely part of Shakespeare, and so confident in my belief that I understood what was the nature of the effect he had on me, as I did at the production of *A Midsummer Night's Dream* which Peter Brook directed for the Royal Shakespeare Company in 1970. Here is an absurd test: if I were asked to select one single production of one single work on the dramatic or lyric stage as the richest and most profound experience I have ever had in any kind of theatre, I would choose that one. From the clash of cymbals to which the characters of the opening scene entered through the swing doors in the bare, white back wall, to the almost unbearably affecting yet gloriously appropriate final gesture of the cast making their exit through the auditorium, shaking hands with us as they went, it constituted the most complete and fruitful interpretation of any work of art I had, and have, ever seen interpreted. I mention it for a particular reason: when the production opened, Brook gave an interview in which, discussing Shakespeare's use of the comic play-within-the-play as the climax of the work rather than as an interlude in the serious business of love, he said, 'By now, Shakespeare did nothing by accident.'

It is a haunting phrase, and it is surely true. Shakespeare's self-consciousness was greater than any other artist who ever lived; not Beethoven himself saw more deeply into his own heart. And he takes this to lengths that would be very dangerous in the hands of lesser men:

> Not marble, nor the gilded monuments
> Of princes, shall outlive this powerful rhyme

So long as men can breathe, or eyes can see,
So long lives this, and this gives life to thee.

   . . . How many ages hence
Shall this our lofty scene be acted o'er,
In states unborn and accents yet unknown!

         . . . I have bedimm'd
The noontide sun, call'd forth the mutinous winds,
And 'twixt the green sea and the azur'd vault
Set roaring war; to the dread-rattling thunder
Have I given fire and rifted Jove's stout oak
With his own bolt: the strong-bas'd promontory
Have I made shake; and by the spurs pluck'd up
The pine and cedar: graves at my command
Have wak'd their sleepers, op'd, and let them forth
By my so potent art . . .

The last of those extraordinary claims to immortality
provides a clear test of Shakespeare's pre-eminence, for the
passage is a reworking of part of a translation of Ovid's
Metamorphoses by Arthur Golding, published in 1567, and
although Golding certainly had great gifts, the difference
between his talent and Shakespeare's transcendent genius
becomes at once apparent when we watch him striking fire
from Golding's clay. It is worth quoting the original at some
length for a true comparison:

   . . . Ye Elves of Hilles, of Brookes, of Woods alone,
Of standing Lakes, and of the Night approche ye
   everychone.
Through helpe of whom (the crooked banks much
   wondering at the thing)
I have compelled streames to run cleane backward to their
   spring.
By charmes I make the calme seas rough, & make the
   rough Seas plaine

And cover all the Skie with Cloudes, and chase them
   thence againe.
By charmes I raise and lay the windes, and burst the Vipers
   jawe:
And from the bowels of the Earth both stones and trees do
   drawe.
Whole woods and Forests I remove: I make the
   mountaines shake,
And even the Earth itselfe to grone and fearfully to quàke.
I call up dead men from their graves: and Thee O
   lightsome Moone
I darken oft . . .

No wonder that Shakespeare, contemplating Golding's earthbound lines and his own soaring imagination, dared to claim immortality. But many a lesser artist, many a poet and playwright without even a slight gift, might put forward such a claim; indeed, many have, and it is not enough to say, though it is true, that he has made good his claim for four centuries, and will continue to do so for many more centuries to come. He based his certainty that he was immortal on something far deeper and more important than his under-standing of the magnitude of his genius, and not only had he no need of Jonson's epitaph to understand that he 'was not for an age, but for all time'; he knew precisely why.

If he knew why, it seems likely that, whether deliberately or not, he communicated the reason to us, his readers and audiences. And to do so he had no occasion to resort to ciphers concealed in the text, nor to publish accounts of his aims and methods, nor to commit such reflections to diaries now lost. The mystery is explained in the works themselves, which is where we would expect it to be explained, and the explanation is not at all difficult to find, nor to understand when found.

My own most striking experience of the discovery was also the most striking Shakespearean experience I have ever had; it was much more powerful than anything I have ever

154

felt in any other performance or study of his work, not excluding the magical *Midsummer Night's Dream*, and could hardly fail to be so, given the circumstances.

It has always been my practice, whenever going to see any Shakespeare play, to read it before setting out for the theatre, however many times I have seen it and however well I know it. Many years ago, I was due to see *Love's Labour's Lost* for the first time; it was the only one of the canon that I had never seen staged, for I had by then collected even the rarely-performed *Titus Andronicus*, in an astonishing production, also by Peter Brook, with Olivier in the title role, which raised it from its gory gutter to the status of a true Roman tragedy, and thus provided me with a valuable early lesson in the truth that if we think little of any play of Shakespeare's, even the slightest, the misunderstanding is more likely to be in us than in him. (The production also included a most striking *coup de théâtre*, still fresh in my mind decades later. In one of the battle scenes the action was shaped to suggest that the enemy was in the audience, and to our amazement the suggestion was suddenly borne out by a shower of arrows embedding themselves in the proscenium arch and the scenery. Brook had had the arrows fixed to their targets and painted so as to be invisible; then, at the moment they were to be 'fired', the unseen wires were all twitched simultaneously and the arrows instantly stood out at right angles, hypnotizing the audience into the belief that they had been shot off from behind us and passed over our heads to do their work.)

In the afternoon, following my custom, I took down *Love's Labour's Lost* from the shelf and began to read. Before I had finished Act I, scene i, I had shut the book and put it away. For I had realized that not only had I never seen the play; I had never read it either. Now of course that is true for everyone, and for every play of Shakespeare's at some point; every Shakespeare-lover, from the most occasional theatre-goer to the editors of the *Variorum*, has had to discover the plays, one by one, and to be ignorant of them before doing so. But in this case, I was already familiar, to a greater or lesser degree, with all the other thirty-six; many I had known for years, and some intimately, both in performance and on the page. I could by then, for instance, recite some thousands of lines from the canon, and could tell you not only who Voltimand and Cornelius are, and in what play they appear, but could do the same for such far more recondite figures as Rugby, Capucius, Boult, Philario and Sir Oliver Martext, and in addition say where to find, as stage directions, both the famous *Exit, pursued by a bear* and the much less famous *Enter, and pass across the stage; a sewer.*

How *Love's Labour's Lost*, and that one alone, had escaped me I could not guess, and still cannot, but there lay the fact before me, and I knew at once what I was to do. That night, I had the pleasure (though the word is far too familiar to describe what I experienced) of seeing a new play of Shakespeare's as his contempories saw it when they were already familar with his work in general. For me, that night, it was entirely new, just written and never before performed; I could measure it against his other plays but not against previous recollections of itself, as it unfolded on my delighted ear and eye and mind, and found there no preconceptions, no knowledge, no previous acquaintance with the characters or even the plot, to get in the way of its force, beauty and effect.

It so chanced that the production itself was a thing of vibrant imagination and loveliness; it was directed by David William, in the Open-Air Theatre at Regent's Park, and even the weather was perfect. The entrance of Mercade in the final scene of the play – and remember that until he spoke I did not know what he had come to announce – was miraculously staged. Dressed entirely in black, he emerged from the bushes at the back of the acting area; the scene of the Worthies had ended in a full-sized Court Ball, and for some time the messenger was unobserved. One by one, the revellers noticed him as he stood, silent and unmoving, surveying the mirth that he was so soon to bring to an end;

one by one, they stopped their dancing, and eventually the whole stage was still, staring at him as the music faltered and died away. Then he advanced a few steps into the silence, and bowed to the new Queen:

'God save you, madam!'

'Welcome, Mercade;
But that thou interrupt'st our merriment.'

'I am sorry, madam; for the news I bring
Is heavy in my tongue. The king your father – '

'Dead, for my life!'

'Even so: my tale is told.'

Did even Shakespeare ever give a character so few words (twenty-eight, for Mercade says nothing else and appears in no other scene) yet establish him instantly as a recognizable individual and at the heart of the drama? (Yes, he did. Popilius Lena, who appears only in Act III, scene i of *Julius Caesar*, has only *ten* words – 'I wish your enterprise today may thrive . . . fare you well' – spoken to Cassius immediately before the assassination, yet epitomizing all those who speak ambiguously in dangerous affairs of state in order to ensure that whatever happens they may plausibly claim to have supported the winning side.)

Even at this point, of course, I did not know what was to follow, the vows demanded and given, the song – which I had long known as a poem without knowing its provenance or even its authorship – and that final, conclusive, eternally echoing curtain line:

The words of Mercury are harsh after the songs of
    Apollo. You, that way; we, this way.

As I left the park, and made my way home through the silent night, I was being borne along on the extraordinary intensity of what had just happened to me, the experience of new-minted Shakespeare; and that river of glory, as it swept me, unresisting, with it, taught me, and teaches me still, whenever I conjure up the feelings I had that night, what is the greatest of all the pleasures and wonders and beauties and insights that Shakespeare provides.

No other writer, and with the exception of Mozart no other artist, has brought us so close to the heart of the ultimate mystery of the universe and of man's place in it; no other has felt and presented the numinous with such certainty and power, no other penetrated so deeply into the source from which he derived his genius and from which we all, including him, derive our humanity. The ultimate wonder of Shakespeare is the deep, sustaining realization that his work, in addition to all its other qualities – poetical, dramatic, philosophical, psychological – is above all *true*. It is hardly surprising that he, alone among mortals, has conquered mortality, and still speaks directly to us from lips that have been dust for hundreds of years, and a heart that stopped beating to mortal rhythms on St George's Day, 1616. He alone has defeated the last enemy, that pitiless foe which he called 'cormorant devouring time'; no wonder that he knew it, and thought it no shame – 'Not marble, nor the gilded monuments Of princes shall outlive this powerful rhyme' – to proclaim it.

Think of the old definition of tragedy: a man brought down by the quality that made him great. Then think of what it means in symbolic terms; the imperfection that lies within us all, and that we are on earth to work at until – perhaps, as the Buddhists believe, through many thousands of lifetimes – we wear it away entirely and become one with the perfection of the universe. Surely there is hardly an important character (and in Shakespeare *every* character is important, including Mercade and Popilius Lena) who does not in some way reflect back to us the principle that informs the universe.

Why is Macbeth a villain? Because he commits murder? But what is the murder he commits, apart from being specially heinous as the murder of one to whom he owes the

158

loyalty both of a subject and a host? It is an insult, in the sense of the word as it was used on Dylan Thomas's death certificate – 'an insult to the brain' – to the universe, a deliberate attempt to disturb its order, its flow and its purpose. Why, unless we are psychopathically deranged, do we *always* know when we are doing wrong, whether we thereupon stay our hands or not? Because we are all attuned, deny it though we may, to the harmony of the spheres ('There's not the smallest orb which thou behold'st, But in his motion like an angel sings, Still quiring to the young-eyed cherubins'), and we know instantly when we have introduced a discord into this harmony ('But while this muddy vesture of decay Doth close us in, we cannot hear it'). The 'order' speech of Ulysses in *Troilus and Cressida* is a statement, perhaps the noblest in the entire canon, of Shakespeare's own horror of anarchy and disorder. Shakespeare, however, was rarely quite so literal, and never two-dimensional; the speech, which in any case is obviously – more obviously than anything except Prospero's farewell and lines like Falstaff's 'I am not only witty in myself but the cause that wit is in other men' – Shakespeare himself speaking, is a statement of *why* he felt that horror.

Troilus and Cressida was written little more than a century after the Battle of Bosworth; when he was a boy there must have been men and women in Stratford whose fathers had fought there and told them of it, and of what it meant for their country, racked so long with civil war. That war, for Shakespeare, reflected the other, greater war in man's soul, which will continue until man makes his own peace by learning how to heal the split between those inner factions of White Rose and Red, and Ulysses describes precisely what must happen until that peace is made:

> . . . untune that string
> And, hark! what discord follows; each thing meets
> In mere oppugnancy: the bounded waters
> Should lift their bosoms higher than the shores,

And make a sop of all this solid globe:
Strength should be lord of imbecility,
And the rude son should strike his father dead:
Force should be right; or rather, right and wrong –
Between whose endless jar justice resides –
Should lose their names, and so should justice too.
Then every thing includes itself in power,
Power into will, will into appetite;
And appetite, an universal wolf,
So doubly seconded with will and power,
Must make perforce an universal prey,
And last eat up himself . . .

The Bosworth within us all is real: 'Two loves I have of comfort and despair . . . I guess one angel in another's hell'. Again and again, Shakespeare strikes the agonized balance between contrary impulses; he wrestled throughout his life with the Divine Right of Kings, and in *Richard II*, most perfectly balanced of all the Histories, he stated the human dilemma in terms of Richard and Bolingbroke, king and subject, allegiance to an oath and allegiance to a country. He did it constantly, this offering of the stark choice we all have: what else is *Hamlet* but another such battlefield, on which the regiments are mother, father, the canon 'gainst self-slaughter *and* against murder, and on which the same interior dynastic struggle is being waged?

Aeschylus could solve the insoluble problem and free Orestes from the Furies by a *deus ex machina*; Wagner could square the circle of Wotan's impossible bargain by the creation of a new order out of the resultant chaos; Shakespeare knew better than both of them, and Lear must drain the cup to the last drop once the bitter wine is poured.

We are here to learn, and there is nothing we cannot learn from Shakespeare if we will only trust him. The feminine principle, yin for yang, he saw as the indispensable healing agent in the masculine, three centuries before modern psychology saw it too, and it is never stronger in Shakespeare than when it is literally disguised: there are no more complete women in all art than Rosalind-Ganymede, Viola-Cesario, Imogen-Fidele, Portia-Bellario, emphasizing as they don their jerkins the incompleteness of one sex without the other, which is in turn another clue to our duty to be whole:

> . . . Men must endure
> Their going hence, even as their coming hither;
> Ripeness is all.

There is no play of his that will not, in the hands of a sufficiently imaginative director, yield up the same secret. When Trevor Nunn directed *The Comedy of Errors* for the Royal Shakespeare Company in the late 1970s, he knew that the play is almost always thought of as a feeble and unworthy work, thrown off without labour, and consequently incapable of making a modern audience laugh, or indeed of conveying anything but boredom. But Nunn knew also that fifteen years earlier, at Stratford, Clifford Williams had succeeded in making it an airy, delicate comedy, which suddenly, in the scene of reconciliation at the end, presided over by the Abbess (a true *dea ex machina*, conjured up by the deep necessity of the play's witness, not the shallower need of its plot), struck an entirely different note. This note was born of the pain that lay behind the comic confusions of the drama, and of the terrible threat to the fundamental regime of harmony and order that the unresolvable mystery poses until, when all the missing parts of the whole are assembled for the first time, we can see that there is no mystery and never was one; there was no more than a fragmentation, which needed only to be made whole.

That is what Clifford Williams did with the play; he divined what Shakespeare had done with it, and managed to convey that to the audience in unmistakable conviction. How was Trevor Nunn to do the same, to work the miracle again? At first sight, he seemed to have solved the problem by fleeing from it, by making the play only a ripe and dazzling farce, larded with such imaginative and pleasing business that we could do nothing but laugh helplessly throughout. But in that case, why did we feel not merely the benign warmth of laughter, but a sensation of extraordinary harmony even amid the whirling absurdities? Because he also had divined Shakespeare's purpose, and interpreted it by making the spinning farce truly centripetal, so that the reconciliation scene became, incredibly but undoubtedly, the only logical – the only *true* – way out of the impasse. It so happened that at the time of the first of these productions of *The Comedy of Errors* I was just coming to the end of a period of some years as a newspaper theatre critic, and at the time of the second I was just embarking on another such period. Of the first I wrote that 'at the end, it was like taking leave of a group of friends': of the second that if he could have seen it 'Shakespeare would have gone his way rejoicing, and so did I'. Both comments were reactions to the quality that Williams and Nunn, in their very different styles, had found in the play. But obviously they had only been able to find it because it was there. And if it is to be found in a play as slight as *The Comedy of Errors*, how much more clearly can it be seen in the principal tragedies, comedies and histories!

If we seek something in Shakespeare and cannot find it, it is not because what we seek is not there; it is because we have not sought it diligently enough.

I started reading *Much Ado About Nothing* when I was a schoolboy, and seeing it not much later, and I always enjoyed Benedick's catalogue of the attributes of his ideal woman – rich, wise, mild, noble, musical – ending with a shrug and the casual line, indicating his indifference to such considerations, 'And her hair shall be of what colour it please God'. Then I saw Robert Donat play it; he struck the last word a delicate blow, his voice falling half an octave on it – 'her hair shall be of what colour it please *God*' – and instantly a joke, at the expense of women who touch up the silver with gold, that had lain buried for three and a half centuries, sprang to life. No wonder Mercutio dies punning.

The laughter of Shakespeare must not be rated low; if we think of it as no more than decoration we are in danger of missing not only the point of the laughter but the point of Shakespeare himself. Laughter is one of the deepest essences of mankind, one of the most significant clues to our humanity, for no other animal has the gift. Nobody has yet discovered what it is, not even physiologically, and we can only guess at the purpose it serves. But Shakespeare understood, and portrays, every variety of it, from the earthiness of Falstaff and Sir Toby Belch to the delicate raillery of Beatrice and Benedick and all the way to the bitter truth in the jests of Lear's Fool:

'Dost thou call me fool, boy?'

'All thy other titles thou hast given
away; that thou wast born with.'

The first Falstaff I saw was Ralph Richardson; the finest, Hugh Griffith (said to be the most difficult and uncolleaguely actor on the stage, though this characteristic never communicated itself to the audience – another proof that Shakespeare was right when he said 'There's no art to find the mind's construction in the face'); both gave performances that vibrate still in the memory, because they went straight through theory ('How do I get this laugh, why is this line funny?') into Shakespeare's own understanding of the nature of laughter. It is a truth not yet universally acknowledged that an actor who trusts Shakespeare to know his business will have taken the greatest single step towards success; this also applies, even more strongly, to directors, though they are even further away from understanding the necessity for the rule ('Shakespeare does nothing by accident') than the actors are.

I can remember my laughter at Shakespeare before any other of my responses; Stanley Holloway was First Gravedigger to that Gielgud Hamlet, and made me realize, again without understanding what the realization meant, that laughter is valuable at a level far deeper than the enjoyment of the moment; young and unknown actors with any sense ought to leap at the chance of playing Osric, or the Porter, or the Clown in *Antony and Cleopatra*. (Though directors with any sense will not let them do so, knowing that such tiny but vital parts must be put in surer hands.)

Close behind the laughter came the excitement. There were no Histories in that month of Wolfit, and only the two *Henry IV*s in those early seasons of the Old Vic, though it is true that they gave me Olivier's Hotspur; I did not see *Henry V* until the young Richard Burton, afire with youthful promise that was doomed never to be fulfilled, played it at the Old Vic when the company had moved back across the river to its own home at Waterloo, nor *Richard II* until I saw it at Stratford with the young Guinness as Richard facing the young Harry Andrews as Bolingbroke, nor *Henry VIII* until Tyrone Guthrie directed it as a loyal salute to the monarch in Coronation year, 1953, nor any of the *Henry VI*s until the Birmingham Repertory Company brought them to London for a brief season. But even collecting performances of them one by one over so long a period I could realize what an important part of Shakespeare's life and work the Histories constitute.

There has been too much silly, modish chatter about 'Tudor propaganda' from critics and dons who seem incapable of sensing the greatness of the events the cycle of history plays depicts. There is carnage as well as splendour, treachery as well as honour, cowardice (though astonishingly little of it) as well as courage; but what we see is the forging of England on the anvil of history, and anyone who is, or, worse, affects to be, not at all stirred by pride as the metal is shaped and toughened has no idea of what a nation is, or why it matters to the people of it. Some day, a leading theatre company should stage all the ten Histories in a single season. I can think of no better way of explaining the first four of the most crucial five centuries of this country's history (alas, there was no Shakespeare to finish off the cycle with the Civil War and the Glorious Revolution, only the Restoration dramatists with their febrile, mincing wit) than by watching Shakespeare's immense tapestry unroll. When the R.S.C. gave us *The Wars of the Roses* I recall that even the scenery entered into the spirit of the plays and their didactic purpose, its great slabs and joists of English oak and English steel making Shakespeare's point as vividly as Shakespeare's words did, and suffusing the theatre with the pleasure the audience took in its fitness.

And that is only the Histories: what of the excitement of *Macbeth*, of which Keats said that he didn't know how anyone alone in the house at two o'clock in the morning could even dare to read it? That first *Macbeth*, with Wolfit, seared my feelings with the power and electricity of the tale and the language in which it is clothed; who, however often he has seen it (and I suppose I must have seen it more than a score of times now), does not experience in himself, and not just vicariously, the sickened realization that the witches are false when Macduff declares that he was from his mother's womb untimely ripped, or does not feel the hair rising on the back of his neck when the servant announces that Birnam Wood is on the march to Dunsinane, or at the appearance of Banquo's ghost?

There is not a play of the thirty-seven without this excitement, the excitement that comes from seeing human beings facing apparently insoluble clashes between irresistible force and immovable object, whether these take the form of kingship and usurpation, or jealousy and fidelity, or belief and duty, or fathers and children, or cruelty and forgiveness, or dignity and humiliation, or truth and falsehood, or love and misunderstanding, or life and death.

Line after line rolls echoing round the mind on wheels of passion and arousal:

> How all occasions do inform against me
> And spur my dull revenge!

> 'Tis one thing to be tempted, Escalus,
> Another thing to fall.

165

There was a man . . . dwelt by a churchyard.

I was not angry since I came to France,
Until this instant.

There is a world elsewhere.

                                  Perdition catch my soul
But I do love thee! and when I love thee not,
Chaos is come again.

Kill Claudio!

And the imperial votaress passed on,
In maiden meditation, fancy-free.

If every ducat in six thousand ducats
Were in six parts and every part a ducat,
I would not draw them: I would have my bond.

Good shepherd, tell this youth what 'tis to love.

I dare do all that may become a man;
Who dares do more is none.

'Tis the times' plague, when madmen lead the blind.

The last of all the Romans, fare thee well!

We feel the terror of Macbeth's cry 'Which of you have done
this?', even if we know the play intimately, and even if the
director or actor is clumsy, so that we see Banquo slipping
into his place at the table, we still feel it undiminished. But
why do we feel it so? Because for a moment we *are* Macbeth.
That is why the question that works with all other playwrights and novelists – with which character do we identify?
– simply makes no sense with Shakespeare, whose genius
ensures that we are Iago as well as Othello, Hamlet and
Claudius, Lear and his daughters, Montagues and Capulets,
Posthumus and Iachimo, Shylock and Antonio, the Dark

Lady and the lovely boy. And for the best of all reasons: these are all aspects of ourselves, and no man can contain Prospero without also encompassing Caliban.

And yet whatever of Shakespeare resides in his laughter, his excitement, his characters, his sense of history, his balance, his understanding, his universality, it is his poetry that provides the sea on which all these proud vessels sail; his music provides the most immediate, complete and enduring of all the pleasures he offers. There is no mood it cannot reflect or evoke, no feeling it cannot recall or inspire, no thought it cannot brighten, no sound it cannot make sweeter. In the words of Henry the Fifth it is always bright as noon; in the speeches of Iago it is dark and smoky as hell; in the ghostly tones of Oberon we are well-met by moonlight. And just as Shakespeare never ceases to remind us that we are at once king and rebel, Caesar and assassin, Leontes and Hermione, Timon and Athens, so the limitless flood of his verse is poured out for the knaves as well as the upright, the poltroons as well as the heroes, the corrupt as well as the pure, the solemn and the light-hearted, servant and master, countryman and courtier, clown and sexton, rich and poor, old and young, beautiful and ill-favoured.

Why do we smile at the story of the old lady who saw *Hamlet* for the first time and came out complaining that it was full of quotations? Shakespeare's unique ability was to convey a thought, original or familiar, profound or casual, in words that have rooted themselves in the innermost consciousness of millions, because his thoughts correspond to what is already, unexpressed, to be found there. If it were not so his words, however magnificent, could not have struck roots so deep and so tenacious; he found the soil fertile, and through his genius it has borne fruit.

'Truism' is a word of abuse, but it should not be, for the whole point of a truism is that it is true, and those Shakespearean phrases that have been worn away almost to dust remain alive in his mouth even if they do not in ours. If you cannot understand my argument, and declare 'It's Greek to me', you are quoting Shakespeare; if you claim to be more sinned against than sinning, you are quoting Shakespeare; if you recall your salad days, you are quoting Shakespeare; if you act more in sorrow than in anger, if your wish is father to the thought, if your lost property has vanished into thin air, you are quoting Shakespeare; if you have ever refused to budge an inch or suffered from green-eyed jealousy, if you have played fast and loose, if you have been tongue-tied, a tower of strength, hoodwinked or in a pickle, if you have knitted your brows, made a virtue of necessity, insisted on fair play, slept not one wink, stood on ceremony, danced attendance (on your lord and master), laughed yourself into stitches, had short shrift, cold comfort or too much of a good thing, if you have seen better days or lived in a fool's paradise – why, be that as it may, the more fool you, for it is a foregone conclusion that you are (as good luck would have it) quoting Shakespeare; if you think it is early days and clear out bag and baggage, if you think it is high time and that that is the long and short of it, if you believe that the game is up and that truth will out even if it involves your own flesh and blood, if you lie low till the crack of doom because you suspect foul play, if you have your teeth set on edge (at one fell swoop) without rhyme or reason, then – to give the devil his due – if the truth were known (for surely you have a tongue in your head) you are quoting Shakespeare; even if you bid me good riddance and send me packing, if you wish I was dead as a doornail, if you think I am an eyesore, a laughing stock, the devil incarnate, a stony-hearted villain, bloody-minded or a blinking idiot, then – by Jove! O Lord! Tut, tut! for goodness' sake! what the dickens! but me no buts – it is all one to me, for you are quoting Shakespeare.

And the pleasure of Shakespeare's language is inextricably interwoven with what he says in it. His mind is an instrument of such stupendous understanding, depth and creativity that it towers over the human race, and to hear the contents of that mind clothed in that poetry provides a pleasure which consumes like fire.

> Take him and cut him out in little stars,
> And he will make the face of heaven so fine
> That all the world will be in love with night,
> And pay no worship to the garish sun.

When I hear those words spoken by a Juliet who knows how to ring Shakespeare's chimes (it happens, alas, all too rarely), I shiver in the ecstasy they provoke. But so I do when Coriolanus begins 'You common cry of curs', or Hotspur 'My lord, I did deny no prisoners', or Dogberry 'Dost thou not suspect my place?', or Petruchio 'Have I not in my time heard lions roar?', or Wolsey 'Farewell, a long farewell, to all my greatness'. For the ecstasy wells up from a level far below the ecstasy that comes from beauty or passion; it comes from the same spring as that which gives us life and meaning, which defines our humanity and our divinity, which makes us what we are and Shakespeare what he is. And that is why his last words apply to everything in the universe except him and what he serves:

> The cloud-capped towers, the gorgeous palaces,
> The solemn temples, the great globe itself,
> Yea, all which it inherit, shall dissolve,
> And like this insubstantial pageant faded,
> Leave not a wrack behind. We are such stuff
> As dreams are made on; and our little life
> Is rounded with a sleep.

Seven

Some are born to music, some achieve music, and some have music thrust upon them. I am of the second category.

The more I think about my love of music, the more mysterious it becomes. I have no gift for it, in that I cannot write music, or play any instrument, or sing in tune; I can hear a theme in my head, and identify it, but I have not got absolute pitch, and I know very well, and can prove it by putting the thing on the gramophone, that I am not remembering it accurately. Nor have I even much musical talent as a listener. My attention often wanders at a concert or an opera, and I am almost as unobservant aurally as I am visually; I often miss important points to which the composer or performer is trying to draw my attention. So what do I mean when I say that music has been, for most of my life, one of the foundations of that life, giving me not only greater and deeper satisfaction than almost any other experience, but opening windows on a realm of the spirit in such a way as to suggest that music's true home is in that world rather than in ours, and enables us to cross the chasm between this side and that, borne, literally, on wings of song? And whatever I mean by that, why does the effect that music has on me have it, and how does it work its effect? What is it in me that responds thus to music, and how did it get into me?

Apart from the horror of my attempts as a child to learn to play the violin, which I have recounted elsewhere, the first music in my life consisted of a series of vast, improvised oratorios composed with my sister. I did not know they were oratorios, indeed did not know they were music (nor were they, except in the most desperately literal sense), and they were all concerned with the life and times of a character by the name of Chumchi Chaddik, clearly of Slav origin. The name was used by our mother when she wanted to attribute something anonymous, say a proverb or a trait of character, to a specific but non-existent individual; neighbouring mothers, not themselves born of Russian parents, were no doubt at the time using Whatsisname or Father Christmas or Mr Nobody for this purpose, but in my home it was Chumchi Chaddik. Where she got the name from I have no idea, and certainly he had no wider existence for her, but the infant inventiveness of my sister and myself fleshed him out and provided him with a series of picaresque adventures, all couched in a kind of hideous plainsong made up, like the texts and the plot, as we went along.

When that palled, music vanished from my life, to run underground like a hidden river until it emerged, years later, and rapidly took hold. I have a faint recollection of going in a school party to some kind of musical lecture and concert, but the violin-lesson inoculation was then still working in my blood, and the bacillus was presumably resisted, for nothing came of it and I cannot remember repeating the experience. Yet ever since the sacred river began to flow above ground, getting on for forty years ago now, I have been to some musical performance almost exactly once a week, and if I add the time spent listening to music on gramophone or radio, I suppose it must add up to something like 10,000 hours. What have I got to show for it?

In the beginning were the Proms. An eighteen-year-old youth, hearing the *Egmont* Overture for the first time, does not stop to wonder about the nature or effects of music, nor what it means for his life, let alone how he may be able to understand what life itself means by looking at its reflection in music; all I wanted to do, as those three amazing chords brought that most thrilling of codas to an end, was to rush out and liberate the Low Countries single-handed. But that was only partly due to Beethoven; a good deal of the feeling

171

sprang from the fact that I was already half delirious with the discovery of music itself. I think that there is very little in life to compare with that discovery and the subsequent feasting on what has been revealed; apart from love, perhaps nothing at all. And I count myself fortunate rather than deprived to have had the floodwaters held back as long as they were.

Most people, I think, would say that it is best for a child to get the musical habit early, and so it is if it is only a matter of ensuring that the habit is acquired. But though the child in a musical family, who is led gently by the hand into musical understanding, starts on his road to joy years before the one who has to take the first steps for himself, the self-taught music-lover has an intensity of rapture when the dam breaks that one who has been gradually familiarized with the effect of music cannot hope to experience.

Of course I was fortunate also to be a Londoner, and thus to have the Proms available at first hand in return for nothing but a few hours of queueing and a florin. The extraordinary *tour d'horizon* of all the greatest landmarks in the world of concert music that the Proms then provided every year was indispensable to one who, like me, was desperate to make up for those musicless years and to fill the vast deserts of musical ignorance that stretched before me.

I am glad that I knew so little about Beethoven before that concert with the *Egmont* Overture in the summer of 1946 when my journey into music began. It was followed by his Third Piano Concerto and Seventh Symphony, and that alone fixes the day of the week, for when I was first a Promenader, Friday nights were consecrated to Beethoven, and every Promenade season included all his symphonies and concertos. (I was fortunate in that, though I came of a Jewish home, it was not Orthodox. Otherwise, since going to concerts on the Sabbath eve would have been forbidden, I might never have discovered Beethoven at all.) That has long ceased to be true; the advent of the cheap long-playing record, and the cheap equipment for reproducing it with great fidelity, means that the Proms no longer need to repeat the whole catalogue of standard classics each year, as these are so readily available in other forms. But the weekly supply of Beethoven – and Beethoven must surely always be the heart of anyone's discovery of music, gradual or abrupt – was in those days a matter of course, and my memories are full of him.

The pianist on that first occasion was Solomon, one of the noblest musicians this country has ever produced; his career was to be tragically cut short, a few years later, by a disabling stroke, though as I write these words at the end of 1982 he is still alive. I cannot see the conductor in my mind's eye; I think it must have been Sargent, for the first Promenade season I went to was the first without Henry Wood, and Sargent was his successor. Sargent was an immensely thorough and hard-working musical carthorse rather than a Derby winner, but he was fiercely devoted to his Promenaders and his duty to bring them music. (Once, as he began the slow movement of the Choral Symphony, he saw a newspaper photographer clamber in among the back row of the orchestra and prepare to take pictures of the young music-lovers packed against the rail at the front of the Promenade; Sargent at once stopped the music and had the man removed; he explained afterwards that 'some of the Promenaders would have had rapt expressions on their faces', and he clearly felt this to be an intensely private communication of their feelings, not to be made public.) But however uninspired Sargent was as a conductor, it made no difference to me; in those days the music might have been conducted by Chumchi Chaddik himself for all I knew or cared.

Solomon was short, bald, square, very undemonstrative in his platform manner. Not long after that Beethoven Friday I began to hear the piano played by José Iturbi, whose platform manner suggested strongly that he was under the direct patronage of St Vitus. There was a similar contrast between the conducting style of Adrian Boult, restrained to a point only just this side of total immobility, and Victor de Sabata, who leaped and danced and writhed upon the podium like a man demented. Or there was Bruno Walter, getting the music from his players by coaxing, wheedling, imploring, and Furtwängler, getting it by contriving to suggest that he would have a nervous breakdown if he didn't, and, later, Klemperer, by the hypnotic force of the will that glared out of his twisted body, or Beecham, by insisting that they were all doing it for fun (which, given Beecham's attitude to his financial obligations, was quite often, for the orchestra, true), or Toscanini, by making it quite clear that he would break the players' instruments over their heads if they fell short of the standards he demanded.

None of this mattered in the least while I was shovelling down music with indiscriminate haste and unassuageable appetite. I once heard the Beethoven Violin Concerto played in successive weeks by Menuhin and Heifetz – warm gold followed by blue steel – and the Fourth Piano Concerto played in the space of a month by Schnabel, Backhaus and Gieseking, and all the Symphonies in two successive seasons by the Vienna Philharmonic under Furtwängler and the Amsterdam Concertgebouw under van Beinum. Still I craved more, still I fed the devouring furnace at the Albert Hall, the Wigmore, the Conway.

Out of the Promenade season, the Albert Hall always involved a gamble. Deprived of the standing-room Arena, the unmoneyed were compelled to fall back on the Gallery, where there were, and no doubt still are, a very few seats, right at the front, with a commanding view of the platform far below. To be sure of one of these, it was necessary for the gallery-goer to be early in the queue, and, when the doors were unlocked and the cavalry charge up the interminable stairs began, to abandon all thoughts of chivalry and to rely upon fleetness of foot, soundness of wind and readiness of elbow. But the gamble was inescapable for even the hardiest athlete and most merciless warrior, for the Albert Hall, being symmetrical, has matching pairs of doors on each side (the hall, incidentally, is not round, though an optical illusion suggests that it is), but only one attendant to fling the portals wide. Would he start on our side or the other? There was no means of telling, and sometimes it chanced that a record-breaking sprint up the stairs, involving the trampling under-foot of many a feebler rival, resulted only in our bursting through the doors at the top to be greeted by the sight of the other army ensconced in the precious chairs, the turnkey's caprice having led him to begin his door opening on the side that favoured the enemy.

Nothing mattered. One night there was a gigantic, freak thunderstorm, accompanied by massive cannonades of hail, in the middle of the Brahms Violin Concerto, half of which was completely inaudible in consequence; another enchanted evening included a notoriously drunken conductor falling off the podium into the orchestra during Borodin's *Polovtsian Dances* (there was another, later, at Covent Garden, who at one point in the *Ring* turned right round and began to conduct the audience); there was the fuel-crisis winter of 1947, when all heating of public buildings was banned, and the sensible Eileen Joyce, playing the Grieg Piano Concerto, appeared on the platform of the Albert Hall with a huge fur muff (containing a hot-water bottle), in which she buried her hands during the orchestral *tutti*.

Still the furnace raged, still I sought out more musical fuel to feed it. I was far too shy to strike up a conversation with the girl beside me in the queue; I didn't like the Fourth Symphony of Vaughan Williams; on a hot night in the Proms, I fainted during one of those extended moanings, the musical equivalent of blancmange, that constitute much of the *oeuvre* of Delius, so long and so fruitlessly championed by Beecham; I heard the piano played by Frederick Lamond, the last surviving pupil of Liszt, and the concert version of the waltzes from *Der Rosenkavalier* conducted by the composer, and the farewell recital of Alfred Cortot, in which he played all twenty-four Chopin Preludes before the interval, and all twenty-four Études after it.

The Royal Festival Hall was opened in 1951, its copper roof, long since oxydized to a kind of bird-droppings blue,

175

giving brilliant and blazing promise of more delights to come; those visits to it in its early days were like the discovery of music itself all over again, so dazzling in its splendour was the new hall's interior. That will sound odd in the ears of those who do not remember it from its infancy and their own youth, for it has long ceased to be advanced in its architecture or its internal design, and has lately also become very shabby; in those days, however, it was a revelation, and quite literally, too. Not only did it make so striking a contrast to the concert rooms I was used to; it was the first important postwar public building I had seen, and obviously one of the very first to be built. I suppose it must have been the first new building of *any* kind I could remember seeing, and as I dwell on that thought, it occurs to me that I can hardly then have begun to think consciously about architecture at all; perhaps the years of the war, when buildings were being knocked down rather than put up, made the subject too remote. But the glittering brightness of the Festival Hall, and the lavish use of space in its interior, the beauty of shining new wood, metal, marble, the explosive shock of the brand-new auditorium, with those boxes that look like half-opened drawers and the pale beauty of the sycamore baffle over the orchestra – that experience has taken its place for me beside the first intoxicated tastings of the music itself, and its effect in my memory glows no less brightly.

The Festival Hall was, of course, the centrepiece of the 1951 Festival of Britain, and the only building in the South Bank Exhibition complex that was destined to remain. (Or at any rate that did remain, for the Dome of Discovery, a remarkable structure designed by Ralph Tubbs, and some of the smaller pavilions, were originally intended to endure, until the voice of commerce spoke and they were all demolished to make way for the Shell Building, possibly the ugliest, nastiest and most inappropriately obtrusive large building erected in London between the construction of the Windsor Hotel – now, happily, demolished – and the Hayward Gallery – still, unhappily, not.) Today, 'South Bank', as a term for design and architecture, is used only pejoratively, and certainly some of its elements have proved ephemeral, though the best of the style has had a lasting influence, most notably in Sir Basil Spence's Coventry Cathedral, perhaps the only real masterpiece of architecture built in Britain since the end of the Second World War. But in any case, no such pro and contra entered into the feelings of those who, like myself, were open and eager to new experiences and sensations in every aspect of life at the time the South Bank Exhibition and the Festival Hall burst upon us, and I wandered round both of them open-mouthed with astonishment and joy.

The astonishment and joy pervaded the whole place; I remember that Lord Beaverbrook was conducting one of his lunatic vendettas against the Festival, and poor devils employed by him were sent out to find misery and failure where there was nothing but happiness and success. And the happiness was at its most intense in the Festival Hall. At the end of a concert, the audience could not bear to leave, to go from this beauty and opulence into the drab world of postwar Britain, still exhausted, shabby and rationed; we wandered about the corridors and walkways, clearly determined to remain there all night. After a few days of this the attendants, dressed for the opening month of the new hall in resplendent red and green tailcoated uniforms, improvised a solution; they went to the top of the building, linked arms, and moved slowly down from level to level, very gently shepherding us all into the main foyer, and thence, even more gently, into the reality outside.

It was like being in a spaceship, and if a disembodied voice had announced that the Festival Hall would shortly be leaving for Betelgeuse or Aldebaran, we would not have been at all surprised, and most of us would have stayed aboard for the ride. Wandering about the foyer before the concert on my first visit, there passed through my mind the thought that it would be incongruous and disappointing to hear, amid the gleaming future of the surroundings, the old-fashioned sound of a nagging bell summoning us to our seats; just as the thought struck me, the Festival Hall's ethereal gong, which sounds like a much magnified *celeste*, began to beat out its pure A (chosen because that is the first sound the audience will hear inside the auditorium as the orchestra begins to tune). Friends with absolute pitch assert that the A is nowadays sometimes flat, but I still think the idea beautiful and appropriate, and I never hear it without being reminded of the days of my youth when the Festival Hall, and music, and all the world, was new.

Even before the A began to chime on that first evening, another memory was safely tucked away. The architects and designers might have been able, with all the excitement and glitter, to turn my impressionable head, but I was there with a lady who had a practical streak in her character, and was not to be diverted from putting first things first. She disappeared for a few minutes, then returned rubbing her hands and with eyes agleam, to announce that the Royal Festival Hall had been tested and had passed the test: 'Smashing Ladies!'

Just as the Festival Hall's interval bell always revives for me the feelings of awe and wonder with which I contemplated the new surroundings in which I was to hear music, so the music itself never ceases to remind me of the way it stirred my blood when I was just getting to know it. There is a crucial, and wonderful, sense in which we never lose our first enthusiasm for those sights and sounds and feelings that have the stuff of eternity in them; who could get to the point of never again wanting to see a production of *The Tempest* or the interior of the Jeu de Paume, to look at a rainbow or a waterfall, to fall asleep in doubt and wake in hope? Why, then, should anyone think it strange if a music-lover claims to recapture at every hearing something of the feelings he experienced when the hearing, and the feelings themselves, were new? For the music has not changed over the years.

When the pianist emerges, half-drowned in the spray, from that thunderous chord which begins the Emperor

Concerto, and launches into a titanic arpeggio that sounds like God Almighty flexing his fingers before embarking on a recital of some of the noisier keyboard works of Liszt, I now know the passage so well that I could play it myself if I were God Almighty; when the strange, dark, adagio introduction to Beethoven's Fourth Symphony explodes within a single bar into movement of dancing gaiety infused with ferocious energy, it does not come as a surprise to me now, because I know that it is coming, and I know precisely where it happens; the same applies to the transition from the third movement to the fourth of the Fifth Symphony, as the ominous, threatening notes of the drum give way to that mysterious, veiled modulation, which – again within a bar – changes fear and denial into courage and affirmation, as the whole orchestra leaps into the blazing sunlight of C major.

Nevertheless, in all these instances the shock of the unexpected is as great, and as exciting, as when I first heard the works, and I will go so far as to say that the fact that I now know in advance what is going to happen makes the experience more thrilling, not less; it would ruin the enjoyment of a visitor to *The Mousetrap* to enter the theatre knowing the identity of the murderer, but the same cannot be said about *Hamlet*.

Moreover, no newborn music-lover, however indiscriminate, meets all his loves at once. There are some he *cannot* meet when young, because the responses are simply not formed until later in life. It would be a singularly precocious eighteen-year-old who could claim to fathom the mystery of the last quartets of Beethoven, or even to understand that the mystery in question is one of the greatest and deepest in the universe; indeed, I think that the very idea of chamber music appeals less to the young, and there are some composers – Gluck, for instance, and Bruckner – who are best left in their entirety until later. As for Mozart, his depths cannot be fully sounded by any human being, much less by any young one, for Mozart goes down to a level from which no traveller returns, or wishes to; for one who has really understood

Mozart, life can never be the same again. Almost as great a claim can be made for Schubert; when I was young, I thought the C major Symphony the most exciting piece of music ever written, and so indeed it is, and I once heard it played by the Vienna Philharmonic Orchestra under Bruno Walter, as a reward for my esteem. But the keyboard music meant little to me then, even when played by Schnabel or Casadesus; now it means infinity to me, especially when played by Serkin or Brendel.

Si la jeunesse savait . . . Why should it be surprising that the more understanding – of ourselves, of life, of the meaning of meaning – that we bring to art, the more of the artist's understanding of those very mysteries we shall take from it? *La vieillesse peut*; in music, I think, especially. But there is another, less general question to be asked about music, which is also unlikely to occur to the youth afire with the newly discovered *Egmont* Overture. The sheer oddness of music has been too little remarked.

The origins of the drama in religious beliefs and their expression, and its development into the depiction of characters, stories and scenes that the audience can either recognize or readily imagine, is not difficult to comprehend; nor is the growth of the visual arts, for from the cave paintings of Lascaux to very recently indeed it has followed a course parallel to the drama, in depicting a recognizable reality as a record, a tribute, a celebration, a stimulus or an imaginative reconstruction. And literature, from the Homeric bards to the present, needs even less explanation or defence. But what impelled the first man who noticed that different conch shells made different sounds when blown into to blow into several in succession, and then start to vary the order in which they were blown? And how did mankind discover that when it wanted to raise its voice in praise, supplication or triumph, the voice was more effective in song than in speech, and what did the first men to sing think they were doing?

Whatever the answers to these questions, another and much more pressing one arises from them: why was music, alone among the arts, so late a starter? The fourth century B.C. in Athens produced drama, architecture, sculpture, science, philosophy and politics at a level of sophistication and glory that set standards for human achievement still valid today; why was there nothing comparable in music among those achievements? When Medici Florence, two millennia later, produced an outpouring of the arts and sciences next only to the Athenian century, why was music so conspicuously absent from that feast also? Where is the composer contemporary with Giotto who is his equal? Why was Beethoven not born two hundred years or so earlier?

All this suggests strongly that there is something about music that distinguishes it from the other arts. And perhaps the quality which distinguishes it most sharply is what I have called its oddness. Without the intelligible words of literature and drama, the recognizable images of painting or sculpture, the obviously practical masses and shapes of architecture, music, well before opera was invented, set out to conquer the heart of man by combining a variety of sounds, and by this means alone. Why should anyone have bothered, why should anyone bother now, to attend upon, and be deeply affected by, a proceeding that is literally meaningless? How does an art that denies itself all acknowledged forms of communication none the less communicate its meaning with such power?

The implication of these questions is so extraordinary that it has led to the denial of the premise on which they are based. It is held by some that the *Egmont* Overture is a series of sounds which strike the ear pleasurably (that begs another question immediately), and any emotion we feel when we listen to those sounds is in us, not them. This is great nonsense, to be sure, but saying so brings us no nearer to understanding what it means to feel emotion produced by a series of sounds. And perhaps in order to approach that understanding it is necessary to recognize the compromise music made when the paradox unconsciously began to trouble its creators; if the effect of abstract music could not be

181

explained, then music would add words that would explain themselves. Opera was born.

Of course there had been words attached to music before opera, and some of the early works of liturgy and worship, even if not the songs of the troubadours, are among the greatest of all music's achievements. But when music was married to drama no one could deny that it was trying to say something to its audiences. It has been doing so ever since.

I discovered opera at almost the same moment as I stumbled upon concert music; there had been no opera at Covent Garden during the war, and it took some time for a company to be assembled even when the argument over who should run the Opera House, and on what basis, had been settled. Before a regular opera season was established there, however, the San Carlo Opera of Naples (on which thousands of previously musicless servicemen stationed in Italy had cut their operatic teeth) paid a brief visit to Britain, and in the horrible old gallery at Covent Garden, long since gone, where the benches were brutally hard and narrow and the heat on a warm night suffocating, I heard my first *Barber of Seville*, my first *Traviata*, my first *Bohème*, and soon I was clattering up Rosebery Avenue on the tram to the old Sadler's Wells Theatre and my first *Rigoletto*, my first *Bartered Bride*, my first *Tosca*, my first *Carmen*, my first *Figaro*, *Don Giovanni* and *Magic Flute*. The operatic revelation was not so abrupt as the concert-hall one; some operas took me years to appreciate. But I nevertheless sought out opera whenever it was to be found.

Absurdity, even when nothing is going wrong on the stage, is never far from opera. The assumptions it demands are so great, the suspension of disbelief required so difficult to attain, that reality is always lurking in the wings, waiting an opportunity to set in and destroy the fragile illusion. Of course, it is no longer true that the size of opera singers makes the trouble worse; for twenty years or more it has been possible to spot the critic of opera who never sets foot in an opera house by his complaint that the singers are so fat it is impossible to believe in them. Indeed, some of the loveliest women of our time – Elisabeth Schwarzkopf, Victoria de los Angeles, Christa Ludwig, Irmgard Seefried, Lisa della Casa, Elisabeth Söderström, Kiri te Kanawa, Frederica von Stade, Grace Bumbry, Janet Baker, Shirley Verrett – have been opera singers, and there is now only one really fat man among the world's leading opera singers (Luciano Pavarotti) and only four or five women.

The absurdity, certainly, is always near, even if not always quite so near as in the famous exchange of distinctly unoperatic sentiments in *Madame Butterfly*:

> 'Milk-punch or whisky?'
> 'Whisky.'

But all opera-lovers know that the absurdity provides a vital clue to the truth about opera, and about much else, too. Let us seek that clue, and let us begin by seeking it in Verdi's *Falstaff*, for no better reason than that, when I began this chapter, it was the opera I had seen most recently. Forget Shakespeare, forget the conventions of drama, forget melody; let us just watch what happens. A fat man hides in a laundry basket and is thrown into the river, amid much horseplay; young lovers elope and the girl's rival suitor is tricked into thinking he has married her himself, though in fact going through a wedding ceremony with another man, and a red-nosed drunk into the bargain; the fat man, despite his earlier misfortunes, allows himself to be persuaded to don a huge pair of false antlers, after which he has his bottom pinched by the rest of the characters dressed up as fairies; there is a woman who is always curtseying and accompanying her curtseys with the same remark, like a television comedian with a catchphrase; and the opera ends with a chorus of which the chief sentiment is a repeated insistence that everyone is mad. Who, after all that, would disagree?

Few, probably. Why, then, is the pleasure that this work gives me whenever I see it – and I have seen it more than a score of times, the first of them with Mariano Stabile, greatest of modern Falstaffs – as enduringly enriching as any of the delights that this world affords, giving me in addition a haunting sense of the immanent presence of the next? How can absurdity become profundity, triviality significance, nonsense wisdom, sugared confections the bread of life?

Perhaps I chose unfairly. True, *The Merry Wives of Windsor* is very far from being Shakespeare's most sophisticated comedy, in either its plot or its language. All the same, it is not entirely without real Shakespearean quality, and Verdi, when he came to write the opera, had in addition not only his own genius for the music, but Boito, best of the nineteenth-century Italian librettists (and himself a composer of distinction) for the adaptation. Let us make the test harder. Let us take *Fidelio*.

Fidelio is one of the greatest glories of opera; it is one of the greatest glories of the creative human spirit. The pleasure *Fidelio* gives, even in an indifferent production and performance, is as deep and affecting as any human experience can be; anyone capable of appreciating through music the wonders and the mysteries of the human soul cannot fail to emerge from *Fidelio* in a state of spiritual exaltation. Nor is that all, though it is the greatest thing; after *Fidelio* we are strengthened in our faith in human nature and its capacity for self-sacrifice, we are re-dedicated to the cause of human liberty and confirmed in our conviction that no tyranny can endure for ever, we understand better both the dilemma of human beings compelled by force to behave worse than they wish to and the ability of others to behave better than they thought they could, and – a thing not to be altogether despised at a performance of opera – we have listened to some of the most beautiful and thrilling music ever written for the human voice and the standard instruments of the orchestra. If the performance has been a good one, and the production one which shows an understanding of Beethoven and of what he was conveying in *Fidelio*, all those pleasures will be redoubled. If, in addition, the external circumstances surrounding the performance are themselves directly relevant to the plot, the pleasure is increased again, to the point at which it becomes almost unendurable in its intensity.

I saw just such a performance of *Fidelio* in Salzburg, in 1948. The war, and the Nazi *Anschluss*, had ended only three years before; this was the first performance at the Salzburg Festival, since the nightmare had ended, of Beethoven's great hymn to liberty. The audience must have included many men and women who had suffered under the Nazis for their race, their opinions or their resistance to tyranny; among them, sitting next to them perhaps, there must also have been Nazis who caused such suffering. Certainly, there was at least one prominent Nazi on the stage, together with one Nazi collaborator and one who had suffered from Nazism. The conductor was Wilhelm Furtwängler, the most tragic figure in German music of the Nazi era; detesting Nazism and everything about it, he had nevertheless stayed in Germany (despite countless opportunities to get out) in order, as he put it himself, 'to look after German music', and had been ultimately reduced, in his increasingly desperate search for something to help him believe that he was carrying out that self-imposed but imaginary task, to keeping the baton in his right hand when taking his bow on the concert platform, in order to have a plausible excuse for not giving the Nazi salute.

Nazis and their victims; anti-Nazis and their oppressors; in the middle, Furtwängler, who must have found it almost impossible to look at the stage when his *Doppelgänger* in the opera, Rocco the jailer, was digging the grave of an innocent man, shortly to be done to death by a tyrant who could not bear the thought that an honest and upright opponent of tyranny and corruption should go on living, even in darkness and chains. Everyone in the opera house was, must have been, conscious throughout of the extra dimension given to the work by the place, the date and the participants, and the effect of those circumstances was to produce a performance, musically also the finest I have ever heard, that I have

185

remembered for more than thirty years, and shall remember for as many more years as I have before me.

And yet the text of *Fidelio*, on which four writers successively worked (with results that could easily have been predicted from such an attempt to create a work of art by committee), never rises even to the level of second-rate poetry, and the plot is a crude and obviously implausible melodrama, in which the audience is obliged to believe, among other things, that the wife of a political prisoner could, disguised as a man, get a job in the prison that holds her husband, that the daughter of the head jailer would fall in love with her under the impression that she *is* a man, that the jailer, no less convinced by the disguise, would give his daughter's hand in marriage to the sexual impostor and name the day for the wedding, and that when, at the end of the opera, the disguise is thrown off, those astonished at the revelation should include the disguised woman's own husband.

Now those who do not know *Fidelio*, particularly if they do know something about music, including Beethoven's, will reply that there is nothing surprising about that. Music-lovers, they will say, accept the nonsense of the story and the feebleness of the text because Beethoven's musical genius so dwarfs the other two elements in the work that the disparity does not matter; Beethoven simply used the story and the words in order to express himself through the music, and these therefore had, and needed, no other function. Those who do know *Fidelio*, and have really understood it, will know also that the most extraordinary fact about the opera is that that is not true. We do *not* accept, let alone ignore, the plot and the words only for the sake of Beethoven's music; it is not even that Beethoven's magic fire lights their dry wood into a noble blaze. The truth is much more amazing. It is that, out there in the auditorium, a sacrament takes place; the clay is transformed, it becomes a musical Eucharist, and as we watch and listen in the darkness, the story and the words, in that transformation, attain a stature commensurate with the genius of the composer.

186

What has happened? The words I have used provide the explanation; 'darkness', 'transformed', 'sacrament'. *Fidelio* is a story of the passage from tyranny to freedom, but it is much more than that; it is also a story of the journey from darkness to light (the dungeon scene, which is the first half of the last Act, is in darkness, the scene of liberation outside the prison, which is the second half, in bright daylight), but it is much more than *that*, too. The darkness, in psychological terms, symbolizes the unconscious, the light represents full wholeness and knowledge. Beethoven wrote no other opera, and was in a position to choose among plots; he chose that one precisely because it was a story of transformation, and of a journey into full realization.

Now, however, there will be objections, at any rate from those who already know more than a very little about opera. *Fidelio* and *Falstaff* are among the greatest masterpieces of the operatic stage, the finest fruits of the sublime union of the arts – music, drama, poetry – which opera represents. (There are far more operas with good music than with good words, but it is through the fusion of the arts, even when the partners are unequal, that a higher art is born and the pleasure of opera generated.) The obvious objection to a defence of opera's absurdity based on the testimony of its greatest examples, which will naturally transcend the art's limitations, is that the effect of works like *Fidelio* and *Falstaff* is not typical.

The reader who knows a little more still about opera will be able to compile a list of those works which will always and understandably overcome the limitations of opera itself through the power of genius alone, and it will not be a very long list. To *Fidelio* and *Falstaff* add *The Marriage of Figaro, Don Giovanni, Così fan Tutte, The Magic Flute, The Mastersingers, Tristan, Parsifal, The Ring, Otello, Rosenkavalier, The Barber of Seville, Fledermaus, Boris Godunov* and a dozen or so more: say thirty-odd altogether. Anyone who is capable of deriving pleasure from this essentially unnatural entertainment at all must obtain it from these, as any lover of the drama must take delight in Shakespeare. But there are bad plays, and worse operas. If the opera-lover is willing to put aside prejudice or the protection owed to an old favourite, he cannot deny that many of the operas that fill the standard repertoires are wretched stuff – plot, words *and* music.

Il Trovatore, calmly considered, is bilge with good tunes; *Medea* is bilge without good tunes; *Tosca* is no more than what Joseph Kerman, one of the most perceptive of modern writers on opera, called it – a shabby little shocker; no first-rate conductor would dream of directing Donizetti or Bellini with any frequency or regularity, and most never do so at all. The terrible truth is that if four-fifths or more of the operas that are regularly performed, and to full houses, had never been written, the world, and music, would not be discernibly worse off. How, then, can pleasure of more than the most superficial and fleeting kind be gained from such stuff?

The answer lies in a proposition even more remarkable than the contrast between the absurdities of opera and the effect that some absurd operas can have. Opera, alone among the arts, and perhaps alone among all human activities, has a quality that makes it possible to derive from it not just entertainment and amusement but deep, valuable and enduring pleasure, without the source of that pleasure requiring us to take it seriously. So extraordinary a state of affairs requires consideration.

As it happens, really bad operas are far fewer than might be supposed; for every one I dislike so much that I will never enter an opera house where it is playing, I can find among my own acquaintance half-a-dozen opera-goers who place it among their favourites, and many of my fondest operatic loves raise grimaces at best and cries of horror at worst among other opera-lovers (in some cases the same ones) no less passionate about the art than I. Operas that nobody wants to hear are very rare, certainly (and not surprisingly) on the stage of most opera houses. There are many operas, though, which have obvious and undeniable faults, faults which ought to render them unfit for staging, and even more for visiting when staged, which nevertheless *are* staged and visited, frequently and with enthusiasm, even by those most conscious of their limitations.

Cavalleria Rusticana is unbearably sentimental, and its usual companion, *I Pagliacci*, just as sentimental and more obviously hollow. Both of Ravel's operas, *L'Enfant et les Sortilèges* and *L'Heure Espagnole*, are so arch that they set the teeth on edge, and the latter has quite exceptionally ugly music as well. The music of Berg's *Wozzeck* is much, much uglier, and its ugliness is largely the point of it. *L'Africaine*, like all Meyerbeer's operas, is bloated, bloodshot and gross. *Lucia di Lammermoor* could reasonably be thought, even more than most of Donizetti's operas (and he wrote at least sixty), fit to appeal only to idiots. *Carmen* is about as authentically Spanish as the Rue de Rivoli. *Hansel and Gretel* has bored more children into a lifelong detestation of opera than any other work children are regularly taken to.

The list could be considerably extended. But the point of it is that none of those faults in any way lessens the pleasure the works are capable of giving.

If that is so, what is the source of the pleasure? What is it that makes Isolde and Norma sisters under the skin, puts *The Bartered Bride* on a footing with *The Marriage of Figaro*, ranks *Emilia di Liverpool*★ alongside *The Mastersingers of Nuremberg*? Where, in the world of opera, is the factor common to them all, the quality that I love when I love opera?

Opera exists, obviously, *to convey feeling and understanding through sound*; I know no opera that does not attempt to do that, and no opera with even a modest place in the repertoire and the opera-going public's heart that fails to achieve it. Of course, the level at which it is achieved varies, from the greatest heights man has ever attained in the arts to a plateau on which nothing more ambitious is attempted than a few hours of gentle stimulation or amusement, but at both levels opera works the same effect by the same means, and at

★ Donizetti thought Liverpool was in Kent.

both levels that is its express function. The feeling may be superficial and unreal, as in *I Puritani*, or touch the finest and deepest qualities of which we are capable, as in *Alceste*, and the understanding may be only that of the identity of the body in the sack, which is what we learn from the last scene of *Rigoletto*, or may give us a glimpse of the truth of why we were born and what we live by, which is what we take away from the last scene of *The Magic Flute*, but the principle is the same; · we are pierced, sometimes even to the soul's depths, by that trident of sound, feeling and illumination, and as we sit in the darkness of the auditorium, blind to opera's absurdities and deaf to its crudities, the emotion and understanding steal into us along a network of instincts and responses that cannot be measured, cannot even be located, but which are there so that we may absorb the pleasure that opera gives us – absorb and retain, so that the pleasure is not limited to the few hours of the evening, but lingers to warm us, uplift us, vivify us and, at the best and last, transform us.

How does this happen? In the first place, it is certainly no coincidence that the stories of opera, at least until very recent operatic history, are almost all of an edifying nature, and are intended to be. Opera is full of treachery, murder, tyranny, adultery; as full of those shadows as is history itself (countless operas, from *Don Carlos* and *Boris Godunov* to *Salome* and *Maria Stuarda*, have been based, however distantly, on real events and characters),* but opera is extraordinarily free, unlike history, of stories of tyranny triumphant or villainy unavenged. On the contrary, though operatic villains, like real ones, may and do rob, defile and kill, they themselves come to a bad end with a much greater frequency than their real-life equivalents, and even when they do not the audience is left in

* Verdi's *The Masked Ball* has the unique distinction of containing a scene that is less operatic than the historical reality. The assassins of Gustavus III agreed to wear identical black and white dominos at the ball, so that they could instantly recognize one another. When they got there, they discovered that they were only three of *nineteen* masked revellers thus attired. Verdi omitted the other sixteen.

no doubt as to where right and justice lie. Apart from Monteverdi's *L'Incoronazione di Poppea*, I know of no operatic work in the highest category, and astonishingly few in any category, that leaves the villains in unquestioned possession of the fruits of their villainy and untroubled even by conscience, without at the very least the clear disapproval of the composer.

This refusal to countenance moral ambiguity is one of the most striking features of opera; though it also exists in the drama, it is found there in a much less direct form and by no means so widely. And it provides one of the most important elements in the power and pleasure of opera: the feeling that the world is run on principles of morality and justice. Hearts are broken in opera, from *La Traviata* to *Rosenkavalier*, but they are broken so exaltedly that the result is to leave us not downcast but uplifted; the innocent die, from *Rigoletto* to *Rheingold*, but the spirit of justice is present even as they do so; villains spin the plot, from *Otello* to *Lohengrin*, but our feelings go out to sustain the heroes. We may leave an opera house in a state of dejection caused by the inadequacies of the performance, but we never emerge depressed by the tragic story we have seen and heard unfold.

And there is a positive side to this aspect of opera, too. Although there are more tragedies than comedies in opera, more operas with unhappy endings than happy, the themes that run through opera are almost invariably affirmative. Opera tells us that human beings *are* capable of nobility, heroism and self-sacrifice, that evil *can* be conquered by good, that – above all – it *is* love that makes the world go round.

La Bohème is not one of the most majestic of operatic masterpieces, though understandably one of the most popular works in the repertoire. The four struggling artists are unsuccessful and penniless at the beginning of the first Act, and they are no better off at the end of the fourth. The love between Rodolfo and Mimi, born in an instant, is not destined to endure; nor does it, destroyed as it is by jealousy.

The heroine's cough is obviously, from the start, bound to prove fatal; in the last scene she duly dies of consumption in her lover's arms, reunited too late. A recipe for inevitable gloom, it would seem. But it is not; even a lesser composer like Puccini could not escape (not that he wanted to) from the power of opera to transcend the superficial; *La Bohème* becomes a beautiful and encouraging hymn to true and lasting love and friendship, and tells us that there is a reward of joy awaiting lovers and friends that is far greater than the sum of all their pains.

And if that is the effect of *La Bohème,* imagine it multiplied a thousandfold – *ten* thousandfold – at *The Marriage of Figaro* or *Tristan and Isolde* or *Fidelio.* And then imagine something else, something greater even than that great clue to the source of operatic pleasure. Throughout history many composers have written their most beautiful and exciting music for opera. That is not surprising; if the emotions and attitudes of operatic characters (to say nothing of the plots) are full of love and heroism, ardour and nobility, composers must always have striven to match those qualities in their music, but they have consistently succeeded beyond the dreams of the drama; few playwrights other than Shakespeare have really, in their language, risen to the challenge of what they were portraying, but in opera this has been achieved not just by the musical equivalent of Shakespeare – Mozart, Beethoven, Wagner, the Verdi of *Falstaff*, the Strauss of *Die Frau Ohne Schatten* – or by the operatic parallels to Ben Jonson or Schiller – the Verdi of *Otello* and *Don Carlos*, Monteverdi, the Strauss of *Rosenkavalier* and *Capriccio*, the Mussorgsky of *Boris* and *Khovanshchina* – but by the opera composers who are no more than the peers of Galsworthy, Victor Hugo or even Bertolt Brecht.

Take *The Barber of Seville*, hardly a work to plead for opera before the bar of the eternal verities. It contains no moral, it serves no lofty purpose, it advances the evolution of humanity not a whit. Its plot is not merely absurd, but predictably so, for it is obvious from the first scene that young love will triumph, and from the second that crabbed age will fail to thwart it; it is hardly too much to say that that can all be deduced from the Overture alone. The only thing to be said for *The Barber of Seville* is that it is enjoyable: but that is enough. For it is enjoyable, not to the same *extent*, but for the same *reason*, that *Parsifal* is enjoyable. *The Barber of Seville* tells us that young love will triumph, *Parsifal* that Christ has already done so; but both convey what they have to convey in music which lives up to its ambitions.

If the pages of a book could sing, my task would be considerably easier, for I could then lay down my pen and let them sing to you, starting their programme with the Quintet from Act Three of *The Mastersingers*. How many times have I seen that work? Thirty, perhaps; yet every time, as the five voices blend, part, exchange themes, blend again, soar, swoop, exult, dream, rise, fall, and finally come to a climax and die away, I find tears filling my eyes. Four of the five voices are singing of love, the fifth of wisdom; and the orchestra, which knows everything they know and more, makes the sixth voice. Imagine being so locked against feeling as to be unable to respond to such beauty in sound, conveying feelings so deep! It is not even necessary to have loved to respond to the *Mastersingers* Quintet; it explains – with its sound, not with its words – what love is, in terms that enable even the most inexperienced to comprehend.

I think that is even more true of Susanna's final aria in Act Four of *The Marriage of Figaro*. I must have seen that work twice as many times as I have seen *The Mastersingers*, yet the feelings induced in me by *Deh vieni, non tardar* still grow stronger every time, as I discover in it new glories, fresh beauties, more pleasures, unsuspected truths. There is raillery in the love between Susanna and Figaro; there is even real jealousy; there is fear – the worst fear love can inspire, the fear of loss. By that point in the opera, however, all those darknesses have been put aside, along with disguise; now the brimming heart speaks.

It speaks of pure love, selflessness, faith and trust; and it

193

speaks of these with such power and such beauty that we know it is so, that it must be so for ever. We know that in the real world such propositions are by no means invariably or eternally true; we know of love that has been false, love that has died, that has been blighted, that has turned to hate. Yet the untruth inside the opera house is truer than the truth outside it, and John Press has enshrined that knowledge in a haunting poem about this very work, 'After *Le Nozze di Figaro*':

> It did not last. Before the year was out
> The Count was once again a slave to women.
> Susanna was untrue to Figaro,
> The Countess had a child by Cherubino,
> Young gallants went to bed with Barbarina.
> But for a moment, till the music stopped,
> They all were ravished by a glimpse of Heaven,
> Where everything is known and yet forgiven,
> And all that is not music is pure silence.

There is a sense, and the most important sense, in which that applies not only to *Figaro*, not only to opera generally, not only to the *Egmont* Overture, but to all music, however austere, however far removed from our earthly concerns, not excluding *The Art of Fugue* itself. It is certainly true that although the art of opera has constantly brought out the best in opera composers, there are few operas which attain the greatest heights that music, that art, that humankind, are capable of. Even if we extend my list of operas that are the fruits of the highest genius to encompass fifty, I can still think without any difficulty of five hundred works of music for the concert hall that attain the same exalted level. Perhaps it is because opera, being able to rely on words to communicate its quality, has never had to strive as hard as concert music to achieve that goal of conveying feeling and understanding through sound, but certainly there are far more operas that go only as deep as, say, Mendelssohn's Italian Symphony than penetrate as far as, say, the Seventh Symphony of Bruckner or the First of Brahms.

To say nothing of the last quartets of Beethoven or the *Lieder* of Schubert. In such works, the power of music is concentrated like the atoms in those stars of which astronomers tell us that a single grain of their earth would weigh thousands of tons, and it is not surprising that the full understanding of such works must wait until our lives have shown themselves in their true colours, until disappointment has been not only experienced but assimilated, until our hearts are quiet enough to hear the secret harmonies which were so long inaudible. If we have truly understood that our lives are journeys that never end, then even if we do not know where the journey began or where it is leading us, we shall have understood also what holy function music serves, and we shall even, if we are fortunate, be ready one day for Mozart.

'The rot', remarked Benjamin Britten, 'started with Beethoven', by which he meant, I take it, that Beethoven personalized music, insisted that it did and should affect us in the most direct way, teach us lessons it is necessary for us to learn, reach into our souls and hearts to show us what infinite treasures are there. Britten was doubly wrong, first because Beethoven did not start it (if anybody did, it was probably Bach, but it is much more likely that it was inherent in the very nature of music from the start), and second because it is a rot only in the sense that the seed must rot to produce the flower, the flower die to produce the seed. But of course I see what Britten meant, and like the drowning man whose past life flashed before his eyes, my musical life can be plotted along the course which Britten was speaking of.

Beethoven first, for the boy who wanted to put the world to rights; Wagner next, for the man unable to put himself to rights; Mozart at last, as the shadows lengthen, to confirm the growing belief that there is a realm 'where everything is known and yet forgiven'.

Music hath charms to soothe the savage breast; the rites of passage celebrated in *Fidelio*, or on the bridge between the last two movements of the Fifth Symphony, or in the touch of the spear in *Parsifal* that heals the world's eternal wound, or the benediction of forgiveness in the garden at the end of *Figaro*, or the apotheosis of Gerontius, or the heaped-up splendour in which Bruckner ends his Eighth Symphony, or the release from his prison of stone of the Emperor in *Die Frau Ohne Schatten* – all these and hundreds more musical examples point the way to our human understanding of our human duty, the duty to be transformed, to rise from darkness into light, to pursue the will-o'-the-wisp of integration and completeness until it turns out to be no will-o'-the-wisp but the shining sun of eternal truth.

Perhaps the greatest of all the musical masterpieces which speak of transformation is *The Magic Flute*. There is fear in the opera, but it is cast out by perfect love; there is temptation, but it is resisted with the aid of a power which never fails; there are ordeals to endure, but they are accepted as part of the journey from this world to another; there is evil, but it is overcome by good.

Many years ago, I dreamed that I was talking to a group of people who were about to set off on holiday; they were staying, they told me, with a most hospitable man in his most beautiful house, and there would be many others there. Why, they asked, did not I come too? I protested that I hardly knew *them*, and their host not at all – how could I possibly impose myself on him? Nonsense, they replied, he would welcome me as he welcomed everybody, whether known to him or not. I went along, tormented by the fear of being rejected when I arrived, especially if everyone else was allowed in.

We arrived by water; there was a huge crowd on the boat, and more crowds on the shore, all making for the same paragon of hospitality. The more impatient leaped to the shore; some missed their footing and fell between boat and ground, but it made no difference, for they all still landed safely, intact but sprawling, greeted by a wave of happy laughter from those already on firm ground. I made my way cautiously down the gangway, ashamed of my cowardice,

196

but fell none the less as I stepped ashore; I was not hurt, but I, too, was engulfed in laughter, and the laughter, I found, did not hurt either.

We arrived at the house; all was as I had been promised. Crowds mingled in vast rooms bathed in light, all with vast windows looking on to beautiful scenery. Our benign host pressed us to eat, to drink, to be happy. Presently we set forth; it was understood that we were going to his other house. On the walk, I found myself left behind and alone; the fears returned. Not far away there were lions, white ones, beneath a clump of trees; my fears vanished, of the lions and of being alone, for I recognized the animals as the beasts from *The Magic Flute*, gravely nodding their heads in time to the divine spell. I never got to the other house, but it did not matter, and presently we were all back where we had started, where more and more guests were arriving, and all were welcome. We began to drift back to the water's edge; we reboarded the boat. I knew nobody around me, and talked to none, but that did not matter either. Amid more laughter, the boat set off.

I awoke bathed in tears of joy, knowing where I had been, what door had been flung wide for me; the music of *The Magic Flute*, not just the spell, echoed in my head:

> In diesen heil'gen Hallen
> Kennt man die Rache nicht;
> Und ist ein Mensch gefallen,
> Führt Liebe ihn zur Pflicht.

I knew then what music was, why its strangeness and its absurdity had been devised; I knew also what it meant in my empty life, and how it could show me the way to fullness:

> . . . and then, in dreaming,
> The clouds methought would open and show riches
> Ready to drop on me; that, when I wak'd,
> I cried to dream again.

Eight

I cannot get out of my head the belief that when I peel a banana, if I do not, before eating it, remove also the fine stringy threads that run along the divisions between the segments of the fruit, I shall contract leprosy. I am quite unable to remember when and how this extraordinary idea got into me; usually, such beliefs stem from a superstition current in the holder's childhood, but I have never met anyone, whether my contemporary or older than I, who has ever heard of it, much less held it. Possibly it was based on a misunderstood remark of my mother's, though it is so specific I cannot well see how that could be. Certainly she did hold a wide variety of superstitious beliefs, as most women of her time and background did; I remember being taken to see a family friend, a woman always spoken of at home in a somewhat reserved tone, and before we set out my mother took a tiny fragment of coal, wrapped it in a scrap of paper and thrust it into my pocket, bidding me leave it there until we returned and to say nothing about it. I had not the slightest idea of the purpose of this action, nor did she explain it, but in the trusting way of childhood I assumed that it must mean *something*, and since the burden of the coal and the simultaneously enjoined secrecy was not great, I made no objection.

It was many years later, and not from my mother, that I learned the meaning of the strange ceremony; apparently, the woman whom we were to visit was reputed to have the Evil Eye, and the coal, it seemed, was a charm against it. In the instant of my discovery, I remembered another inexplicable moment from that afternoon – one so puzzling that memory had until then suppressed it altogether. On leaving the home of the *malocchio*, my mother turned first to her left, then to her right, spitting each time on the pavement as she did so; this action, familiar in some form in many primitive cultures, is likewise reputed to keep evil spirits at bay. I also believe, as firmly as I hold the leprosy-inducing banana-strings theory, that a cut between the thumb and forefinger will lead inevitably to lockjaw.

The belief about the banana, even though its origins are undiscoverable, is my earliest memory of anything to do with food; it even antedates my first recollections of the food I ate as a child. But next to it in time is the memory of an episode so painful that, as I embarked on this sentence, I had to break off and occupy myself in something altogether different for an hour, before I could feel calm enough to tell the story, and as I put these words on paper I live again the hour of that day, more than forty years ago, as though it had only just happened.

The unleavened bread called *matzo*, which Jews eat instead of ordinary bread at Passover, was to be found in my home, on and off, throughout the year; I loved it, and still do. But it has – or had in my childhood home – culinary uses wider than as a substitute for bread. A dish which my mother used to cook quite frequently was based upon it; I have remembered the recipe well, despite the trauma it led to, and often cook it myself when I am eating at home alone. For those who are interested in having the taste experience without the trauma I give the recipe:

Break four or five large *matzos* into small pieces in a sieve, then pour boiling water over them, until they become limp; shake the surplus water through the seive. Beat three eggs, well salted, in a bowl, then put the soaked matzo pieces in the egg batter, separating and turning them with two forks so that they are all thoroughly coated with egg and, as far as possible, not stuck together. Heat some butter – quite a lot of it, for the egg-and-*matzo* is very absorbent – omelette-hot in a large frying pan, and fry the coated *matzo* in it on a high flame, stirring it frequently to keep it from forming chunks made of several layers. You will almost certainly find that you have not used enough butter; if so, make a hole in the panful of *matzo* and put more butter in it, repeating this action every time the butter vanishes – when you finally remove the *matzo*, browned, crisp and cooked through, it will be dry and the pan perfectly clean, but you will almost certainly find that it still needs more salt when you are eating it, which you do unaccompanied by anything in the way of vegetables.

I assure you that, done properly, this is delicious; it might be called a Jewish *fondue*, and has the additional advantage that it disproves two of the most passionately held beliefs of dieticians – as hopelessly superstitious as my mother's trick with the coal – that butter and salt, taken in large quantities, are dangerous for the heart. I have been eating and enjoying this dish all my life, never sparing either of the dieticians' two poisons, and my heart beats still.

The dish was called *matzobrei*, the 'brei' being from the Yiddish (and before that from the German) and meaning something like a mash or puree. At my elementary school, the day began, before any lessons were embarked upon, with an assembly of all the pupils. It is possible that there was a hymn or other collective activity, but this I have forgotten: I do remember, though, that the assembly concluded with any special or general announcements, before we dispersed to the classrooms.

On the fateful day, the announcements were not the end of assembly. Whether some sociologist was conducting an experiment, whether there were fears (as well there might have been in those days and in that neighbourhood) that many children were not getting enough to eat at home, whether somebody had had a bright idea in the staff common-room, I do not know, and nobody explained. Nor did it matter. What happened was that each child was invited to stand up, in turn, and say before all the others what he or she had had, that day, for breakfast. This did not, when it was announced, strike me as alarming or strange, and I patiently awaited my turn, halfway through the alphabetical order. When it came, I said that my breakfast had been a *matzobrei*.

It had not occurred to me that a word with which I was perfectly familiar, which described a simple and customary dish, would be utterly unknown to three hundred other children and the entire staff of the school. I was asked to repeat what I had said, the teacher in charge assuming that he had not heard correctly. I repeated it. I was asked to repeat it again, and did so. By now murmurs were breaking out throughout the hall; everybody had heard clearly what I said, but it conveyed no meaning to any mind there. I was asked to come from my place, to the front of the hall, *on to the platform*, and say it again. I did so; there was a pause, during which I stood where I was, alone and in full and prominent view, while the staff held a whispered conference, trying to make out what I was talking about. One of them then advanced to the centre of the stage – the questioning had been conducted throughout with the greatest mildness and tact – and bent his head gently to my face, asking me to say it once more, close to his ear. I did so. He straightened up, shook his head, patted my shoulder, and motioned me to go back to my place. The next child was asked to say what he had had for breakfast.

The episode took perhaps six or seven minutes; in that time, any meaning the world might have held for me had vanished. I could think of no explanation whatever that would make sense at all of the experience I had just been through. Had I misheard the word at home? Of course not. Had they misheard the word from me at school? Not after three repetitions. Was everybody mad? Was I mad? Was the Devil in charge of the universe after all?

I went back to my place in the hall; my schoolfellows instinctively moved away from me as I passed among them, lest the contagion should come upon them; they were as baffled as I was but safe, and I don't think any of them had even laughed. When I got back to my row the children on either side of me stared straight ahead as though I was not there at all; the breakfast call-over finished, assembly ended, the school day began. I went through the day's lessons in a trance; I said nothing when I got home, and from that day until this hour, I have never said a single word about it to any human being.

It was a long time ago, and nothing much to get excited about. The explanation is, and was when it occurred to me only a year or two later, obvious: no one not familiar with Yiddish could have known the word or even guessed at its meaning. Children have had far worse experiences and survived them smiling. And yet I, a middle-aged man not at all given to dwelling in the past or keening over my inability to rewrite it, can bring back, instantly and completely, the experience I have described, and in doing so can feel all the pain I felt that day, and all the terror of its inexplicability.

It is a wonder I ever ate breakfast again, or anything else. But there were good things to eat in my childhood home, though, as I learned only later, and then gradually, it was sometimes touch and go whether there would be anything at all; I cannot remember noticing, or if I did being puzzled by the fact, that the silver candlesticks, and sometimes my mother's rings, would vanish from their accustomed place for a few weeks, returning as mysteriously as they had gone. My mother was not a natural cook, much less a trained one; but she had learned a small repertoire, mainly from her own mother, of standard Jewish dishes, and those she did well and with complete consistency. I don't think she ever thought of what she was doing as cooking at all, much less as 'cuisine'; she was simply making dinner for the family. I cannot recall ever seeing a cookery book, for instance, or any wine except once a year with the Passover dinner, when it was invariably something called Palwin.

This may well still exist, though I hope not, for a more

202

powerful force for instilling the idea that wine is disgusting I cannot imagine; the first time I drank real wine, many years later, I could not believe my taste buds, and I have no doubt that many children exposed to Palwin grew up as lifelong teetotallers in consequence. It was made in Palestine, as its name suggests, and tasted like very heavily over-sweetened prune juice; I have no recollection of any alcohol content in it at all, though there must have been some, I suppose, for my mother, who had the lightest head of anyone I have ever known, would never take a second glass for fear of the consequences, or more than a sip or two of my grand-mother's cherry brandy, though that I recall as being very powerful. The only other drink I can recall clearly, apart from endless cups of tea (coffee was unknown, though I seem to remember a bottled concentrate called Camp, which bore much the same relation to coffee as Palwin did to wine, and must have had much the same effect on those exposed to it early), was a patent juice called Lucozade, most devoutly believed in my home to have almost miraculous medicinal properties, and another called Tizer, similar to Lucozade but not believed capable of restoring the dead to life.

If there was nothing interesting to drink, there was a short but interesting menu, and the taste it gave me for Jewish cooking has lasted the rest of my life. Grilling was unknown; practically everything was fried, and most of what wasn't was roasted. The heart of the repertoire was fried fish, more often plaice than anything else, but with cod a good second and occasionally halibut. Fresh salmon was of course unknown, being far too expensive (so was carp, though important to classic Jewish cuisine, if there is such a thing); it came only in the tinned form, which was certainly not salmon but a variety of inferior fish, and out of this my mother would make fried rissoles, of which I was particularly fond. The fried fish was always done in batter, and always accompanied by *chren*, in the making of which my grandmother was the acknowledged family expert (as she was with the cherry brandy I have mentioned, which I suppose – I did not understand the process – she must have made in an illicit still). *Chren* was home-made horseradish sauce; it was mixed with beetroot, partly to make it milder and partly to make it taste and look more interesting. I loved to watch as my grandmother grated the horseradish, cooked and prepared the beetroot, added the sugar and combined the ingredients in the correct proportions; no witches' cauldron was ever more carefully tended.

The result, however, was, and was meant to be, enormously strong, even toned down by the beetroot. Sniffing the *chren* jar had exactly the same effect as the most powerful smelling-salts, and I remember one of my uncles daring the other to put his nose right into the jar and breathe in sharply; the dare was accepted, and a moment later the experimenter was flat on his back on the floor, semi-conscious and gasping for breath. I have not tasted the real thing for years; even good Jewish restaurants serve a feeble diluted version, and the bottled kind is beneath the contempt of anyone who ever tasted any Jewish grandmother's. There was also *gefillte* fish, a kind of *quenelle*, served cold.

The fish was always accompanied by chips, fine-cut and done to crisp perfection; olive oil was too expensive to be the sole cooking-medium, and was therefore eked out by kosher lard. Sometimes, when money was even shorter than usual, and both the candlesticks and the rings were on holiday, the fried fish became a tin of sardines ('a makeshift' was my mother's term for such a meal), but the chips were never cancelled.

As fried fish was the left hand, so the right was boiled chicken, or, more rarely, roast. When it was boiled, there would, naturally, be chicken soup, which – if any single dish may claim the title – must be regarded as the staple of Jewish cookery. The broth was rarely served clear; it contained *lokshen*, a kind of very fine vermicelli, or *kreplach*, a similarly superior cousin to *tortelloni*, or *kneidlach*, which were dumplings. The roast chicken was invariably accompanied by oven-roast potatoes. Meat of any kind was unusual; I do not think there was ever roast beef *à l'anglaise*, let alone lamb, or even veal, and strangely enough I do not think I can remember salt beef. Occasionally there was a steak, though since nothing was grilled (I think it possible that my mother had never encountered the technique at all), this was always done in a frying pan and, bizarre though it may sound, doused and recooked in boiling water, in the same pan, before being served. It thus became – not that I knew it at the time – a kind of *Tafelspitz*. I enjoyed it greatly, and never met a real steak until years later.

Chopped liver; a mixture of chopped egg and fried onions; a kind of pancake, made from a mixture of potato flour and *matzo* meal (the fine-ground kind was the equivalent of flour and the coarser was used for the batter in which the fried fish was coated), which was called a *luttke*, and was my mother's speciality, much in demand at family gatherings (my sister and I gave her a surprise party for her eightieth birthday, and arranged with the Dorchester, where it was held, for a stove and the utensils to be provided, while we got the ingredients, and at a given signal drew back the curtain behind which all was in readiness, whereupon, after we had draped a monster apron round her finery, she turned to and cooked 'Rosie's *luttkes*' for all); baked apples; these are among the other dishes I recollect from my childhood with pleasure. There was virtually nothing cooked in my childhood home that I did not enjoy, except *lokshen* pudding; this was a dessert, made from the same vermicelli that went into the soup, but in this form compacted, sweetened and baked. My favourite dish, though, was a sweetmeat that went by the name of *taygelach*, and its making was the highlight of the year: it did not appear more often than annually, because it was very expensive to make, using prodigious quantities of Tate and Lyle's Golden Syrup. I dare say that that delectable, viscous substance still exists, and if it doesn't I would be perfectly happy, should Tate and Lyle wish to revive it, to shut my eyes and draw the old tin from memory; it had a lion on it, for reasons which will be known to those familiar with the zoologically improbable story of Samson and the lion in *Judges*, chapter 14, a story which incidentally includes the first nagging wife in recorded history.

The *taygelach* were made of a kind of dough, rolled out into cylinders somewhat thicker than a pencil; these were then lightly baked and dropped into a huge saucepan in which the syrup was boiling. Removed from the liquid, the strips were laid side by side on greaseproof paper, and cut diagonally into rhomboids about the size of a domino. They were then sprinkled with ginger, and left to set hard. The result was an incomparable form of toffee; as the teeth crunched into it they went through the coating of hardened syrup and encountered the dough, which crumbled at once; the ginger was the perfect spice, hot but sweet. When she was making it, my mother would use just enough dough to absorb the syrup, but inevitably there were bits of dough left over, and the saucepan was still coated, so my sister and I were allowed to mop the scraps in the still warm liquid.

Vegetables, apart from potatoes, were rare; there were carrots with the boiled chicken and the cold *gefillte* fish, peas (I can remember helping my mother to shell them) and buckwheat, called *kasha*, which I loved, though I have not seen it these many years. There was cabbage, though only in the form of the wrapping for forcemeat, and I have a very faint memory of runner beans also, but I am sure there was never any spinach, broccoli, haricots or mushrooms, and as for the now common courgettes, aubergines, artichokes and the like, they would have been considered as exotic as ortolans' tongues or first-growth claret. There were no shellfish, and no crustaceans; the former were banned under the faint vestiges of obedience to the Jewish dietary laws that reigned at home, and the latter in addition were too expensive and viewed with intense suspicion as likely to cause food-poisoning. I have grown up unable to eat oysters, mussels or clams, but devoted to every kind of crustacean from the tiniest shrimp, as served in the *crevettes Alfonso* at L'Epicure, in Soho, to the vastest lobster, as served in the Hostellerie du Moulin du Maine Brun at Angoulême.

Over the simple pleasures of my infant dinner table a cloud was forming, though I did not know it and could not possibly have guessed what lay ahead, nor done anything about it if I had. Only those who attended an English public school as boarders during the Second World War can truly say that they have experienced the very lowest level that food can reach and still be classified as food. If the memory of the *matzobrei* is too painful to think about, that of the food served at my school is too nauseating; there were the usual school-boy rumours that the meat, invariably in the form of a glutinous and quite extraordinarily disgusting stew, came from the rotted carcases of beasts gathered from the hedgerows in which they had perished of disease, or from zoos which were culling their less edible specimens, and none of us would have been in the least surprised if the rumours had turned out to be true.

I was clearly in danger of starving to death from the effect of the food served and the culture shock it would have given me even if it had been the finest *haute cuisine*, for I had never eaten anything except the cooking of my home; of most of what faced me I was quite literally unable to swallow a mouthful (the school had a most sensible rule that, although we had to finish anything we took, we were not obliged to take anything we did not want), and I lived almost entirely off potatoes and bread, and later off peanut butter, which I think I got from a shop in the nearby town.

The horrors of school food might have been thought likely to lead to a complete lack of interest in the subject (I have just remembered some filth described as liver, though what animal it came from I dare not guess, and I know that I would not touch liver thereafter until I was in my late twenties); I think, however, that instead it encouraged a taste for food.

It meant that I could not, as I might otherwise have done, come to believe that the narrow range of Jewish cooking I was used to was the only kind that existed; in addition, from the fact that the muck at school could not possibly be the

207

only other kind of food there was I derived an interest in discovering what else there might be in a world elsewhere. This was an almost fully conscious feeling, which seems odd now, because it meant that I was interested in seeking out something of which I had had no experience at all, and I cannot remember reading about food, or even coming across descriptions of banquets or meals in fiction.

I cannot remember quite how I began to explore for myself the pleasure of eating. The earliest restaurant meals I can recall must have been eaten when I was a student; the first restaurant I can recall patronizing was a little Soho place, long since vanished, called Fava, and some at least, if not a great proportion, of the meals I ate there and in similar places were taken with my cousin Clive, with whom I shared the discovery of music as well as, to a large extent, that of food and wine.

Not far from Fava was another restaurant that disappeared many years ago, called Maurer's; it was run, as I recall, by a plump German *patronne*, and served – this, I am sure, was its attraction in those days – meals of the most gargantuan size, including a dish called 'Transylvanian Mixed Grill', which was for two people, but off which six could have dined richly, and eight adequately.

I am not at all sure what a palate, a taste for food and wine, is. Is it something, like an ear for music or an eye for painting, that is innate in those who have it but that may be encouraged, cultivated and extended? Or do we all have it, and need only to learn to use it? Or can it be taught? If it can be taught, I am sure it can only be taught by experience; of all the experiences of the senses, the kind most difficult to convey in words is that which comes from the sense of taste; even smell, notoriously difficult to describe except by direct comparison, can be more easily passed on.

This truth I must somehow have acquired, for I simply used to eat as many good meals as possible on a limited budget; no grand, or even moderately expensive, restaurant could be visited, but in those days, even before the *trattoria* movement began, Soho was full of places where an interesting meal could be had for a few shillings, accompanied by wine which, though again nothing of any fame, was not just *vin de table*. By the time I took my degree, I must have acquired some knowledge of the subject, for a group of us planned a great feast to celebrate our graduation, and I was deputed to buy the wine.

Alas, my reputation among my fellow students must have been much greater than my knowledge, for in the Old Compton Street wine merchants I went to with my request, I was persuaded (the assistant who served me must have been as ignorant as I was, but with far less excuse, and should never have been allowed behind a wine merchant's counter without better training) to buy a magnum of 1945 Domaine-bottled Richebourg. Now a magnum of Domaine-bottled 1945 Richebourg is something that today I would go a long way to find, though I dare say I could only afford to look at it now; but the year of the graduation feast was 1949. Obviously – except that of course it was not obvious to me then – a Richebourg of that *annus mirabilis* could not possibly have been ready, or even nearly ready, in a mere four years, and as we smacked our lips over it, and pronounced it excellent, we little knew what rich, red blood we were so innocently spilling. (Nearly three decades later, I set out to buy the wine for a rather different kind of celebratory feast. In 1978, three friends born within a few weeks of each other – William Rees-Mogg, then Editor of *The Times*, for which I was writing, Harold Evans, then Editor of the *Sunday Times*, the other newspaper for which I was writing regularly, and myself – were fifty years old. I invited the other two to lunch on a day near to our three birthdays, and set out to find some 1928 wine to accompany the meal. I could find no claret, but the cellar master at the Café Royal kindly came up with two bottles of Grands Echézeaux; I was, however, determined that we should start with champagne, and where to find 1928 champagne was a question I could not begin to answer. So I rang Patrick Forbes, Moët et Chandon's man in London, and a prince among friends as well as among wine-bibbers, and asked him if 1928 was a vintage year for Moët, and if so whether the Château had any, and if so whether they would let me have a couple of bottles. The answer to all three questions was yes, whereupon I drew a deep breath and asked Patrick to ask the Château what I had to pay for them – the Burgundy had set me back a pretty penny, but 1928 champagne must have been beyond price. So it was, for as requested he consulted the Château, and the magnificent reply was 'Nothing – the Château wishes the three of you to accept it as their birthday-present.')

The Richebourg experience taught me nothing, except in retrospect, but there are very few culinary experiences from which knowledge cannot be derived. In the art of eating, perhaps more than in most of the other arts, the best teacher is experience. The wider the range of it, the greater is the opportunity for learning, and the faster the apt scholar will increase in knowledge and understanding; of course, he would be a foolish student who neglected to take advice from the more practised, or who failed to exchange and compare information with others engaged in the same pursuit, but just as only he who has experienced the taste can enjoy it, so only the enjoying of it can provide the experience.

I realized this truth, happily, very early indeed in my own study of the pleasures of the table, and took much comfort, when I surveyed the vast expanse of unmapped territory that faced me, in the story of the small boy at the circus who is so entranced by the performance of the sword swallower that his father, in response to the child's importunities, needs must take him backstage, where the sword swallower meets his new fan. 'Please, mister,' says the boy; 'how do you become a sword swallower?' The performer shrugs. 'You swallow a sword. If you live, you're a sword swallower.'

So it is with the art of food swallowing. I have called it an art, but is it one? Surely it is, though I am well aware that this view is fiercely contested by many who would accept the word in the case of music even though they were themselves tone-deaf, or in regard to painting if they suffered from colour-blindness, or as applied to literature despite a condition of illiteracy. The art of food, and that alone, is cast out from the protection of the Muses. More; to take pleasure in good food and wine, and to express that pleasure, is by some considered altogether impermissible, and even arouses the most unbridled hostility.

I have better reason than most to know this. For thirty years or so I have been writing about the arts, among many other subjects. I have tried to convey the pleasure I take, both in general and in relation to particular experiences, in music, in painting and sculpture, in architecture, in the drama, in books, in food and wine. No journalist with a substantial and regular output can remain long in ignorance of his readers' view of what he writes, and I have had, for as long as I can remember, a large postbag, not least when I write about the arts. In all other areas of the subject, I hear from readers who agree or disagree with particular judgments, who confess themselves, often with very deep regret, unable to respond at all to what moves me profoundly, who wish me to know that I have succeeded in conveying to them the quality of what I had heard or seen or read, who inquire of me for information that will help them to develop their own understanding and appreciation. In writing about the art of the table, and that alone, I get in addition letters of passionate hatred – the word is not too strong – condemning not my taste, my opinions, my attitudes or my errors, but the very fact that I enjoy food and make my enjoyment known.

Why should this be so? There are people with no feeling for music, but they do not hate it, nor me for loving it; when I write that *The Brothers Karamazov* and York Minster are mighty works of art from which I derive immense pleasure and solace nobody who disagrees flies into a rage; those who are invariably bored at the theatre are content to stay away rather than stand outside and throw stones at the playgoers as they arrive. I have repeatedly asked to be told *why* the pleasures of the table are regarded as more culpable than

211

those of Sodom and Gomorrah; no one has ever obliged me by explaining.

Pleasure in the arts comes in many forms, and it would be senseless to try to arrange them in order of moral worth; moreover, no pleasure precludes any other pleasure, and in this it is certainly not true that *le mieux est l'ennemi du bien*. All the same, the claims of the table must not be pitched too high. The pleasure a fine meal gives can be intense and memorable, but for me at least it cannot be compared to the experience offered by the most profound works of music, of the graphic arts, of the drama or the novel.

No meal I have ever eaten could be truly compared to a performance of Schubert's *Death and the Maiden* quartet by the Amadeus on their finest form, not even *chez* Girardet in the suburbs of Lausanne, where they make a tea sorbet out of their own blend of Darjeeling and Earl Grey, nor *chez* Hure in Avallon, where Napoleon stopped on the way north from Elba to meet his Waterloo at Waterloo, and would have done well to stop longer even if he had not been bound for disaster, nor *chez* Chapel at Mionnay, where just as you think you have finished there arrives a cornucopia of desserts that is like an entire orchestra of silver trumpets, nor *chez* Brazier, last of that noble breed the *mères* of Lyon, who used to dissect the *poussin demi-deuil*, so called from the slivers of truffle under the skin, with four swift flashes of the knife, and to whose branch establishment in the hills above the city I once asked directions from a traffic policeman, whereupon he not only provided them but held up the traffic for me to proceed and wished me 'Bon appétit' as I did so, which I do not think would happen in the outer suburbs of Liverpool or Birmingham, nor *chez* Point thirty years ago, when the shade of the old man still hovered over the table, nor *chez* Jérôme in La Turbie, where there is a Roman well, and where the chef once asked me at the end of dinner why I had eaten two successive main courses rich with cream, and when I replied 'Parce que j'ai un foie de fer' (which is true, incidentally), he shook my hand gravely and said 'Mes félicitations', nor *chez*

Barrier in Tours, where the tradesman's entrance has a weighing-machine fitted into the entire width of the doorway, so that nothing can get in without being weighed and at the same time inspected, nor *chez* La Petite Auberge at Noves, where the head waiter once asked whether I wanted wine, and when I said I did inquired further as to whether I wanted *good* wine, and when I said yes to that question too, replied 'Bon – vous voyez, nous avons le mauvais, mais nous n'aimons pas le servir', nor *chez* Pangaud, in Boulogne-Billancourt, that suburb of Paris where all those French films of the 1930s seem to be taking place, nor *chez* Le Moulin d'Ivry in the rue Henri Quatre at Ivry-la-Bataille, where I once held the place spellbound by reciting the whole of Macaulay's poem ('Oh, how our hearts were beating, when at the break of day, We saw the army of the League drawn out in full array . . .'), though that was nothing to what I did to the customers of a tiny restaurant in an alleyway in London's Little Venice, which was, for a bet, to sing the whole of the *Tannhäuser* Overture as a duet with a friend, standing on the table, nor *chez* Haeberlin at Illhauesern, where I had just chosen a bottle of Hugel Gewürztraminer to go with my *soufflé de saumon* when a tall, handsome man walked in and the *sommelier* said, 'C'est M. Hugel même', nor *chez* Guérard at Eugénie-les-Bains, where Tito left without paying the bill, doubtless used at home to restaurateurs who would not dare to present it to him or complain, if they did, when he bilked them, nor *chez* l'Hostellerie du Château at Chaumont-sur-Loire, where the salmon leaps straight out of the water, through the window and into the pan, I think, nor *chez* Parveaux in the Château de Castel Novel at Brive-la-Gaillarde, which is where Colette lived with the horrible Willy, and where every day they make an ice cream two feet high in the shape of the main tower of the castle, nor *chez* La Reserve at l'Alouette outside Bordeaux, where the mosquitoes feasted on me all night, doubtless in revenge for the various beasts I had feasted on all evening, nor *chez* Le Chèvre d'Or at Èze, a village that is wrapped round the top of a mountain and where no wheeled thing may pass, and not many things with fewer legs and less agility than a goat, nor *chez* Garcin in Talloires, to which I would retreat for some rough *pâté de campagne* and a steak with the marks of the grill criss-crossing it, after a few days of royal banquets down the hill *chez* Bise, nor chez Dorange at the Reine Pédauque in Cannes, where I dare say the *mousseline de rascasse* flourishes still, and where I once drank the most astounding 1959 Gruaud Larose in the company of no fewer than seven of my dearest friends, nor *chez* Terrail at the Tour d'Argent, where I once pleased M. Terrail *même* by telling him that *le restaurant de la Cathédrale est la Cathédrale des restaurants*, nor *bei* Schwarzwälder in Munich, where the *Hirschgoulasch* is served with cranberries, and so it should be, though it often isn't elsewhere, nor *bei* the old Ritz in Berlin, where they specialized in exotic meats and could get you a crocodile steak at a week's notice, nor *bei* the Gasthof Adler in Watzenegg, where on a whim we asked for *Salzburger Nockerl* to finish, and when we complimented the chef he confessed that he had never done one before, but was so pleased to be asked for something other than hamburgers and chips that he had done it from the cookery book, nor *da* Morino in Orvieto, where they serve kid of miraculous delicacy, nor *dalla* Locanda Cipriani on the island of Torcello, where, after visiting that extraordinary basilica, which feels as though it had slept for a thousand years beneath the sea, you are served the only serious roast chicken in the whole of Italy, nor *dalla* Mamma Gina's in Florence, where the *tortelloni verdi* make me understand why it is that sheep, if they have a never-failing supply of fodder and are allowed to stay by it, will go on eating until they have eaten themselves to death, or so I have heard, nor *da* Bagutta in Milan, where they have heard all possible versions of all possible jokes about the 'Last Supper', nor *bij* the Indrapoera in Amsterdam, where they serve a *rijstafel* of thirty-six dishes, nor at Le Dôme in Los Angeles, where I once took to dinner a lady on a diet so strict that all she would have was some hot water (with which she made her own herbal infusion) and a plate (from which she ate the special kind of mango that she had brought with her, wrapped in a clean white handkerchief borrowed, the purpose carefully unstated, from me), and the staff smiled on the whole performance, which I also do not think would happen in the outer suburbs of Liverpool or Birmingham, nor at the Chinese restaurant in the Taj Mahal Hotel in Bombay, where I ate the finest Chinese meal of my life, not excluding those I had eaten in Hong Kong, nor at the Slipped Disc Restaurant in the same city, where I confess I did not eat at all, though I took a photograph of the signboard in case no one at home would believe me, and then lost the photograph, so that no one ever does, nor at the *sukiyaki* restaurant in the old Imperial Hotel in Tokyo, which was built by Frank Lloyd Wright so that it would not fall down in earthquakes and remained undamaged in the cataclysm of 1924 and indeed throughout the bombing of the Second World War, but finally succumbed to the more powerful assaults of commerce, when it was pulled down by property developers who wanted to build something uglier in its place, nor at Kenneth Bell's Thornbury Castle, where once the *patron* had prepared a special *menu surprise*, accompanied by divers *vins surprises*, for the participants in a B.B.C. programme taking place in the vicinity and where the meal was so splendid that I was not even put off by the fact that Mr Anthony Wedgwood Benn would drink nothing but barley water (I believe he explains his teetotalism by his wish to keep his head clear), nor at the Hole in the Wall in Bath in the days of George Perry-Smith, who started an entire generation of English cooking, nor at Popjoys in the same city, from which Stephen and Penny Ross removed to Freshford, just outside it, and opened a country-house hotel not very unlike what I imagine Paradise to be and warmly hope is, and where most of this book was written, nor at Boulestin in Covent Garden in the old days and the recent days, the days in between being best forgotten, nor at the Cosmo in Edinburgh, where they spend their time thinking of more ways to please their customers, which is a great deal more than can be said for many a rival restaurant in that fair city, nor at Le Petit Savoyard in Soho, long since vanished, where I used to go and drink a bottle of 1928 Beychevelle every year on my birthday, until one year I arrived for the annual ceremony and was told that at some point in the twelvemonth the last bottle they had of it had been drunk *by somebody else*, nor at the Pike Grill in the Talbot Hotel in Wexford, where the bacon and eggs are the best in the world and can be eaten at two o'clock in the morning, nor at a place in France about which I have forgotten everything except that I ate a lobster for lunch there, and then, feeling that if the world came to an end in the course of the afternoon it would be a pity if I had left it at that, had another lobster, and then, finding that my fear about the possible ending of the world had still not left me, had still another; nor anywhere else, for that matter.

That does not displace the art of eating from the table of the Muses; at worst, it moves a few places down. If I have never eaten a meal that has corresponded, in the depth of satisfaction it provides, to the greatest experiences offered by the other arts, I can say, hand on heart or better still on stomach, that I have eaten many which are the equivalent of the next best thing – say a concert consisting of the Carnival Overture of Dvořák, the Schumann Piano Concerto and the Italian Symphony of Mendelssohn, or a performance of one of the plays of Sheridan or Wycherley, or an exhibition of the etchings of Piranesi or the sculpture of Houdon, a set of the novels of Meredith or the poetry of Browning.

No one, I think, will deny that those achievements, comparable with the achievements of the table, are art. They are not the highest form that art can take, and we know they are not because they do not instantly leap the gap between earth and stars, body and soul, man and God, as the very highest art always does. By the same token, we know that the pleasure of a fine meal can never take us across that chasm, but must for ever remain earthbound instead of heaven-sent. True; but the corollary is true also, for if such an

216

experience can give us everything except what only the highest art can provide, I cannot see how we can deny to food made and served at the level of Chapel, Girardet or Bocuse the title of art which we would not, and could not, withhold from Rachmaninov, Seurat, Trollope or Herrick.

There is, then, an art of eating. Oddly, the context is more important in this art than in any of the others, and the pleasure to be derived from food, though separate from the ambience in which it is eaten, is very easily enhanced or diminished by it; the decor and costumes of an opera are not more integral and essential to the pleasure of the music than is the quality of the place and its atmosphere to the enjoyment of the meal.

A restaurant should be pleasantly decorated (if it is too beautiful it can be distracting, which is why I am never really happy at Ledoyen, in the Champs Elysées, where I cannot help feeling that the lace tablecloths and massive cutlery ought really to be in the Victoria and Albert Museum), it should offer fair linen and shining glass, comfortable and handsome chairs, an air of bustle without hurry, meticulousness without fanaticism, dignity without solemnity – these are the things I look for in a restaurant before I open the menu, and they are to be found in the humblest *estaminet* if someone is making an effort as much as in the temples of *grand luxe* with five crossed knives and forks in the *Guide Michelin*.

Pour manger bien il faut savoir attendre. But that admirable precept must be interpreted in the widest possible sense. Unlike all the other arts, eating demands, and provides, relaxation. To go to a restaurant in a state of excited expectation is a dangerous mistake, and if it is not corrected can lead to disappointment. Fortunately, if the restaurant knows its business, the mistake can be corrected easily. The purpose of the aperitif and the leisurely study of the menu while sipping it is precisely to enable the diner to relax, to put away all the cares of the preceding hours and of the impending morrow, and to get into the right mood for the greatest

217

possible enjoyment of the pleasure of the meal. From time to time, when I feel like a good dinner but not company, I go alone to one of my favourite restaurants; I even don a dinner jacket for the occasion. Then I eat and drink slowly, reflectively and silently, and invariably find, as the evening goes by, the calm, the solace and the strength that I have obviously been seeking. Friends to whom I have mentioned this curious habit have mostly been bewildered; even for one who loves solitude, it seems to them to be rather extreme behaviour. The most understanding restaurateurs think it not odd at all, for they know that it is not only food and drink that they dispense, but that balm of hurt minds, which is also the death of each day's life and sore labour's bath (and, incidentally, great nature's second course) attributed by Shakespeare to sleep, the innocent sleep, but which can also be obtained from a fine meal approached in the right spirit.

It is the French who know this best, for it is part of the wider philosophy of gastronomy that has made them for so long the best cooks in the world. You can eat well in almost all of the civilized countries of the world, and even many of the uncivilized; in some – Italy and Austria, for instance – you can eat well anywhere in the country, from the biggest city to the smallest village. But only in France, a nation so devoid of aesthetic sensibility that they think Victor Hugo a great poet, can you find the year-round consistency that alone can make a memorable and significant cuisine.

For the glory of French cooking does not lie in the famous establishments run by the great chefs and patronized by gourmets from all over the world. The tallest mountain peak must have a mountain below it, and the truth about the great restaurants of France is that they rest upon a secure foundation of thousands of unsung little places serving excellent but simple meals to a knowledgeable and demanding French clientele.

It is no longer possible, if it ever was, to discover which is the chicken and which the egg. Do French diners know about food because the restaurants are good, or are the restaurants good because the diners know about food? Certainly the restaurants *remain* good because the customers are knowing, for the ultimate sanction is, in France, a very real one: a dissatisfied diner will rise from his place, go to the kitchen, and empty the offending plate over the chef's head. How that started is not now to be known, and we must remember that not many years ago as human history reckons it was English food that visitors praised. It has been said that the Industrial Revolution, herding millions into cities which had no real purpose other than to receive the herded millions, destroyed English cooking, unable to survive the horrible conditions; nations which followed more slowly in England's footsteps were spared this fate. It is a tempting belief, but does not really answer the question, which is why are the French so much better at gastronomy than any other nation?

At Eugénie-les-Bains, in southwest France, there is the establishment of Michel Guérard, the man who developed *cuisine minceur*. On my visits there I have eaten superbly at every meal, not only from the *menu minceur* but also from the more traditional *menu gourmand*; I have no doubt at all that Guérard is one of the most distinguished and creative chefs of our time. But just down the road from this rightly venerated shrine is a tiny village called Luppé-Violles. Staying at Guérard's a year or two ago, we felt like playing truant, and wandered off to Luppé-Violles, where we found the Relais de l'Armagnac. We found it more or less by accident, for it has no stars in the Good Book for its cuisine, no reputation outside the area as somewhere to be sought out, no lines of cars moving purposefully in its direction. It has a menu shorter by far than Guérard's (and cheaper by a lot further, though it must be said that Guérard is by no means the most expensive of the three-starred French restaurants, and his *menu minceur* is astonishingly reasonable), it has plain chairs and tables, copper pots hanging on the walls, red-and-white check tablecloths, no tourists (we were the only foreigners in the place the night we went there), nothing that could really be called cuisine at all, let alone what would be recognized by the word just up the road at Eugénie.

Yet I remember the Relais and the taste of what I ate there – ending with an astounding dessert that consisted of no more than unfermented goat's cheese from the farm next door with white *armagnac* beaten into it – as well as I remember what I ate at Guérard's palace. And the locals who filled it showed by their expression, to say nothing of their *embonpoint*, that the food had passed their critical inspection, based on a lifetime of demanding the best at the prices they could afford, and refusing to accept anything less.

I communicated the news of the Relais to my penfriend, the Professor. And a true penfriend he is, for although I have never met him, and would understand nothing of his recondite scientific discipline, we have been corresponding for some years about our mutual love of good food, signalling our discoveries to each other, and recommending particular dishes at particular restaurants; his epistolary encouragement is most welcome to me, especially at times when the food-haters are particularly active, which is, naturally enough, whenever I have just published an article on the subject implying that I have just enjoyed a meal. Happily, the food-haters do not trouble the Professor or me when we are at table.

I can discern no very clear pattern in the dishes I most enjoy, and I cannot deny that I am cautious in the discovery of new ones. On the whole, I am not an instinctive lover of fish, though I am not often, on the other hand, to be found demanding huge quantities of red meat. Poultry and most gamebirds, except those like snipe which are too high for me, figure largely in my personal repertoire; I do not think I know of a more perfect dish than Bise's *poularde braisée à la crème d'estragon*, with its accompanying rice, though I return again and again to the White Tower for that crisp bird, with its savoury stuffing, that has given John Stais, one of the greatest restaurateurs London has known in my time, his invariable greeting to the regulars: 'There's a duckling in the oven.' Liver in almost all its forms I learned to love when the memory of the horror at my boarding school finally faded; at the Hostellerie du Château Servin, in Belfort, where they keep colour photographs of all the bedrooms at the reception desk, so that the arriving client may choose, from among those which are free, the one which most takes his fancy, they serve an *escalope de foie gras* poached in raspberry vinegar, which transforms that usually over-bland meat into a thing of fascination. Veal I also find uninteresting, except in that excellent and robust Swiss dish called *Züriches geschnetzeltes*, which is really a *boeuf Stroganoff* with the wrong meat, and of course in the great *Wienerschnitzel* itself. Truffles, in their place, I dote upon; when sated with richness, I am content – more than content – with some tiny lamb cutlets and no less so with a classic *coq au vin*, the *sole Cardinal* at the Tour d'Argent, the *canard aux olives* at Allard, on the left bank, the *pâté en brioche* at the Pyramide (though it is not what it was) – but my correspondence with the Professor would really require a volume to itself. (With another separate volume for cheese, on which I could live happily for the rest of my life.)

I have never managed to like white Burgundy, though some of its humbler cousins from the Loire, especially Sancerre, please me greatly; the limitless world of German wine would take several score lifetimes to explore properly, but I have been doing what I can in thirty-odd years of my present span; though I will often seek an excuse to order red Burgundy (O that Richebourg, and my youth, long ago!), in the end I will always turn to claret, the noblest family in the great people of wine.

It sounds like a concession to the pleasure-haters, but I must say that as I contemplate the meals I have had, or better still one I am actually having, I do not make the mistake of believing that my pleasure in food elevates me above those who have no interest in what they eat, though I feel sorry for them, as I feel sorry for those who have no ear for music or eye for painting. But I have no regard at all for those who hold, consciously or unconsciously, the view that because eating is something we all have to do, it is somehow wrong to enjoy a universal necessity. There is no logic in this argument, but the pleasure-haters take comfort from it, clearly, and even find it convincing; I am not at all surprised, for instance, that the prigs of *Private Eye* hate food even more than they hate homosexuals, Jews and art.

'Bless thy good creatures to our use, and us to thy table.' That was the grace before meals at my school, and it seems to me to sum up admirably a truly balanced attitude to the pleasures of food and drink. We must keep those pleasures in proper perspective; we must indulge them reasonably, not grossly; we must try to understand what they say to us that it is necessary for us to know, even though they say it much more quietly than the proclaimed witness of music, painting, architecture, books. But the savour of good food and good wine is one of the elements of true civilization, and no man who embarks on a fine meal in that knowledge can rise from it without thinking that something real has been added to his nature. I am sure my friend the Professor would agree.

Nine

At a large boys' boarding school it is almost impossible to miss a lesson by accident, let alone two consecutive ones. I managed this feat one day, with predictably appalling consequences, because I was so absorbed in the book I was reading that I entirely failed to notice the passage of time or even the bell that summoned to class. Karel Čapek is forgotten today; not even the best-read European in a hundred is likely to remember *The Insect Play*, and not one in a thousand knows that he invented the word robot. But he was one of the authors I read in my adolescence, and he had upon me an effect almost as powerful as that of Chesterton, indeed in one respect more so, for it was his *The Absolute at Large* that I was reading with such fascination on that fateful summer's day.

It is science fiction; Čapek wrote a good many books in the genre, and this one is remarkably prophetic, for the 'absolute' of the title is the energy trapped in the innermost core of the atom. Even more far-seeing among his novels was one called *Krakatoa*, which makes the connection with nuclear fission still more direct; yet both books were written well before the Second World War. (He died in 1938; it was said of a broken heart, when the Nazis marched into Prague, his native city.)

I read *The Absolute at Large* for the ingenious and imaginative tale it was, and it had no wider meaning that I could see at the time; moreover, when I reread it more than thirty years later, it proved to be a much slighter and less subtle work than I had supposed it. Yet it has had an extraordinary effect on my life, though not for decades did the effect make itself consciously felt, for one incident in the book struck me, even as a schoolboy, with such force that I never forgot it, and it pursued me down the years and down the days, invisible as an underground river, until its waters broke surface at last and began to rise about me. I shall return to the theme – it is in a sense the subject of this chapter – but first I must think about the terrain beneath which the sacred river ran.

As I have said, my childhood home, though Jewish, paid virtually no attention to any Jewish observances. I have mentioned the occasional nod in the direction of the dietary laws, and the candles that were lit on the Sabbath eve, though these were not the only ones, for the candle that burns for twenty-four hours on the anniversary of a loved one's death was a regular ritual; memories of my childhood are punctuated with these tiny flames that marked the day consecrated first to my Aunt Lily, then to my grandfather. He died at home, which was customary in those days, though even if it had not been I am sure he would have refused to go to a hospital, for he had a calmness as he saw death approaching (the night before he died he dreamed of his father, who had beckoned him, smiling and saying 'Come') that the Stoics would have recognized; I recall my mother opening the window of the room in which he died, and turning to the wall all the mirrors in the house, customs enjoined upon Jews. (The window is opened to let the soul go free; the mirrors are covered as the first act of mourning, an immediate denial of vanity in the presence of eternity.)

I have my grandfather's hairbrush to this day, still in perfect condition, without a bristle gone, after thirty-five years of use by me, following I know not how many by him. I also have a photograph of him, and sustaining memories of his gentle and patient character; only years later did I begin to understand his full quality, and to wish I had known him even better. (I was eighteen when he died, but very young indeed for my years; I shall never cease to regret that I failed to understand how rich were his memories of Tsarist Russia, and what treasure I could have stored up if I had only had the wit to sit him down and question

224

him about the world of his youth with a pile of notebooks beside me.)

He and I used to play cards, sometimes a form of two-handed whist and sometimes a simpler game from his native land, called (presumably in child-Yiddish) *pisha-paysha*; he also played patience, always the same one (I think it is called Prince Albert), which I learned from watching him. We played draughts, too, though when I came back from school having discovered chess and tried to teach him, he found it beyond him.

He would go to the synagogue on the high days, and occasionally on an ordinary Sabbath. Sometimes he would take me, but I got very little from the experience, apart from a sense that the climax of the mystery had been reached at the moment when the Ark of the Covenant is opened by the rabbi, and the scrolls of the Law removed; of the mystery itself, however, I sensed nothing, and neither he nor anybody else tried to tell me anything about the Jewish faith, or about any other kind of faith either. I suppose there must have been a Scripture class at my elementary school, but I have no recollection of it at all; presumably there would have been an option for non-Christian children to be withdrawn from such teaching, and possibly my mother had exercised it on my behalf.

Certainly I had never set foot in any kind of Christian place of worship before I went away to school, and had not the slightest knowledge of what went on in a church. I speedily learned, for we went to the school chapel morning and evening every day, the morning service being before break-fast; non-Christian boys (there were only four or five of us) could be excused, but either my mother decided not to exercise the right on my behalf, or I refused to accept the exemption. If it was the latter, I know why, for I enjoyed chapel more than almost anything else at school.

At first the enjoyment came from the fascination of exploring a world so strange, though this feeling was mixed with some anxiety, for I had no idea what I was supposed to be doing. That was a problem easily solved, for all I had to do was to watch what the others did, and do the same. Thus, I had no notion of what a hymnal was, let alone a psalter, but it was easy enough to see from what everybody else was doing when it was time to pick up the green book or the black, and to turn to the appropriate number. I discovered at once that I enjoyed singing hymns; I still do, having a very large repertoire learned at school. For the rest, I knelt when others knelt, stood when they stood, turned to the altar for the Creed when they did. One mystery alone defied solution by such pragmatic methods; the words of the Psalms were before me in the black book, and the tune was easily enough picked up by ear. But the Gloria was not printed; I was surprised when I found that although I had finished singing, the others went on for another few moments (I recovered quickly enough, even on the first occasion, to keep moving my lips until the music stopped). But for the life of me I could not pick up the words, though I had learned the Creed in that fashion within a week; I dared not admit that I had no idea what the others were singing, because I dared not admit that I was not familiar with Christian church practice, and I went through my entire boarding-school days without finding the key to the lock. I cannot remember how I did in the end discover what I had been pretending to sing twice a day for six years, but I know it came as a delightful surprise:

Glory be to the Father, and to the Son, and to the Holy Ghost; as it was in the beginning, is now, and ever shall be, world without end, Amen.

Even after the novelty of chapel wore off, I continued to enjoy my visits to it, for the singing (we used to do the *Messiah* every year, with the whole school as Chorus), the sometimes very interesting sermons, and the gratifying feeling of being one with my schoolfellows, which was not a sensation that I felt very often otherwise. We used to sing improper words to some of the hymns, and I recall the

226

exquisite pleasure we had when a group of us were collectively called in one day and severely rebuked by a master whose place was opposite that of my House, and who had deduced from our gleeful grins that we were not singing

> Glorious things of thee are spoken,
> Zion, City of our God

to the tune of *Deutschland Über Alles*, but *Deutschland Über Alles* itself. The pleasure, and the difficulty we had in keeping our faces straight while we were being lectured, came from the fact that although we were not singing the hymn, we were not singing the enemy National Anthem either, but a ditty which began

> Auntie Jane has been aborted,
> For the forty-second time;
> Uncle Jim has been deported,
> For a homosexual crime . . .

The chapel was decorated with paintings of Biblical scenes by Frank Brangwyn; they were almost unimaginably ugly and lifeless, and must have given many generations of schoolboys an instant aversion to both Christianity and art. What is strange, though I did not realize it at the time, was that although I became interested in the Christian religion, nothing recognizable as any kind of religious feeling entered into me. The experience was (though of course I did not realize that at the time either) entirely aesthetic; I not only felt nothing at all of the numinous, I did not even understand that there was something to be felt, and I left school having sampled two of the world's great religions and derived nothing of importance from either. There followed many years in which I gave no thought at all to the most important question, and when I finally started to do so the process started, as it does for many, through art. But at this point I must explain the long, slow-growing effect on me of Karel Čapek's *The Absolute at Large*.

The book, as I say, describes the discovery of a scientific process akin to splitting the atom, and in doing so freeing the ultimate essence of energy. This force comes to be called 'the Absolute', and it has two principal effects. The first is the release of the physical energy itself, which is virtually infinite; there is a hilarious scene, typical of the results of this release, in which the energy is channelled into the working of a factory making tintacks, and the tintacks begin to pour out in such torrential quantities that the system of removing the finished product breaks down completely, so that gigantic mountains of tintacks form all round the factory.

In addition to unchaining the Sorcerer's Apprentice, the Absolute has another, very different, property. With the energy there pours out an equally limitless benevolence; anyone near the workings of the Absolute-releasing machines is engulfed in love, purity and selflessness, and soon it seems as though all mankind must turn saint. There is a catch in it, of course, which leads not to a reign of universal peace and brotherhood, but to an almost infinitely destructive war; that, however, is not what I took away from my first reading of the book and have carried with me all my life, even though for most of that life in ignorance of the treasure in my pocket.

For one man, and one alone, resists the Absolute; resists, that is, not the physical energy but the psychic. As the goodness of the universe pours over him, he fights against its effect; weakened almost to death in the struggle, he flees to Switzerland, where, in an isolated spot, he recovers his strength and his intact personality.

The reason he gives for his rejection of divinity is not important to my theme, for I did not identify with him. It was the attitude he adopted that entered my bloodstream: *he would not be made good against his will*. For the character in the book, that meant no more (but no less) than a free man's refusal to resign control over himself at the bidding of anything outside him. For me, it means – at last – understanding that whatever the Absolute is, it is inside us, whatever our lives are, we make them so, whatever God bids us do, we bid ourselves, whatever enlightenment we attain, we are our own light, whatever goal we have of being ultimately woven into the fabric of the universe, we ply the needle, whatever revelations we experience, we do the revealing, whatever voice whispers in our ears, it is our lips that form the words, whatever the lever that moves the world, we are the fulcrum, whatever the Kingdom of Heaven may be, it is within us.

Is that too much to derive from a little book of science fiction based on an ingenious idea? I cannot say; but there must be some reason why, although I gradually forgot everything else in the book over the years until I reread it, I remembered, perfectly and vividly, the man who says No while everyone and everything, even the Absolute itself, says Yes:

> The last temptation is the greatest treason:
> To do the right deed for the wrong reason.

Besides, it was *The Absolute at Large*, and no other book, that seized my schoolboy attention so fiercely that I forgot everything else in the world that afternoon, even the very fact that I was at school and the bell had gone for lessons. Could *that* have been an accident?

I suppose it could; but I do not see how Mozart could be an accident. I said that my disposition for wondering – the wondering that constitutes the most important element in our lives, and may be the most important element in the universe – began with art, and so it did. Of course 'Mozart cannot be an accident' is a conscious statement, an attempt to put in words what grows in us as a sensation; but it is the sensation that is important, not the words.

And what is that sensation? What words are there to put it in, since the inexpressible cannot be expressed? I am not talking about revelation; I have never had such an experience, and on the principle of the man in *The Absolute at Large* I am not sure I want one. But what I feel as I am listening to a

229

performance of the last three Schubert piano sonatas, or standing before Rembrandt's 'Self-Portrait as the Apostle Paul', or contemplating the equestrian statue in Bamberg Cathedral, or reading the poem which François Villon wrote on the eve of his execution, before he knew that he was after all to be reprieved, is an unmistakable understanding that the work of art, the artist and I are all three bound together like the particles of the atom, and that – like the bound atom itself – we are part of something which is vastly greater than ourselves, *and which makes sense*. What the sense is that it makes I cannot tell, any more than an individual atom knows what it is part of; but the secret harmonies that invariably sound when we are before transcendent genius (though not only then, of course) cannot be seriously denied by anyone capable of believing in something greater and more mysterious than what can be detected with the five physical senses, or indeed by anyone capable of feeling the transcendent genius itself.

The most important element in the feeling is the sense of being part of something greater. I first felt it in the Musée Rodin in Paris; I could not have been much more than twenty years old, if that, and I certainly did not know until many years later what it was that I had felt. I have never lost the love for Rodin that I acquired on that occasion. He is out of fashion now, accused of the gravest crime on the artistic Statute Book: he is said to be sentimental. So he is, in exactly the same way that Beethoven is sentimental; he feels, and causes others to feel. What is more, both Rodin and Beethoven would have maintained that nothing else made sense of their art; seized by the impulse to express a feeling that had arisen unbidden, they passed that feeling through the template of their genius, shaping, harmonizing and enriching it, until it was ready to be released and to work its effect upon us.

The genius of Rodin lies in his ability to liberate the energy in stone or bronze, as the inventor in Čapek's book liberated the energy in the atom. The image of 'liberation' is the key to the feeling Rodin inspires, and which presumably inspired me all those years ago. How did the energy get into the stone? How did it get into the atom? How did it get into the first movement of the Eroica? These are more important questions than 'How was the energy liberated?', though that is important enough. Whatever the answers may be, they cannot be provided by anyone who believes that Beethoven and Rodin were the result of nothing more purposeful than millions of years of evolutionary dice-throwing, and that Beethoven's Third Symphony is only a series of sounds by which Beethoven did not mean to convey any news of any kind, let alone the greatest news of all, or that Rodin's 'The Prodigal Son' is likewise an attractively symmetrical shape which reminds us of an interesting old legend.

This, I think, is what I mean when I say that wondering what is the answer to the most important question, or indeed wondering what the question itself is, often begins with art, and did for me. But it does not end there. It is very rare indeed for a book to change the entire world-view of a man in his mid-forties, though of course it happens once a week when he is just coming of age. Oliver Sacks's *Awakenings*, however, showed me beyond doubt that the body is nothing, nothing but a receptacle for the mind and the spirit, and from there it is only a step to Oliver Lodge's argument

> that we are spirits here and now, operating on material bodies, being, so to speak, incarnate in matter for a time, but that our real existence does not depend on association with matter, although the index and demonstration of our activity does,

which I suppose is as close to a definition of what I now believe as it is possible for me to get for the time being.

Only a fool would assert that there is no more on Rembrandt's canvas than paint, nothing on Mozart's music-paper but notes. We can go further. The secret harmonies that we hear in the greatest art, and in whatever

231

there is that is greater than the greatest art, have another property altogether: we have only to hear them clearly once to be able to recognize them every time thereafter. Obviously I could not hear them clearly that day in the Musée Rodin, or even at the first performance I heard of *The Mastersingers of Nuremberg*, which must have been at much the same time, and had much the same delayed effect. So although I cannot say exactly when my ears were opened, I know beyond doubt that they were already open when I first went to Oslo, and there heard the celestial music more clearly and more strongly than ever before.

I had heard those sounds, as I have made clear, in my response to art; I had even understood what they were, and why art transmits them. There is, though, a category which stands above even art, which does not rely upon the transforming effect of creative genius, though that effect may be incorporated in it, which transmits its power and truth directly into the mind and heart, indeed into the soul. With the phenomena in this category, the secret harmonies can be heard more easily, just as the stars, barely visible through the smoke and haze of a city, can be seen in all their glory from a vantage point far away from the habitation of man.

I am a stargazer *manqué*. Not an astronomer; it would have been an attractive profession for me in the days of Kepler, Copernicus or Galileo, and perhaps as late as Sir James Jeans, but the Einsteinian world of quarks and quasars, pulsars and black holes, or particles that arrive before they leave and space-travellers who journey through the heavens for a year only to return and find that on earth a century has gone by – this is no world for the man whose pleasure in the heavens is derived entirely from the mystery and beauty of what he can see when he gazes upwards on a cloudless night.

Perhaps I do the astronomers of today an injustice; perhaps they, too, feel that mystery and beauty, and at once forget their appallingly complex calculations of the incalculable. I would like to think so, for to me the pleasure of the stars begins where the possibility of understanding them ends.

And surely there is no mystery in the universe more mysterious than this one.

The distances, to start with; these alone will make the head swim. A light-year is 5,865,696,000,000 miles – even more in a leap-year – and some objects in the visible universe are *millions* of light-years away; where is the sheet of paper that could accommodate the noughts in a single line, and where the mind that can grasp such numbers? The astronomers talk of closed worlds, of strange curves that mean that the universe is endless though finite, of big bangs and steady states; none of this can be grasped, or indeed should be grasped, by the man who merely wants to look up at the sky with his imagination intact. And any man who does so must at once collide with the terrible paradox. If the universe is finite, what is outside it? If it is infinite, how *can* it be? The human mind cannot grasp infinity or finity, yet it cannot grasp, either, a universe which is not the one nor the other.

I suppose there are people who can, or who claim they can, look up at a sky filled with stars and not wonder who put them there and why; I am sure the members of the National Secular Society could field such a team, and argue, with no conception at all of their argument's daftness, that what they see above them can be explained on purely materialist grounds, and deny that such a faith ever wavers, or that they feel awe when they put it to the test. For me, the pleasure lies first in the awe, in thinking about the vastness of space, in realizing that each of those twinkling points of light, which are strewn in places as thick as dust, is distant from its nearest neighbours by all the journeys of ten thousand lifetimes. No one can see the sky as three-dimensional, despite the fact that we know it is, that the stars of Orion or Cassiopeia do not lie all in one plane, that the Plough would be invisible if we were able to take ship and sail through it. That is why we think of the night sky as a tapestry, a decorated canopy over our heads, a domed ceiling, anything that our feeble, sense-bound thoughts can grasp as easily as we can grasp the fact that there is a roof to every room in a house.

233

Next to the distances come the sizes. We are told that there are stars which are many millions of miles across, and that their year is hundreds of times as long as ours, that our sun is a mere candle-flame beside some of the roaring furnaces of space, that the galaxies are so huge that they constitute in themselves entire universes, and that there are millions upon millions of them. The awe deepens; it is the awe felt before something we cannot understand, something of which we cannot understand even how we should go about trying to understand it. Marco Polo in Cathay must have felt some twinge of this feeling, but the stargazer feels it on, literally, a cosmic scale.

I suppose that those who deny the mystery would also deny the beauty. Throughout history the two have gone hand in hand; men have speculated on the nature and significance of the stars and at the same time have coined names for them, names to fit their beauty, have written poems and made speeches to them, have invested them with magical properties, and ultimately, at a point where the mystery and the beauty join, have worshipped them. I do not find this at all surprising.

Orion is my favourite. God only knows how far apart the jewels of his belt are, how many millions of centuries separate the creation of the blade and the hilt of his sword, how many times the dog at his heels would fit into his shoulder-knot. At the first stirrings of human consciousness Orion was there, though he has moved gradually through the ages; it was impossible that men would not invest him with magical, with supernatural, qualities and powers. But all the most primitive and deep-rooted beliefs are rooted in something that corresponds to the reality around the emerging consciousness that brings them, blinking, into the light, and the worship of the moon as a goddess was not only understandable, it was fully justified, and based on the same conception of the universe as all the later religions held and hold: the belief that the universe must make sense, because it would not and could not exist if it did not, and that if it makes sense there must be some power in relation to which it does so. There is an unbroken succession from the Signs of the Zodiac to Paley's Watch, and the primitive man who worshipped bears or trees or thunderstorms had understood the meaning of the universe much better than many an eminent physicist of our time.

The beauty above us on a clear night, with the stars scattered across the sky as though all the chamois-leather bags in Hatton Garden and Amsterdam had simultaneously burst, has inspired generations of poets, as long as poetry has existed; but through the celebrations of the poets there runs a strain that cannot be matched in similar poetry inspired by battles and heroes, saints and martyrs. Which is the more important lesson for human beings to remember: that we die, or that we live?

It is strange that the stars, most of which are dead, should give us so powerful a feeling of life. This feeling does not come from the fact that as we watch them they seem to move, and that the familiar twinkling means the same as the twinkling of the lights of a city as we come in to land at an airport; nor is it based on our knowledge that each night the stars will be, when we seek them, in a position slightly different from that which they occupied the night before. And only children – though the child's eye on the heavens can often see more than the adult's – believe that a shooting star is a star rather than a fragment of cosmic rock. No, the throbbing life we sense in those icy jewels strewn with such profligacy on black velvet is the life that binds them all, dead or alive, and binds our earth among them. The orbits of the stars, the fixed relations they keep with others, the gravitational pull that ties a planet's moons to their mother's apron-strings and that, as we have recently learned, braids into plaits the bands of dust that surround the head of Saturn – these are not to be understood by any but mathematicians and real astronomers. But we all know it, and understand, with a sense that is not of mathematics, what it means, when we glance up at the night sky:

235

> The heavens themselves, the planets, and this centre
> Observe degree, priority, and place,
> Insisture, course, proportion, season, form,
> Office, and custom, in all line of order;
> And therefore is the glorious planet Sol
> In noble eminence enthron'd and spher'd
> Amidst the other; whose med'cinable eye
> Corrects the ill aspects of planets evil,
> And posts, like the commandment of a king,
> Sans check, to good and bad . . .

The stars hold out a promise as bright as that of the rainbow which tells us that if we keep faith we shall not be drowned again, as beguiling as the Christian pledge that 'whoso believeth on me shall never die'. They are indeed the star to every wandering bark, so indeed shines a good deed in a naughty world. You can tell what the stars mean to us by going to Australia (or coming from Australia if that is where you start): I remember my first glance at the heavens there, and always shall, for I had managed to forget for a moment where I was and what I would see when I looked at the sky on the other side of the world, and the feeling of horror and panic that instantly swept over me gave me a glimpse of what Hell must be like. For if Hell is anything it is a sphere in which logic has been destroyed, causality abandoned, where if one of the damned should drop a stone it is as likely to fly upwards or sideways as down. When I looked up at the Australian sky *I saw the wrong stars*, and chaos was come again:

>   . . . but when the planets
> In evil mixture to disorder wander,
> What plagues, and what portents, what mutiny,
> What raging of the sea, shaking of earth,
> Commotion in the winds, frights, changes, horrors,
> Divert and crack, rend and deracinate
> The unity and married calm of states
> Quite from their fixure! . . .

For all that, for all the lessons we can learn from the stars if we have not rendered ourselves (as some have) incapable of learning them, it is their beauty by which they live in our hearts, and which gives us such pleasure when we contemplate it. I am not one for sleeping out of doors, whether in the wilds of Africa amid lightning and rain or on a friend's lawn in Kent on the balmiest night in a perfect summer. But even I have lain on my back upon the ground, here and there, as night fell and the stars came out, and felt a great joy at the millions of night's candles lit above me. And that metaphor goes deeper than we know. A candle is the earthly simulacrum of the stars in heaven; it is no wonder that candles play so great a part in so many great religions, for it is not absurd to think of them as the heavenly promise made tangible, another set of tablets brought down from another Sinai, and I am sure that the candles in my childhood home remain in my memory because they communicated something of this essence to me.

Gods and goddesses, heroes and giants, homely objects, animals real and mythical, these fill the sky above us, and however many we can see and count we know that they are only the tiniest fraction of all the stars in all the galaxies. It is only very recently that we have begun to wonder whether there is life, of a kind we would recognize, on other worlds, and it is more recently still that we have begun to listen for voices calling across space and watch for messages painted on the sky. Scientists have now begun to tell us that the vastness and multitudinousness of the universe is such that it is overwhelmingly probable that the physical condition in which life began on our own planet must have been repeated again and again; from this they conclude that some of those parallel worlds must have experienced a parallel development. I find this an arid theory, not because it is impossible to test it but because the wonder of the stars would not be sensibly increased for me if I knew that they were strewn with every kind of life from the amoeba to man.

'What is the stars?' asks the Paycock; 'what *is* the stars?' I do not know, nor do I know of anyone who does. There is perhaps a clue, though, in the strange fact that it was not a signpost, a local guide or even an angel that led the Three Wise Men to Bethlehem, but a star.

The Seven Wonders of the World were all man-made, and all modern attempts to compile a similar contemporary list accept the original condition. I really do not see why natural objects should be rejected, though some of them, like the stars themselves, are far more wondrous than even the greatest work of man's hands. And what about the products of man's imagination, those ideas that have never taken on any form more solid and tangible than the thought in which they were conceived?

Plutarch, in his Life of Alexander, says that Alexander's favourite architect, Stasicrates, had offered to carve a statue of the conqueror, 'the most lasting and conspicuous in the world', to serve as a monument to him. Stasicrates did not exaggerate; for what he proposed was to cut Mount Athos (which is, incidentally, 6,350 feet high) into a figure of Alexander, on a scale so huge that in the statue's left hand there would be a city of ten thousand inhabitants, and in its right a river.

The idea of a statue, even one that was never built, more than a mile high, with ten thousand souls nestling in its left hand, produces the catch in the breath that tells us we are in the presence of one of the wonders of the world, those sights and ideas and combinations of sights and ideas which are singled out for awe and reverence in more than ordinary measure.

The catch in the breath at the idea of the statue is so acute that it clears all other feelings out of the way for a long moment, and in the ensuing emptiness we can discern a clue. The clue is necessary, for although there are many wonderful sights in the world, many examples of the work of Nature or man, many cunning combinations of the two – noble buildings and spectacular sunsets, impossible viaducts and

238

mighty rivers, solemn temples and infinite deserts, giant highways and boundless oceans – not all of them are of the blood royal, not all of them produce the unmistakable feeling in us, the feeling that tells us, even as we experience it, that it has reached into the most secret caves and chambers of our being. The clue, I think, lies in the fact that the true wonders of the world produce, in addition to the catch in the breath that marks them out as made of no mortal clay, a stab of the most intense and abiding pleasure.

There is a parallel here in the feeling we have when we hear about, or better still experience at first hand, a really striking coincidence. I do not believe it is possible for anyone of any imagination to come across such a coincidence, even at second hand, without at the same time seeing a curtain drawn back for a moment upon a vista of happiness. And it is that twitch of the curtain, that momentary glimpse into the infinite, which a coincidence shares with the true wonders of the world, for both offer, if we can only accept the offer, an instant of piercing joy at the news that all's right with the world. We have to accept the offer; I am quite unable to understand the nature of a man or woman who could contemplate, without feeling anything but interest, the Taj Mahal or the Pyramids, Niagara Falls or the Sydney Opera House, the Golden Gate Bridge or the Grand Canal, the Wieskirche or Cassiopeia, the Grand Canyon or the Parthenon, the doors of the Baptistery in Florence or the Propositions of Euclid, a pride of lions or the New York skyline, the mind of Erasmus of Rotterdam or a Stradivarius violin, the Lorelei or the Mycenean death-mask, a child's first steps or a snowflake under a microscope, the Himalayas or the landing of the astronauts on the moon, courage or the game of chess, the temperature of the sun or the heart of man.

I have written elsewhere about my first visit to the Taj Mahal, and the effect it had upon me. The effect was the most intense experience of the catch in the breath I had had until then, or ever expected to have; every time I have seen it since, the effect has been no less great – if anything, more.

But it was in Oslo, of all places, that I saw a sight which I sometimes think equals, in the intensity with which it offers the catch in the breath and all that that means, the Taj Mahal itself.

There are times when I think it surpasses it, for the purity and harmony of Shah Jehan's creation are such that they remove the spectator altogether from the earthy world, the world of getting and spending, living and dying, whereas Oslo's treasure, even while it lifts the heart, never lets us forget that we have to live in that world and that it is the way we live in it that gives us all the chance to be our own wonders, to generate the catch in the breath within our own souls. And it was the imagination, vision and faith of the City of Oslo that made possible this mighty telling of a mighty truth.

Gustav Vigeland, who was born in 1869 and died in 1943, is the most celebrated sculptor of Norway, though his fame has not spread abroad as has that of Grieg, Munch, or Ibsen; certainly I had never so much as heard of him before my visit to Oslo, and I have met few people since, however artistically knowledgeable, who even know his name, let alone his work. There is a reason for this ignorance, and it is to be found in the Frogner Park, a little way out of the centre of Oslo, where his masterpiece stands; the reason it is unknown elsewhere lies in its very nature, for not only could it never travel abroad, but it cannot even be photographed in its entirety.

In Frogner Park there is an area some 900 yards long and 140 yards wide at its broadest, which was designed, landscaped and laid out by Vigeland, and which is filled from end to end and from side to side with his sculptures. But this is no mere open-air exhibition of his work, like the mighty array of Henry Moore's sculpture that was held in Florence in 1972, for the 192 sculptures, comprising 650 figures, are laid out to one plan and one design, forming an integrated whole from the monumental wrought-iron gates that guard the entrance to a giant wheel of seven entwined bodies that closes

240

the vista half a mile away, and incorporating a lake, crossed by a bridge a hundred yards long, a giant maze in marble and an obelisk a hundred feet high.

This monumental work was the fruit of a confidence by the City of Oslo in the artist that was greater even than that of Rome in Michelangelo. Three times, over a period of twenty years, he changed the plans drastically; the City Council approved each time, and the people, led by their elected representatives, raised the money no less faithfully. It is still not finished, though it looks perfectly complete and symmetrical; Oslo built an enormous studio for Vigeland near the park, which was intended to become, and did become, a museum of his work after his death, but to the end of his life he went on adding to his giant masterpiece, and there are plaster models in the museum, not yet cast in the bronze for which they were intended, and a place allotted to them in the park.

It sounds like the fever-dream of a megalomaniac, an assertion of the ego over the spirit that brings to mind the claims of a Napoleon or a Hitler. It is nothing of the kind; by all accounts, Vigeland was a modest and dedicated man, but even if nothing was known of his life the visitor to Frogner Park, faced with the dazzling purity of its conception and execution, would be in no doubt that this is the work of a servant of art, not a master of the world, which is another essential test of the man-made wonders as I have defined them (if it were not so, the Empire State Building and Concorde would be on the list).

I have called Vigeland a servant of art, and so he manifestly was. He was also, and no less manifestly, a servant of that which art also serves, and it is plain that his work would have made no sense to him, and would make none to us either, if it were otherwise. The secret harmonies that pulsate throughout this stupendous work of art are what give it its life and its meaning, as they obviously gave him his, and we can therefore hear them as clearly and unmistakably as we can hear them before the Taj Mahal itself.

241

As I say, my ears were already alert for those sounds by the time I first visited Oslo. But I think that the effect of the Frogner Park monument would convince any visitor who had not deliberately shut and locked his heart against conviction that Vigeland and his achievement can no more be thought of in purely human terms than can Mozart or a rainbow; though we know exactly how a rainbow is produced and why it looks as it does, it has its effect on us as though we knew neither, and our knowledge of the materials and tools used by Vigeland, and the effect of the different perspectives of his masterpiece, have nothing at all to do with what we feel when we gaze upon it.

None the less, I must attempt to describe what it looks like for those who have never seen it and have no real hope of ever doing so.

The giant causeway of Vigeland's imagination has two nodes or focuses. The first is a stupendous bronze fountain, in the form of a bowl, set almost exactly halfway along; it is lifted by a group of huge figures, and the water pours from the bowl and beyond these Atlases, so that they are always seen within a curtain of water. This fountain is set on a square plinth; on the sides of the base there are sixty bronze reliefs, of babies, children, foals, men and women, and standing on the edge of the plinth, and thus surrounding and fencing the fountain, are twenty bronze trees, each with figures entwined among the branches, sitting in them, flying through them, even – as in the case of the baby-tree – hanging from them like fruit. Before the fountain is a vast pavement in blocks of black and white marble; it looks perfectly regular, but in fact it is a maze with a unique solution, and a visitor who traces the route from entrance to exit will have walked two miles.

The symbolism in all this is almost overpowering – almost, but not quite, for Vigeland's purpose was to show us the essence of simple humankind as it is by drawing it on a larger than human plan. The bronze reliefs, traced right round the platform, begin with babies and end with skeletons crumbling into dust; the figures lifting the bowl of the

242

fountain are of varying ages, and they are undertaking their share of the labour with varying degrees of effort; among the branches of the bronze trees the human forms merge with those of nature; the labyrinth on the ground is, no less plainly than the succession of bronze reliefs, an account of man's journey from birth to death.

Beyond the fountain the eye is carried to the dominant element of the whole design; a rising series of marble terraces, with the top one supporting a huge circular set of steps culminating in a final platform. Thirty-six sculptured groups stand on the steps, and in the centre of the platform is an obelisk, carved from a single block of stone and consisting of – not decorated with, but literally made out of – 121 human figures, men, women, and children.

The phallic significance of this monolith is obvious; even more obvious is the purpose of that significance. The column symbolizes the eternally renewed creation of humanity; at its root the figures are immobile, but as they spiral towards the sky they grow more and more alive – some thrusting violently upwards, some floating, some helping others. And it ends in a final burst of small children.

The thirty-six sculpture groups on the steps of this vast belvedere, carved in granite, have the same characteristics and the same variety. One is a squirming heap of children; in another a woman, on hands and knees, gives a horseback-ride to her two babies, who are using a plait of her hair as a bridle; another is of two laughing girls standing on their heads, another of an old woman cradled sleeping in the arms of a greybeard, in another a man lifts a corpse; in another an old woman lays her hand in blessing on the head of a young one, in another a couple reach out for each other across their baby, another is a pile of dead bodies, another shows two men in a fierce struggle; the whole teeming profusion of life is here, in its negative as well as its positive aspects, and as we walk round the platform we see humanity embracing, sitting, standing, playing, talking, listening, dying, thinking, celebrating, fighting, loving, suffering, scanning the heavens.

Yet even the fountain with its frieze and its tree groups, the obelisk with its mass of bodies and the sculptures which radiate from it, even these do not exhaust the glory of Gustav Vigeland's creation. About a third of the way along, before the mosaic labyrinth, there is the sunken lake with its hundred-yard bridge. On each of the parapets that run the length of this bridge there stand a further twenty-nine bronze sculptures, and these two sequences are the most human and varied of the whole work. A little boy, his face contorted in childish rage, stamps his foot; a man gives his son a running pick-a-back; an old man walks hand in hand with a small boy; a woman runs, her hair streaming out behind; a man plays with four children, lifting one of them on his foot; a woman carries her sleeping child cradled in her arms. Again, sentimentality is absent, that sentimentality which insists that life is without shadow, without toil, without pain; Vigeland was undoubtedly – the truth leaps from every inch of his creation – on the side of yea against nay, but he never pretends that his side is the only one, nor that it can win without a struggle. And the final symbol of the struggle is provided by the four stone columns that stand, one on each side of each end of the bridge, surmounted by figures of hideous and sinister dragons entwined with men and women. Everywhere else in Vigeland's display the grim reality of the negative side of life is portrayed in human form; the dead children on the steps that lead to the obelisk, the skeletons on the frieze round the fountain, the sufferings of age, the flight from fear, the violence of combat. These dragons are the only non-human shadow figures in the entire masterpiece, and they must be there for no ordinary or casual, let alone unconsidered, purpose.

As I gazed at these dreadful figures I remembered my first visit to the Oberammergau Passion Play, in 1960, and as I did so I also realized why that experience had come into my mind as I looked up at the four dark sentinels. The Oberammergau theatre is open to the sky at the stage end, and the green hills of Bavaria provide a magnificent natural backcloth for the drama. As Christ's journey was moving towards its climax, a fighter plane screamed across those hills, its shadow racing beneath it on the green tableau. In the seconds it took to pass the heart and mystery of the story we were watching were laid bare, and exactly the same revelation was provided by the dragons on Vigeland's bridge. For what is depicted by Christ's life and death, and the Oberammergau telling of it, is the same as what was encapsulated in the whine and flash of the death-dealing aircraft, and no less clearly enshrined in the dragons and their inhuman strength. The dragons are real, as the Cross was real and as the aeroplane was real, because darkness and suffering are real, and *they* are real because evil is real; but the dragons can be overcome, as darkness, suffering and evil can be overcome, *though not without a struggle*.

That overcoming, and the duty laid upon us to undertake the struggle without which the overcoming cannot take place, is the greatest of all the wonders of the world, and perhaps, therefore, we should need none of these reminders, no works of art, none of the creations of man's hand and brain, no visible witness to the grandeur of the earth; for that truth permeates us all, and our very humanity is steeped in it. But the spirit, as well as the flesh, is weak, and it is therefore as well that such signposts should be dotted here and there about the world.

Nor do they have to be as vast as Vigeland's park, let alone Mount Everest. Santa Fe, a town of barely fifty thousand people in the middle of the New Mexico desert, comes close to being one of the wonders of the world in itself; the adobe architecture of the American Indians is the only style the municipal authorities will permit in the central area of the town, but the infinitely varied ingenuity with which it has been used by modern architects makes Santa Fe a living, vibrant centre instead of the museum a visitor would expect from such a decree. On the edge of the historical area is the Chapel of Our Lady of Light, and in it there is a sight that produces the catch in the breath twice; once on seeing it, and again on hearing the story that lies behind it.

The chapel was built in 1878, a simple and unremarkably

functional place of worship. The plan called for a staircase up to the choir loft, but the workmen, having finished everything else, abandoned it, saying that it was impossible to fit one in. The problem was that an ordinary flight of steps would swallow up too much of the space of the church, and a spiral staircase could not be built tightly enough for the height (only seven yards). The Sisters wrung their hands, and prayed, and their prayers were answered in a fashion that has led to the answer being known as the Miraculous Staircase. A stranger appeared in the town, volunteered for the job, completed it in six months, and departed without either giving his name or asking for any payment. He used a variety of woods, some of which do not (and would not) grow anywhere near Santa Fe, though there was no record of his having brought any timber with him; his only tools were a hammer and a saw, together with a constant supply of hot water in which he made pliable the wood that he was to twist into an impossible spiral; he used not a single nail anywhere in the construction, but only joints so perfectly fashioned that they will last for ever; there is not even a central pillar, or any kind of support other than the harmony of its making.

In its seven yards of height, the staircase makes two complete 360° turns, and the grace and delicacy of its beauty, and the contrasting colours of the different woods and of the inlaying the mysterious carpenter used, make it seem to float, not climb, from the chapel floor to the balcony; in all my life I have never seen another such creation from the hands of a craftsman, nor indeed any other work of craft at all which communicates so overpowering a sense of that instinctive reverence which tells us with a certainty beyond argument that we are once again listening to those secret harmonies.

The Miraculous Staircase of Santa Fe is certainly a miracle in the colloquial sense; the Sisters naturally believed that it was a real miracle, the answer to the prayers which they had offered up in their unfinished church, and I do not think that anyone who looks upon the staircase, and has heard the story, can fail to think of one particular carpenter. And if the

Sisters were right, and the stranger *was* that carpenter, it is hardly to be wondered at that he would not hammer nails into wood.

A massive park in the land of the midnight sun; a wooden jewel in a church in the New Mexican desert; a monument to a beloved wife in Agra; Venice, who once did hold the gorgeous east in fee; is there not one of the world's wonders in more homely surroundings? There is, for what could be more homely than London's Haymarket, a few yards from Piccadilly Circus and a few more from Trafalgar Square, with its two cinemas, two theatres and the hard-headed offices of the American Express? At the bottom of that familiar thoroughfare is a glass-fronted skyscraper (sky-scraper by London's modest standards), which is called New Zealand House, and holds that country's diplomatic and trade representation in Britain. In the entrance hall there stands a wooden column, three storeys high. It is a Maori totem pole, called a *poui*, and it is carved, from a single tree, with a richness and profusion comparable with those of Vigeland's obelisk of life. This beautiful and haunting wonder is the work of one man, Inea te Wiata, a great Maori opera-singer who died young a few years ago, and was finishing it in the last days of his life. And it, too, asserts, in the circumstances even more poignantly than Vigeland's masterpiece, the truth in St Paul's words: O Death, where is thy sting? O grave, where is thy victory?

Perhaps that great, confident cry is the ultimate source of the pleasure these jewels of our world induce; if so, it is hardly surprising that the pleasure in question is of particularly deep and affecting kind. So perhaps it is not altogether an accident that the best known of the world's wonders is the Taj Mahal, and that that is the one which works its magic upon millions who have never seen it in reality, and indeed have never seen it except in inadequate photographic reproductions or crude models, but recognize it, even in those debased forms, for something far beyond a beautiful building in a beautiful setting.

On a visit to India a year or two ago, I met two of my friends from England, mother and daughter. The mother was returning to this country, the girl staying for an extended period, possibly a couple of months. I urged her – we were in Bombay – to find time to see the Taj Mahal, but she explained that she was going south to stay with friends until it was time to come home. I pressed my appeal more strongly, trying as I did so to convey some of the literally celestial pleasure I had got from it on my every pilgrimage, and assuring her she would feel it too. Very doubtfully, she said she would try to fit in a visit to Agra if her timetable could be changed; but when we parted, I felt sure she would not get there, and would never know what profound experience of a pleasure, not of this world, she had missed. Some weeks after I returned home, I received a postcard from Agra; the spell of the unimaginable symmetry that the Taj possesses had drawn her there after all, and her card spoke of the joy, the peace, the serenity she had felt sitting at its feet. She, too, had known that catch in the breath.

When I sit high above San Francisco and look down, through the rays of the setting sun, on the Golden Gate; when I toil up the Acropolis to the blinding marble miracle above, or drive out of Athens to the Temple of Poseidon at Sounion; when I look up at the roof of King's College Chapel, Cambridge, when the evening star is bright on the horizon in a velvet sky; when, before I return to my hotel and bed, I stand for the last time in the day with my back to the Campanile and look upon the illuminated darkness of the Piazza San Marco; when I recall how once, high over the Pacific, I saw distinctly the curvature of the earth; then I know once more that unique pleasure, not of art, not of the mind, not of the senses, that comes from hearing the secret harmonies of the world vibrating through that same world's wonders.

Gustav Vigeland heard those harmonies, too; and it was given to him to add one to the number of the wonders of the world. His monument is rooted in his understanding of man, and for all that he wrought in stone and metal, it is the living flesh that he sets before us. He would have no part of non-representational art; how could he deny the human form that was both his inspiration and his achievement? He knew that dragons exist, and are enemies to life; high on those columns at the portals of his bridge he set man and woman to wrestle with them. But when it was put to him that his figurative style was becoming out of date, his reply was simple and conclusive: 'When will human life become out of date?'

Never, I think; and while it continues, human beings will not cease to feel the pleasure of wonderful things, and to sense the meaning that lies behind the wonders of the world, and to guess at the reason for the pleasure they give.

Thus I reflected, sitting on the steps from which Vigeland's mighty obelisk rears aloft, when suddenly there was an abrupt incursion on my peace, though one which turned out to be the perfect complement to the feelings induced by this masterpiece of the human spirit and of the spirit of the universe. A huge procession of children, dressed in vivid national-costume finery of green, red and white, began to make its way across the park, led by a children's band making peacefully martial music. The children in the procession ranged from thirteen years or so to infants who had not long learned to walk, and were holding their mothers' hands; some were even younger, and were travelling in prams. Practically all of the children in the column were carrying Norwegian flags, and the spring sun shone kindly on them all; I decided that it must be Pied Piper's Day in Oslo, though on inquiry I discovered that it was the anniversary of Norway's Independence in 1814. The cheerful scene reminded me, perhaps even more forcefully than the sculptures by which I was surrounded, that the greatest wonder of the world is man himself, in his immeasurable capacity for experience, and it was in contemplating his fellow beings and that capacity of theirs that Vigeland himself felt the catch in the breath which he transmitted to the world in the splendours and truths of Frogner Park.

It was time to go. I crossed Vigeland's bridge, between his two rows of bronze figures, and, with my heart full of the secret harmonies that such wonders sing, turned my head for a last glimpse of his enduring achievement. At that moment I realized what is the greatest truth behind such sights, such creations, such marvels of nature or the work of man's hand. I knew, as we all know, that the dragons will be defeated.

Index

Note: Buildings and parts of London are entered directly; elsewhere, they are found under place.

251